THE COCKTAIL CHRONICLES

NAVIGATING THE COCKTAIL RENAISSANCE WITH JIGGER, SHAKER & GLASS

PAUL CLARKE

Foreword by Jim Meehan

Publisher: Paul McGahren
Editor: Matthew Teague
Art Director: Lindsay Hess
Illustrator: Andrew Vastagh
Layout: Maura Zimmer
Copyeditor: Kerri Grzybicki

Spring House Press
3613 Brush Hill Court
Nashville, TN 37216

ISBN: 978-1-940611-17-4

Library of Congress Control Number: 2015941304

Printed in the United States

First Printing: June 2015

To learn more about Spring House Press books, or to find a retailer near you, email *info@springhousepress.com* or visit us at: *www.springhousepress.com*.

Praise for

THE COCKTAIL CHRONICLES & PAUL CLARKE

"Paul Clarke began writing about the cocktail renaissance when it was still wishful thinking, and has been covering it ever since. I challenge anybody to find somebody who knows it better or, just as important, somebody who can explain it more clearly or genially. He is the ideal guide."
—DAVID WONDRICH, author of *Imbibe!* and *Punch*; *Esquire* drinks correspondent

"The most indispensable cocktail guide in years. Paul Clarke's serious authority never gets in the way of his pleasure. This is the guy you want behind the bar with you."
—JONATHAN MILES, former *New York Times* cocktail columnist

"Whether celebrating the rebirth of The Last Word or comparing an aperitif to Boom Boom Mancini, *The Cocktail Chronicles* is a decade-in-the-making document of Paul Clarke at his finest. He nails that sweet spot of drinks writing, appealing to veteran bartenders and cocktail geeks while expertly demystifying matters for those eager to learn more."
—BRAD THOMAS PARSONS, author of *Bitters: A Spirited History of a Classic Cure-All*

"It's not often that a new cocktail book holds my attention, but I wasn't surprised that Paul's did. *The Cocktail Chronicles* will serve as a wonderful homage to what is perhaps one of the most pivotal times in the history of cocktails."
—AUDREY SAUNDERS, owner of Pegu Club, New York City

"*The Cocktail Chronicles* is not just an engaging inquiry to the classics, but a unique eyewitness account of the contemporary craft-cocktail revolution. It's a lot to drink in, but Paul mixes it perfectly and serves it with a smile."
—JEFF "BEACHBUM" BERRY, author of *Potions of the Caribbean*

"*The Cocktail Chronicles* is an insider's guide to the classic and modern drinks, spirits, bars, and bartenders driving the current cocktail renaissance, from a writer who has been on its front lines for the past decade."
—CAMPER ENGLISH, cocktail journalist and publisher of Alcademics.com

"The Cocktail Chronicles blog was such a big part of my education. This book is long overdue, and will be required reading for the next generation of bartenders."
—JEFFREY MORGENTHALER, bar manager at Clyde Common (Portland, Oregon) and author of *The Bar Book: Elements of Cocktail Technique*

"This book is not only valuable, it's necessary. And while it's replete with cocktails, at Paul Clarke's hand, the writing always wins."
—TED HAIGH, "Dr. Cocktail," author of *Vintage Spirits and Forgotten Cocktails*

"Few people have followed the cocktail revolution as closely as Paul Clarke. And to follow his journey—and look at where it all began, where it's been, and where we've ended up—there's no more entertaining way of discovering all the details than by reading this fine tome."
—GAZ REGAN, author of *The Joy of Mixology*

CONTENTS

RECIPES

CHAPTER 1

NOTES FROM A RENAISSANCE IN PROGRESS

CHAPTER 2

NOT FORGOTTEN

CHAPTER 3

MUSES & BRIDGES

CHAPTER 4

STAYING POWER

FOREWORD

Paul began writing about drinks on his blog, The Cocktail Chronicles, and for *Imbibe* magazine in 2005. That same year, I was hired by Audrey Saunders to tend bar at the Pegu Club, and by *Food & Wine* magazine to edit their annual cocktail book. I'd tended bar for 10 years by that time in my career, and helped edit the *Mr. Boston Bartender's Guide*, but my professional journey may as well have just begun.

A movement—some call it a renaissance—was taking shape in bars across the country, fueled by the same ethos that chefs, winemakers, brewers, distillers, and baristas were pioneering in their workplaces. With the hangover of the fruit-flavored, Martini-fueled '90s still ringing, history-minded cocktailians—a fancy term for people who can name more than three brands of bitters—began to question what a bar and bartender should and could be. Interestingly, many of those driving the dialogue weren't bartenders.

At the time, the Internet was still taking shape, and thanks to chat groups in online forums, like-minded enthusiasts from all over the world found each other. Two notable domains from the city of Seattle were Robert Hess's DrinkBoy and Paul Clarke's Cocktail Chronicles. Spurred on by the exploits of local bartenders such as Murray Stenson and Jamie Boudreau, they used their skills as writers to document their experiments, share their resources, and shed light upon their brethren across the World Wide Web.

A handful of books were published around this time to cement their platform: *Vintage Spirits and Forgotten Cocktails* by Ted Haigh; *Cocktail: The Drinks Bible for the 21st Century* by Paul Harrington; and *The Craft of the Cocktail* by Dale DeGroff. Without sounding melancholy or maudlin, each of these traced the history of the cocktail back to the 19th century, and documented the author's efforts to recreate and source historic ingredients and recreate old recipes that begged more attention from modern audiences.

This was happening at a time when chefs were centering their menus around local ingredients; craft-beer brands were

With the hangover of the fruit-flavored, Martini-fueled '90s still ringing, history-minded cocktailians—a fancy term for people who can name more than three brands of bitters—began to question what a bar and bartender should and could be.

hopping; American winemakers were capturing international acclaim; and baristas were taking Italian coffee culture to new heights. Ingredient-driven cocktails prepared with fresh produce and premium spirits just made sense—so much so, that a Portland, Oregon-based magazine called *Imbibe* was founded to celebrate "liquid culture" in full-color splendor, with Paul as one of the founding contributors for their debut issue in 2006—which brings me to the author of this timely tome.

No one's had a better vantage to chronicle the transformation in American cocktail culture than Paul Clarke. This will date me, but if I had to compare *The Cocktail Chronicles* to an album, it would be the *Singles* soundtrack: a peerless mixtape for a forgettable movie, appropriately set in Seattle, which launched the careers of bands like Pearl Jam, Soundgarden, and Smashing Pumpkins.

Every time I listen to it, I'm transported back to a formative period of my life; reading Paul's book has the same effect. History is tricky, in that its author decides what we should focus on, blurring other angles of the story. For this reason, I couldn't be more enthusiastic about Paul's version, which nimbly portrays the handiwork of bartenders, bars, ingredients, and recipes from cities all over the world.

Each story reinforces not only his mastery of the material, but underscores his relationship with makers of all types whose stories are documented with an intimacy only a select few possess today. And unlike many writers, who vet their perspective by sticking to the popular narrative, Paul sheds light on the work of world-class working bartenders such as Boston's Josey Packard and Chicago's Stephen Cole, whose brilliance tends to fly under the radar of journalists who don't have their fingers on the pulse.

Ever diplomatic, Paul pulls for the West Coast like a presidential candidate establishing his voting record. (The fact of the matter is the vast majority of the country's national media outlets are headquartered in New York City, which skews

most coverage to the handiwork of the cocktail world's capital city.) He's done an admirable job of documenting the contributions of Left Coast bartenders, distillers, and entrepreneurs without his perspective feeling regional in any way.

Left leanings aside, the quality of his writing carries the book. Paul's playful sense of humor, sharp wit, and practical approach to the subject make it impossible not to cheer his choices on. He's critical where it's crucial—in matters ranging from spirit selection, recipe proportions, and environmental concerns—and judgmental without lecturing. His writing steers clear of polemicism, shirks fussy recipes and didactic perspectives, and reinforces the importance of having fun behind the bar; but at no point do you feel like he's casual about the subject after loosening his critical tie.

In addition to being a fantastic history, *The Cocktail Chronicles* is an excellent collection of recipes with everything the reader needs to begin or complete their cocktail education. The author writes for enthusiasts using analogous art forms and pop-cultural phenomena outside the realm of mixology to speak more clearly about those in it. For this, and so much more, I am grateful to Paul for enriching the art of mixing and serving drinks in this lively resource, and heartily cheer him on to continue chronicling his exploits.

— Jim Meehan,
author of *The PDT Cocktail Book*

CHAPTER 1

NOTES FROM A RENAISSANCE IN PROGRESS

Not every revolution requires an insurrection, and not every renaissance begins in salons, galleries or cloistered chambers. The cocktail seemed an unlikely candidate to start either a revolution or a renaissance, but somehow over the past decade, give or take, it has managed to find itself at the center of both.

How unlikely? On a certain level—a big level—it's just a damn drink. But today the cocktail is celebrated at week-long conferences and festivals that draw thousands. The resurgence of the craft cocktail (for lack of a better term) may have started just over a decade ago in faux-speakeasies in New York, London's lux cocktail lounges, and San Francisco's culinary crucible, but today you can order a Last Word at a bar named after the once-forgotten cocktail in Livermore, California (or at bars named for similar purpose in Edinburgh, Christchurch, San Antonio, or Ann Arbor); drink fresh and imaginative riffs on the Old Fashioned or the Tom Collins at an airport bar in Atlanta; or—at the New York City franchise that opened in 2014, anyway—sit back with an Aperol Spritz or a Tommy's Margarita in the uber-Americana environment of Denny's.

Mirroring the wider culinary movement that's been building steam for decades, craft-cocktail bars (and the bartenders and writers who inhabit them) are digging in the depths of the drink's rich (but often shoddily detailed) history. At times, they come back bearing precious nuggets—the Bijou, the Boulevardier, and the felicitously named Corpse Reviver #2, among others. And sometimes, these finds go beyond simple recipes. Techniques and skills have been garnered from the past, dusted off, and deployed in contemporary bars—sometimes with modern-day embellishments and modifications drawn from the molecular-gastronomy kitchens of Wylie Dufresne, Grant Achatz, and Ferran Adria.

Such creativity fuels the renaissance part of the equation. And the revolution? Prior to the resurgence of the cocktail's popularity, the liquor world was dominated by an ever-expanding variety of flavored vodkas and suspicious mixtures designed to appeal to the booze market's lowest common denominator (usually, the 21-to-34-year-old club-goer who's unashamed to ask a perfect stranger for an Adios Motherfucker or a Red-Headed Slut). That's still around, of course—for every teenager who just downloaded a Velvet Underground album, there are thousands of others shelling out for Taylor Swift—and the same rules apply in the drinks world, with sales of whipped cream–flavored vodka eclipsing those of artisanal mezcal by a depressingly enormous margin.

But the cocktail resurgence has changed the way we buy and sell booze. Like ocean liners, the massive liquor-company leviathans are slowly shifting course, recognizing the unexpected and unprecedented surge of demand for cocktail-centric spirits like rye whiskey, complexly flavorful vermouths, interesting gins, and tequilas with a sense of character.

Meanwhile, changes in state liquor laws mean there are now scores of small distilleries popping up in almost every state in the country, making local whiskies, gins, and brandies. These distillers' share of the market is still quantifiable in peanuts, and much of their new liquor is, admittedly, not yet ready for prime time. But these distillers are looking at the experiences of craft brewers and winemakers who, decades earlier, ventured down similar paths.

Some are preparing for the long haul, aiming over time to not only make good booze, but revolutionize the way liquor is made, sold, and marketed. Crass consumption is increasingly out, the garishness of artificially inflected booze about as welcome among craft distillers and bartenders as a Hummer at a Sierra Club conference. Spirits with a sense of virtue are still scarcer than ivory-billed woodpeckers, but there's a prevailing sense that a shift is occurring. If and when that fully happens, the liquor store and the local bar may be fully part of the modern food landscape—places where conversations about ethics and sustainability no longer seem out of place, and where the liquor selection is as locavore as the fruit at the farmer's market.

A dozen-plus years of Prohibition failed to stamp out America's taste for ardent spirits, but it did change the way we drink.

Renaissance and revolution—and all because of a damn drink.

As with any popular movement, the cocktail renaissance (or resurgence, or revolution—none of the nomenclatural hats fit perfectly) involves a cast of thousands, with leading figures such as New York's Pegu Club-owner Audrey Saunders its Leonardo, and writers such as David Wondrich its Dante Alighieri. But before this renaissance could fully get underway, it required the proper alignment of the cocktail planets—in this case, the celestial bodies included such pioneering bartenders as Dick Bradsell in London, Charles Schumann in Munich, and Dale DeGroff in New York.

A few background basics: The 19th century witnessed both the likely advent and the initial zenith of the broad class of drinks we call cocktails. The mixture emerged from the swamp of early American history and flared into full force around the same time as the Civil War. By the 1880s and '90s, the cocktail was a core part of the American character and an increasingly popular export—which was fortunate, as when Prohibition brought the whole thing crashing down a few years later, there were bars in Havana, London, and Paris to which the thirsty (and expatriate bartenders) could flock until everyone came to their senses.

A dozen-plus years of Prohibition failed to stamp out America's taste for ardent spirits, but it did change the way we drink. It fully shifted the emphasis away from carefully rendered balances of flavor and toward a drink's boozy vavoom, its inebriating effects prized above all (a situation that still exists in some ways, as exemplified by fishbowl-sized Martinis in many mainstream bars and the TNT power of drinks like the Long Island Iced Tea). It also eradicated the livelihoods of experienced bartenders, or drove them overseas or into illegal industry—in effect, largely destroying the institutional knowledge that had been acquired in the decades since the cocktail's first mid-19th century surge. The Second World War dealt a further blow, denying American bars imported English gins and French brandies (as well as Italian vermouths and liqueurs), and even domestic liquor was sharply limited due to the war effort.

By the time things seemingly got back to normal—if that term can aptly be applied to the years when impending nuclear Armageddon seemed a certainty—American tastes in drink were already shifting away from the rich, daring, and robust. By the late 1960s, sales of vodka—a neutral spirit easily obscured by the flavor of pretty much

anything—were outpacing those of gin, and by the time of the nation's bicentennial, vodka was surpassing whiskey.

This shift also roughly corresponded with incursions from the food scientists—in the form of commercial sour mix and packaged cocktail preparations—and other labor-saving steps such as soda guns that sprayed tonic, Coca-Cola, or an assortment of other mixers, and other shortcuts that swapped quality and flavor for speed and convenience.

You need only go out for a drink tonight in New York City to experience the lasting beneficence of King Cocktail's reign.

During the 1970s (and well into the '80s), the cocktail was arguably at its weakest point. The country's other cultural touchstones at the time included combovers, platform shoes, and *Muskrat Love*, so perhaps the near-demise of urbane drinking during the '70s isn't so surprising. But by the Fuzzy Navel–era of the mid-1980s, Schumann, DeGroff, and Bradsell were already making moves that would take almost two decades to fully resonate. Bradsell, at Fred's Club and Soho Brasserie; Schumann, at his eponymous Munich bar; and DeGroff (crowned "King Cocktail" in the '90s) heading the bar at Rockefeller Center's Rainbow Room, plumbed the past to look for direction into the future, along the way gathering admirers and acolytes.

They didn't need to look far or wait long. Bradsell drove the British cocktail scene forward with bars such as Match and The Player, and Schumann's *American Bar*—published in 1995—hinted at the direction the larger bar world would soon take.

And DeGroff? You need only go out for a drink tonight in New York City to experience the lasting beneficence of King Cocktail's reign. Dale put the dignity back into drinks from his roost atop Rockefeller Center, and such interest in civilized cocktails quickly spread after the turn of the millennium. Bars such as Milk & Honey, from Sasha Petraske, coined the neo-speakeasy style since imitated worldwide; they also mirrored DeGroff's interest in impeccably rendered cocktails prepared in the mode of the 19th and early 20th century masters of the craft. Audrey Saunders, who worked with DeGroff at Blackbird, first refined her approach at Beacon, The Tonic, and Bemelman's Bar, then—in one of those Apollo mission moments that clearly distinguish what came before from what's happened since—opened her groundbreaking Pegu Club bar on West Houston Street in 2005. And Julie Reiner, who opened Flatiron Lounge in 2003, began to build her own orbit of craft bars, including Clover Club in Brooklyn, which quickly became one of the cocktail world's most beloved following its 2008 debut.

At Petraske's bars (which, in addition to Milk & Honey—currently on hiatus—include Little Branch and Dutch Kills) and those from Saunders and Reiner, New York bartenders built not only solid reputations for these establishments, but honed the talents they'd then take on to a steadily expanding diaspora of bars. Alumni such as Jim Meehan, Philip Ward, and Sam Ross went on to open or to helm such craft-cocktail standards as PDT, Death & Co., Mayahuel, and Attaboy. The reach extended westward, as well, with Petraske sending staff to Los Angeles to help spread the cocktail word there via bars including The Varnish, and Death & Co. owner Dave Kaplan partnering with bartender Alex Day to open the downtown L.A. bar Honeycut, along with a small swarm of additional bars that steadily continues to expand.

But when this East Coast wave first hit the West, it encountered an indigenous cocktail movement already in full flower. San Francisco's mixology heritage extends to the mid-19th century, when Jerry Thomas—the patron saint of today's craft bartenders, and author of the first known bartender's resource, *The Bar-tender's Guide: How to Mix Drinks* or the *Bon Vivant's Companion*, published in 1862—practiced his talents in a city flooded with gold from the Sierra Nevada digs. Restaurants such as Absinthe Brasserie & Bar had begun dabbling with craft cocktails in the late 1990s, and when the cocktail renaissance began to bubble on the East Coast, Bay Area bartenders were already getting into the game.

But while New York bartenders largely embraced the vintage cocktails and approaches, many San Francisco bars functioned a little differently. Most operated within larger restaurants—largely a product of local licensing laws—but this also meant that Bay Area bartenders were often working with chefs in one of the world's most vibrant culinary capitals. Thus restaurants such as Absinthe, Charles Phan's Slanted Door, which opened in 1995, and Tracy Des Jardins' Jardiniere, which opened in 1997, developed bars that also nurtured the city's maturing cocktail identity,

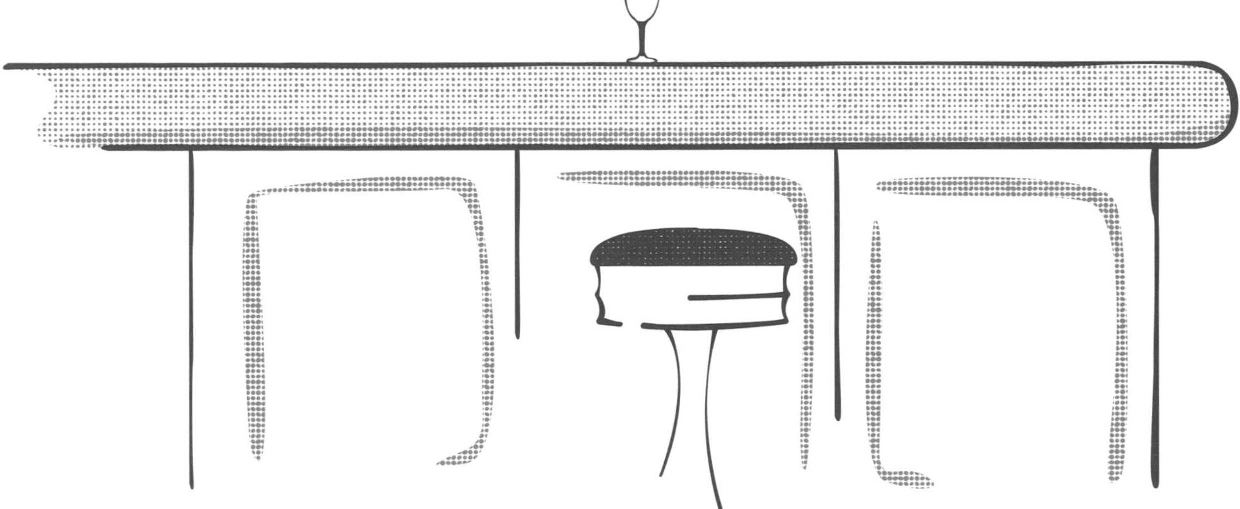

with bartenders such as Erik Adkins, Jennifer Colliau, Marcovaldo Dionysos, and Thad Vogler among those helping San Francisco's cocktail scene grow to rival that of New York.

It's an oversimplification to make too much of the differences between East Coast and West Coast bars, because especially as the cocktail movement appeared in other cities, these broad-stroke regional differences began to blur. Boston's cocktail culture—built by bars such as Eastern Standard, No. 9 Park, and, later, Drink—largely followed the New York model but with a more relaxed style, an approach mirrored in many ways by a West Coast city, Seattle. Zig Zag Café opened in Seattle around the turn of the millennium, eschewing most of the California-style culinary approaches in favor of classically rendered drinks that long ago disappeared from menus, but prepared with a Northwest nonchalance that contrasted with New York's painstakingly staged settings. And regardless of geography, aspects that all craft bars shared included a disdain for commercial mixes and soda-gun shortcuts, and a renewed use of fresh juices and natural ingredients, echoing movements in the culinary world at large.

New York and San Francisco remain the twin U.S. capitals of cocktails today, but it's a realm that's gradually spreading into a vast array of localized fiefdoms. Cities ranging from Sacramento to Charleston, Milwaukee to Louisville, and Houston to Portland now have destination-worthy cocktail scenes, and a once urban-centric scenario is increasingly spreading into suburbs and small towns.

The thirst for great cocktails isn't left behind in the international departure lounge. Under Bradsell's influence, London's cocktail scene developed largely as a contemporary of that in New York, and the cities have dueled—often to London's favor—for the crown of global cocktail capital. Around the same time, bartenders in Hamburg, Berlin and Schumann's home city of Munich were making Germany into an essential stop on any global cocktail crawl. Today, Europe's thirst for great cocktails can be quenched across the continent, as bars in Belfast and Edinburgh, Amsterdam and Paris, Rome and Bratislava have joined the liquid insurrection. Meanwhile, Tokyo establishments such as Star Bar and Bar High Five introduced a painstakingly elegant Japanese approach to the cocktail. And in Australia, Melbourne and Sydney have quietly nurtured imaginative craft-bar scenes that now rival those in London and New York, and the country has taken to exporting such talented bartenders to the U.S. as Naren Young and Sam Ross.

Which is all a long way of saying: this cocktail thing is huge. I hope you're thirsty.

My cocktail enlightenment came satori-like in the summer of 2003. Tasked with making drinks for a dinner party—it was either that, or wash the dishes—I put together an interesting-sounding recipe for a pitcher punch and poured it for my guests: the clouds above parted and the Jesus-light shone down. . . something about the experience just felt right.

Back then, there were few resources and fewer bars that had fallen as fully for cocktails as I just had. I read everything I could find—books both recent (William Grimes' *Straight Up or On the Rocks* was invaluable, as was David Wondrich's *Esquire Drinks* and, later, Ted "Dr. Cocktail" Haigh's *Vintage Spirits and Forgotten Cocktails*) and vintage (David Embury's *The Fine Art of Mixing Drinks* provided me with a cocktail philosophy, and Charles H. Baker, Jr.'s *The Gentleman's Companion* with an aesthetic sense of the art), and scoured Web forums including eGullet and the now-defunct Drinkboy forums (later reborn as The Chanticleer Society).

Eventually, I felt ready to share what I'd learned. But with nothing in the way of a relevant resumé or portfolio, I decided to build my own. Around that time, in 2005, culinary blogs were starting to take off, but nobody, it seemed, was publishing a blog devoted entirely to spirits and cocktails.

The Cocktail Chronicles launched in May of 2005, with a readership of one. As far as I knew (I wasn't tracking things very thoroughly at the start) that's the way it largely remained until two months later, when I received an e-mail from a new reader: Murray Stenson, a bartender in Seattle who'd found my site and shared a common interest in cocktail-nerd figures like Embury and Ted Saucier (the author of a racy cocktail guide titled *Bottoms Up*, published in 1951), and who invited me to come down for a drink.

I knew of Murray, of course—Robert Hess, the namesake moderator of the Drinkboy forums and another Seattle-based cocktail enthusiast, had proclaimed Murray among the best bartenders in the U.S., to little disagreement from others—and Zig Zag Café, where Murray was then working, was developing a reputation (still valid) as among the best cocktail bars in the world.

I'd visited Zig Zag several times, but was hardly a known regular. Murray may have ostensibly asked me down to talk shop (and perhaps to gauge if I had any idea what I was talking about), but he quickly turned that visit—the first of a long series

CORPSE REVIVER #2

¾ oz. gin
¾ oz. lemon juice
¾ oz. Lillet blanc
¾ oz. Cointreau
1 dash absinthe

Glass: cocktail

Garnish: cherry

Method: Shake with ice to chill (see page 24 for details), strain into chilled glass. Garnish.

over the years—into an education session for me much more than it was for him. That first night, we touched on a drink I'd been chewing over on the blog—the Corn 'n' Oil, a combo of rum and falernum (a spiced syrup from the Caribbean), and a drink that nobody as yet seemed to be mixing—and Murray showed me his approach, twisting the rum style and tweaking the drink's acidity, resulting in a ridiculously simple yet disarmingly delicious version much different from mine.

As fascinating as today's artisan-driven or tech-savvy craft-cocktail bars can be, there's also a need for cocktail comfort food—for simple yet exciting drinks that have the benefit of being delicious.

Murray was the first bartender I knew of to read The Cocktail Chronicles, and to engage with me (whether to agree or to argue) about the drinks and perspectives I shared. But what started as an experiment that could easily be abandoned when I got bored turned out a little different. The hoped-for did happen—my blog posts led to paid work, which eventually turned into a career—but the unexpected also happened. The Cocktail Chronicles was among the first small ripples that preceded a huge wave of drink-related blogs and websites that continues to flood the online world, and in the early years, a close community developed among those few of us who bonded over ingredients and recipes online.

Some of the other bloggers were bartenders, like Jamie Boudreau and Jeffrey Morgenthaler, who now own or manage some of the more prestigious bars in cocktaildom (Seattle's Canon: Whiskey and Bitters Emporium and Portland, Oregon's Clyde Common, respectively). Others were tech professionals who dabbled in cocktails and hoped to do so professionally at some point, such as Erik Ellestad, who mixed every drink in the *Savoy Cocktail Book* and more recently tended bar at Heaven's Dog and The Coachman in San Francisco; and Blair Reynolds, now the proprietor of Hale Pele tiki bar in Portland and the producer of an eponymous line of cocktail syrups. Others sought to take a passing interest in cocktails and a part-time college job behind the bar, and turn it into a full-bore profession; one was Bobby Heugel, who finished grad school and launched a cocktail blog while moving to Houston to work as a bartender. With several friends, Heugel soon opened Anvil, now a James Beard Award–nominated bar and a mainstay of Houston's robust culinary scene.

None of us post on our blogs much anymore—the social-media world has shifted, and we've all become busy at the jobs we've built, in part, as a result of those early posts. But as the cocktail renaissance started to bloom in 2006 and 2007, and as more bars and bartenders started looking for information, we were among the first few voices in a now-roaring crowd.

Ten years ago, it was rare to find bartenders who knew a Blood and Sand from a Sex on the Beach, or an Aviation from an Alabama Slammer. Today, you'll find bartenders in Little Rock, Spokane, and Tampa who won't flinch when you ask for an El Presidente or a Vieux Carre, and your Negroni is as apt to come out of a used whiskey barrel—or be served on tap, or carbonated and bottled, or mixed with a house-made vermouth of the bar manager's own design, or selected from an extensive menu of Negroni variations—as it is to be served over a diamond-shaped block of ice hand-carved as part of the bar's ice program.

This is by no means a bad thing. The Zig Zag Café used to be my solitary source of refuge when I was hankering for a balanced, well-considered drink in Seattle (and is still where you'll find me with some regularity), but I'm now within walking distance of places such as Canon—a bar with one of the hemisphere's largest selections of American whiskies—as well as specialized bars with deep rosters of rum (Rumba) or mezcal (Liberty or Barrio—choices!), staffed by bartenders who have intimate understandings of the spirits on hand and how to use them. As overwhelming as the options are becoming, I'm enthusiastic about having them.

But the cocktail experience isn't confined to today's (or tomorrow's) best bars. During Prohibition, America's deeply entrenched drinking patterns were upended; for the first time, it became widely permissible for women to visit bars (or, more accurately, it was no longer more illicit for women to be drinking than it was for men), and also for the first time, people began widely consuming their cocktails at home, behind closed curtains so that nosy neighbors wouldn't see. This wasn't just drinking at home—with all the weights and shadows that implies—but mixing drinks at home, hosting cocktail parties for friends, or simply knocking back a couple with the neighbors at the end of the day, the shoddy or smuggled liquor as intoxicating as the knowledge that taboos were being broken.

As fascinating as today's artisan-driven or tech-savvy craft-cocktail bars can be, there's also a need for cocktail comfort food—for exciting drinks that have the benefit of being delicious, and that can be easily prepared by non-professionals, without the need for a $15,000 centrifuge, a rick of used bourbon barrels in the garage for an elaborate home solera system, or jars full of bespoke bitters crowding the kitchen countertop.

This book is not a lab manual for taking the cocktail experience to a molecular level—there are people much more qualified to write those, and they have (see Resources, page 190). Nor is this an historical monograph tracing the details of our forebears as they developed the drinks we enjoy today (or forgot about long ago)—the cocktail realm already has a David Wondrich and a Jeff Berry, determined and talented writers who are better suited (and wonderfully engaging) at uncovering the stories of drinks and bars past.

What this aims to be is an approachable guide to the cocktail renaissance thus far, an overview as much as a diversion, and—as the name implies—a chronicle of a few of the cocktails that have come along the way. Some are long-established classics, others already on their way to assuming a future crown, and still others perhaps undeservedly overlooked. Regardless of the category, each of the drinks I'm passing along here is worth at least a few minutes of experimental time in your glass.

Sometimes, you want to inspect a rare bird you've never before encountered—an imaginative mix of a locally distilled gin matched with an offbeat Spanish liqueur and an equally surprising (and obscure) Italian aperitif, with the cocktail's flavors brought into focus via a few drops of bitters prepared by your bartender especially for this particular drink. That's awesome—enjoy those birds when you find them, and they are increasingly common.

But sometimes, you just want a decent drink—something that's agreeable enough, and smart enough, to do the job with which you've tasked it, and perhaps interesting enough to break the ice without being so loud or hungry for attention that it spoils the conversation.

A decent, interesting drink? On that point, I've got you covered.

ABOUT THE DRINKS

Any selection of recipes collected during such a vibrant, creative era is bound to come up short. This one is no different.

While choosing the recipes for this book, I plumbed my archives, and my memory, for cocktails that I'd sampled, admired, or meant to try over the past decade of writing about drinks. The recipes collected here are like a photo album of sorts—snapshots of people encountered over the years, with some close friends and family members depicted alongside a few dimly remembered strangers, and an unexpected photobomb popping up here and there.

Just as time can blur during a long night out, the timeline in this book has its fair share of fuzziness. I've split the recipes into chapters of old drinks (Chapter 2) and new drinks (Chapter 4), but a few recipes stray outside their allotted area, drawn tangentially by an issue or a point I'd like to make into a realm where they just seem more at home.

CORN 'N' OIL

2 oz. blackstrap rum
½ oz. falernum (see page 125)
½ oz. lime juice
1-2 dashes Angostura bitters

Glass: rocks

Garnish: lime wedge

Method: Build in ice-filled glass (see page 26 for details); stir to chill. Garnish.

Adapted by Murray Stenson, Seattle

Conversations rarely occur with the topics arranged in alphabetical order, or broken down by commonalities that nevertheless feel arbitrary and irrelevant to the matter at hand. I've embraced this more-or-less randomness with the arrangement of the drinks in this book, following themes and undercurrents that I found more compelling than simple organization based on a drink name's alphabetical order, or the drink's base spirit or general style. Should you desire greater ease of navigation (or simply need to quickly get your drink on), flip to the Recipe Guide on page 6 or the Spirit-Based Index on page 194.

Some of the drinks collected here may seem old hat to those who continually cruise the cutting edge, and there are some favorites and classics, both old and new, that I've managed to snub along the way. But what these drinks share is a common deliciousness, and a role, big or small, in the ongoing cocktail renaissance.

There's another important characteristic these drinks share: they're all reasonably approachable, and replicable by readers playing along at home. Bespoke bitters, shrubs, and syrups are now ubiquitous in craft-cocktail bars, as are centrifuge-separated juices and barrel-aged bells and whistles—and our nights out are usually the better for it. But cocktails should, above all, provide a sense of fun, and demanding that a reader purchase a new product for every recipe or spend hours (or days and weeks) preparing a single ingredient is a sure way to suck the fun right out of it.

There are a few ingredients included that you can make in your kitchen, but where possible, commercial alternatives are recommended. And spirits and ingredients were selected with an eye to utility—there are a few exceptions, but for the most part, any ingredient you see listed may be used in a number of recipes in the book.

When I first embarked on my cocktail quest, I approached written recipes as sacrosanct. In hindsight, that was kind of stupid. All recipes—especially for cocktails—should be adjusted (or abandoned) depending on the tastes of those on the receiving end. The proportions and measurements in this book largely follow established formulae, but are also tweaked to satisfy my own personal preferences. If you like your drinks drier, or sweeter, or stronger than the way I have them presented, then feel free to stray from the written recipes. It's your drink, after all—mix to your tastes, not mine.

Life is complicated—a good drink doesn't have to be. Please, enjoy...

BASIC COCKTAIL TECHNIQUE

Some bartenders spend their careers refining drink-mixing technique, and even after more than a decade of cocktail devotion, I'm still learning new approaches. Here are some basic steps to get you started mixing the drinks in this book—and be sure to look at the Cocktail Gear section (page 173) to get the right tools for the job. To fully matriculate in bar technique, check out Jeffrey Morgenthaler's *The Bar Book*, devoted entirely to the practice.

Measuring

Some bartenders never measure ingredients—instead, they free-pour when mixing a cocktail. They've often honed the skill over hours and years of practice and repetition; when mixing at home (or until you've perfected the technique), it's always best to measure. Precision is needed to achieve a workable balance; jiggers are the time-honored way of measuring ingredients, but they take a little practice—and you may wish to use two jiggers of different sizes to cover the range of measurements you'll encounter. Graduated measures such as the OXO angled measure or the banded jiggers from Cocktail Kingdom are more accurate measurement tools. Regardless of your choice, you should measure cocktail ingredients religiously.

Shaken Cocktails

Shaking chills a drink and adds dilution from the ice—essential requirements for a good cocktail—while also aerating the ingredients for a lively result. The general "shake vs. stir" rule of thumb is to shake drinks that include citrus juice or egg whites, and to stir drinks composed entirely of spirits, wines, and liqueurs (syrups are usually lumped into liqueurs). Regardless of the style of shaker you're using, add the ingredients to the shaker first, then use plenty of ice (fill the shaker at least 3⁄4 full), and shake with vigor for about 10 seconds to reach the full effect.

The "dry shake": If your drink contains egg whites, cream, or other viscous or hard-to-combine ingredients, try the so-called "dry shake": after adding your ingredients to the shaker and before filling it with ice, seal the shaker and give it a good 10-second round of shaking—this can help emulsify the ingredients and boost the froth component—then add the ice and give it another good, solid 10 seconds of shaking.

Straining shaken drinks: Even if you're using a cobbler shaker—the kind that has the little built-in strainer on the top—it's a good idea to invest in a Hawthorne strainer, the perforated, paddle-shaped tool with a spring around the edges. The spring coil should fit snugly inside the lip of your shaker; hold the strainer's body in place with your index and middle fingers, and hold the shaker body with your thumb and remaining fingers; then, without dropping everything on the floor, pour your shaken cocktail into your glass. By scrooNching your fingers back and forth on the strainer, you can make a wider or narrower gap (an "open gate" or "closed gate" in bartender parlance) for the drink to pour through, either speeding up the pour or slowing it down to limit the passage of solids such as ice chips.

Double-straining: For some drinks—those that have mint shaken into them, for example—it's wise to employ the "double strain": shake and strain the drink as usual, except while pouring from the shaker and Hawthorne strainer with one hand, use the other hand to hold a fine-meshed strainer just above the serving glass. This should filter every last solid from the drink.

Stirred Cocktails

Stirring accomplishes the same goals as shaking—chilling and dilution—but limits the aeration, resulting in drinks that have a clearer, more aesthetically pleasing appearance, and that feel smoother on the palate. Combine the ingredients in a mixing glass and fill almost to the top with ice, then slide your bar spoon down the inside of the glass and commence to stir. Because the aim is to chill the drink without bashing it to bits in a shaker, employ restraint. The bar spoon should usher the ice around in a constant circle, the spoon's stem spinning in your fingers as the bowl remains parallel with the curved sides of the glass. It should make barely a sound, aside from a steady whir and stray tinkle of metal against glass—if the ice is rattling and the liquid is splashing, you're doing it wrong. It's best to stir a cocktail longer than you'd shake one—20 to 25 seconds is usually optimal.

Straining stirred drinks: After you've stirred a Martini with effortless grace, it's considered bad form to then strain the drink through your fingers. You could use your Hawthorne strainer, but a better bet is to pick up a julep strainer, which resembles a round, oversized spoon perforated with holes. The strainer should fit inside the glass—position the concave side toward the ice, so it functions as a scoop to hold the ice back—then hold the strainer in place with your index finger while pouring the drink into the serving glass.

Muddling

Fresh herbs, fruits, or spices are sometimes mixed directly into drinks; these are times when you need to muddle. A wooden cocktail muddler is the best tool for the job, but you can also get by with a large wooden spoon or the end of a French rolling pin. There's a lot of common sense about muddling—basically you're just using a hard thing to crush a soft thing—but it requires a little finesse. Mint benefits from a light muddle before mixing a Julep, Smash, or similar drink, but it needs a light hand—too much mashing will turn the herbs to paste, resulting in an unwanted bitterness from the leaves and stems as well as flecks of green in your teeth. Instead, mint and basil benefit more from lightly bruising the leaves with a muddler, and swabbing the glass's interior with the leaves to coat it with the plant's aromatic oils. Other muddle-ables, on the other hand, can stand a little vigor—a sugar cube moistened with bitters and water needs some work in order to dissolve the sugar for an Old Fashioned, and some fruits, spices, and coffee beans only give up most of their flavor after some enthusiastic pounding. When muddling herbs, fruits or spices, it helps to add a bit of liquid—usually the syrup called for in the recipe—as this provides a medium for the muddled ingredient to contribute its flavor.

Building Drinks

Building a cocktail is as simple as it sounds: take the ingredients and skip the shaking and stirring altogether, instead just measuring and pouring directly into the serving glass. *Voila*—mixology.

Swizzling

Some drinks are swizzled with crushed ice until very cold. You'll need a bar spoon (a regular kitchen spoon won't work), or a specialized lele twig (a long stick—wood, plastic, metal, etc.—with several short branches on the end). Build the drink in your tall glass and fill it with crushed ice; stick the bar spoon or swizzle stick all the way to the bottom and position the end of the stem between the palms of your hands. Move your hands in opposite directions, causing the spoon or stick to spin in the drink; continue for at least 30 seconds, adding ice if needed. When frost forms on the outside of the glass, remove the spoon and add more crushed ice to fill.

Citrus Twists

Lemons, oranges, and grapefruits (and, to a much lesser extent, limes) have oils in the zest (the colored part of the peel) that can contribute desirable flavors and aromas; however, the white part of the peel—the pith—carries gnarly, bitter flavors. You can remove a good strip of zest with as little pith as possible using a paring knife, but it's best attempted with a vegetable peeler, which can cut a broad, long (1½ to 2 inches works well) piece of zest with minimal pith. (Channel knives—those with a small, V-shaped blade that cut long, thick, narrow strips of peel—tend to remove too much pith. Besides, those garnishes kind of look like worms.) Use organic, unwaxed fruit if possible, and cut the twist just before serving so it remains fresh and firm. (You can do minor surgery on the twist for aesthetic purposes, trimming the edges and straightening the lines with a knife, if you like.) To express the oil, twist the cut zest into a corkscrew shape while holding it about an inch above the drink's surface and just over the lip of the glass. Use as garnish, or not, depending on your mood and the drink at hand.

Flamed Twists

A few drinks require minor pyrotechnics with the twist, which adds a subtle nudge of flavor from the scorched citrus oils, along with a floor-show component. To flame a twist, hold your prepared citrus twist in one hand while positioning the flame of a lit match about an inch above the rim of the serving glass. Briskly squeeze the citrus twist so the oils spray through the flame and across the drink's surface; blow out the match and proceed as usual.

Other Garnishes

Aside from citrus twists and mint sprigs, most garnishes lend little beyond eye candy to the finished drink. But there's nothing wrong with eye candy—just be sure that the garnish doesn't distract from all your hard work. Supermarket-style maraschino cherries and giant olives stuffed with garlic cloves or blue cheese have no role in a decent cocktail—save those for your kid's sundaes or the snack table. If you wish to use cherries as garnish, opt for the dark, tart Italian cherries (the original maraschino cherries, before the food scientists got in the way) prepared by brands such as Luxardo, or rummage online for a DIY recipe for brandied cherries. Olives and cocktail onions have aesthetic appeal, though their sour salinity and room-temperature storage conditions can ruin an exactingly prepared Martini or Gibson. If you choose to use such garnishes, give them a good rinse—first in water, then in vermouth—and keep chilled until ready to use.

"Wheels" of lime or lemon are exactly what they sound like—thin, round slices of citrus, cut just before serving.

Be Gentle with Bubbles

Drinks such as the French 75 and the Old Cuban have Champagne added to the cocktail. The longstanding practice has been to prepare the cocktail and strain it into the serving glass, then add the Champagne at the end. This is still the usual approach, but in an effort to better combine the ingredients while preserving the bubbles, some bartenders instead add the Champagne to the shaker just before straining, then strain the whole shebang into the prepared glass—while others add the Champagne to the chilled glass first, then strain the cocktail on top. Try 'em all, and see what works best for you.

A Few Words on Freshness

When bartenders get together around a campfire to tell scary stories, one-armed hitchhikers and ghostly figures in the forest rarely inspire much fear. But start telling tales about bartending's bad-old days—a time of sour mix and soda guns, with waxy maraschino cherries as far as the eye can see, and nary a fresh lemon or lime in sight—and even the boldest badass feels a nervous shiver down her spine...

One of the great advances of the cocktail renaissance has been a return to the time when bartenders had little choice but to squeeze their own fruit and utilize fresh produce in order to best serve the throngs of thirsty guests. In a way, this freshness-first embrace mirrors what's long been happening in restaurant kitchens and many homes—but while the bar world may have taken its time to get on board, it's now making up for the delay with overwhelming enthusiasm. Ten years ago, it was still a surprise to find a bar juicing its own citrus before service; today, even my local dive has a Vollrath juicer on the bar, and the idea of serving preservative-packed mixers strikes many as about as appealing as dumping ashtrays (another endangered bar species) into a guest's drinks.

One of the great advances of the cocktail renaissance has been a return to the time when bartenders had little choice but to squeeze their own fruit and utilize fresh produce in order to best serve the throngs of thirsty guests.

If bars that serve hundreds of cocktails each night can deliver on the freshness front, so can any home bartender. Many recipes in this book call for lemon or lime juice; freshness is the norm, and the expectation, and your cocktails will always be better if you squeeze your citrus to order (or no longer than a few hours before serving, if mixing for a party)—pre-bottled citrus juices are crap, and should be avoided at all costs. Other fruits that are occasionally called for—pineapples, raspberries, and the like—also benefit from a fresh approach, as do herbs such as mint and basil; buy them when you need them, and use them promptly. And for reasons that are probably obvious, cocktails that call for eggs, milk, or cream will be ghastly liquid horrorshows if you ignore the importance of freshness.

And freshness extends to the other ingredients that go into your drinks. Wine-based aperitifs such as vermouth and quinquinas benefit from refrigeration after being opened, and should always be properly sealed and consumed within a few weeks, before time and oxidation can take their toll. Eschewing the food scientist's preservative arts means that most homemade syrups also have a limited life span; keep them in the fridge, as well, and toss them after a couple of weeks, before colonies of fuzzy freeloaders start developing in the bottle.

GLASSWARE

Drinking a well-crafted cocktail should at least hint at your civilized side, and that's where proper glassware comes into play. Start with the essentials—a rocks glass, a cocktail glass (the V-shaped style is poorly balanced—it's better to use a classic coupe glass or a Nick and Nora cocktail glass), and a highball glass—and build from there according to your needs and your tastes. (See Resources on p. 190 for suggestions on retailers.) And unless your drink is served with ice in the glass, be sure to chill the serving glass before using.

CHAPTER 2

NOT FORGOTTEN

Familiar classics and back-from-the-dead obscurities

Even during the darkest years of the cocktail-arid 1970s—a time when bar menus were populated by the bibulous equivalents of *Roller Boogie* and *Disco Duck*—old standards like the Old Fashioned or the Martini never really disappeared at all.

Most others, though, weren't so lucky. You could still get a Tom Collins or a Whiskey Sour in most places, to be sure, and New Orleans never gave up on its Sazeracs. But plenty of cocktails made their way into shakers and glasses—and into print—between Jerry Thomas' 1860s heyday and the turned-on, tuned-in, dropped-out 1960s. Most of those drinks had justifiably short life spans; but among the detritus of our cocktail history, there were still a number of gems that were waiting to be uncovered.

In 2004, Los Angeles-based cocktail historian Ted Haigh—known to the libationally literate as "Dr. Cocktail"—published *Vintage Spirits and Forgotten Cocktails*, the product of his extensive forays into the dust-covered shelves of mixology. That book put countless shakers in motion—mine included—as bartenders and cocktail enthusiasts began once again tasting recipes rarely mixed for generations. Along the way, further fueled by the history-tuned work of David Wondrich's *Imbibe!*, many began their own explorations of the lost-booze literature, and today's cocktail menus are filled with some of the trophies of these excursions.

Many of these unearthed drinks are now mainstays of the craft-cocktail renaissance—some enjoying fresh life close to their original form, and others having required a little recipe fine-tuning to bring them fully up to speed. And while this chapter is devoted to drinks that mostly originated before any of today's craft bartenders were born, I've sprinkled in a few newcomers that riff on, and replicate, the style of cocktails we've come to think of as classics.

GIMLET

Comfort sometimes comes in the form of gin and lime.

GIMLET

2 oz. gin
½ oz. lime cordial

Glass: cocktail
Garnish: thin lime wedge
Method: Shake with ice to chill; strain into chilled glass. Garnish.

Nobody celebrates an engagement, a promotion, or a spectacular Saturday with a Gimlet. But a breakup? The end of a workday with no more than the usual screwups? A crappy Wednesday? Those are the times when you need a Gimlet.

The Gimlet was a favored drink of Raymond Chandler, who put many of them in the hands of Philip Marlowe (and the doomed Terry Lennox) in the pages of *The Long Goodbye*. This seems fitting; with a base of gin (you can use vodka, but that'd be like recasting Shia LaBeouf in the role Humphrey Bogart made famous), and lime cordial, and nothing else, the Gimlet has the color of bad luck and resignation, and a character leaning to jaded and slightly seedy, like Robert Mitchum in worn-at-heel wingtips and a suit jacket gone shiny with age.

The Gimlet also has a little problem. As Lennox notes to Marlowe, a real Gimlet is nothing but gin and Rose's Lime Juice ("they beat Martinis hollow," says Lennox, a man who knew his beatings and his booze). But Rose's long ago followed the High Fructose Corn Syrup (HFCS) route, and a drink well-suited to assuaging disappointment now just tastes disappointing.

Some substitute fresh lime juice and sugar, but really, that's just a Gin Sour or a Gin Fix with lime—not bad, but not a Gimlet. Instead, track down some honest lime cordial, which has the tartness of the juice along with a little gamey bitterness from the peel; check the Cocktail Kitchen (page 187) for sources or instructions to make your own.

The Gimlet is more meditative than festive, more brooding than congratulatory. It may never share the Daiquiri's sense of abandon, but on a lonely afternoon, it can be a most suitable companion.

FRENCH 75

Garnish with an artillery barrage.

You might expect that a cocktail named after a deadly piece of World War I field artillery would be a nasty little ass-kicker: some combo of overproof rum, absinthe, and sketchy mezcal, loosened up with a little kerosene and garnished with a cracked rib.

But some guns pack a little glitter into the shell. Sure, the French 75 can carry enough bang to have you singing "How You Gonna Keep 'Em Down on the Farm After They've Seen Paree?" by the third round, but it's such a sultry and approachable drink that it seems to bear little malice until you notice your watch missing the next morning.

Assorted origin stories trace the French 75 to WWI-era London or Paris. The definitive place and date of its original manufacture will likely never be known, but one thing is certain: the French 75 is liquid proof that Champagne makes everything better. In this case, it's nothing more than a basic Gin Sour stretched out and amplified with a dose of bubbles. The drink may be served up, in a cocktail glass or champagne flute, but for better results, aim long—pour it over ice in a highball glass, and sip your way to kingdom come.

The French 75 is liquid proof that Champagne makes everything better.

The French 75 is also ripe for further exploration, as cocktail-renaissance bartenders have shown. For the opening menu for the paradigm-shifting cocktail bar Cure in New Orleans—a city with a bar named for the drink, and known for reinterpreting it with brandy in place of gin—Neal Bodenheimer retooled the cocktail using single-barrel bourbon and peach bitters, dubbing the impressive result the Howitzer.

Fire at will.

FRENCH 75

1 oz. gin
½ oz. lemon juice
½ oz. simple syrup
2 oz. chilled Champagne

Glass: cocktail or highball

Garnish: lemon twist

Method: Shake first three ingredients with ice to chill; strain into chilled cocktail glass or ice-filled highball glass, and top with Champagne; give a light stir to combine. Garnish.

HOWITZER

1½ oz. bourbon
½ oz. lemon juice
½ oz. simple syrup
1 dash peach bitters
2 oz. chilled Champagne

Glass: cocktail

Garnish: lemon twist

Method: Shake first four ingredients with ice to chill; strain into chilled glass. Top with Champagne; give a light stir to combine. Garnish.

Neal Bodenheimer, New Orleans

COCKTAIL ESSENTIALS

GIN

Booze with a backbone.

ALASKA COCKTAIL

2½ oz. gin
¾ oz. yellow Chartreuse
2 dashes orange bitters

Glass: cocktail

Garnish: lemon twist

Method: Stir with ice to chill; strain into chilled glass. Garnish.

Gin's been a favorite among everyone from W.C. Fields to Winston Churchill to Dorothy Parker—and when you consider the rivers of liquor that coursed down those three particular throats, this comes as high endorsement. Julia Child was a fan of gin, too, which speaks to the spirit's culinary qualities, and while it's certainly possible that without gin, cocktails would still exist, the bar would be a place barren of much imagination without the juniper-spiked spirit.

In a grossly overstated sort of way, gin is nothing more than flavored vodka—but what flavors! The only absolute in gin's botanical equation is the presence of juniper. Airy and crisp, and evocative of an alpine arbor (and, thanks to its use in gin, of your Martini-quaffing uncle), juniper has centuries of influence under its belt as both a culinary and an apothecary ingredient. The round, purplish juniper berry (more accurately, a scaly seed cone) crept into the first gin prototypes starting in the 1500s, probably introduced not only for medicinal value but to mask the rougher edges of what surely must have been some very coarse base spirit.

But juniper rarely appears in gin on its own, and this is where much of the dazzling diversity in the spirit can be found. Citrus peel, orris root, and angelica are frequent companions, lending touches ranging from bright and ethereal to deep and earthy; familiar spices such as coriander, cardamom, and licorice are not uncommon, and some contemporary gins utilize everything from almonds to lavender to cucumbers to apples to create distinctive strains of the spirit.

This presents a dilemma. When a recipe says "gin," exactly what kind of gin does it mean? As with Modern art, pornography, and Quentin Tarentino movies, the dividing line between "OMG!" and "WTF?!" will vary according to the user.

In order to determine which gin direction to go for a particular drink, it's helpful to briefly consider the different major styles that are available—but keep in mind, even within each category, there's often lots of variety to be found. Sussing out the differences between individual gins will require plenty of pitchers of Martinis and bottles of tonic water, but this kind of research is what makes cocktail exploration so fun.

LEAVE IT TO ME

1½ oz. Old Tom gin
1 Tbsp. lemon juice
2 tsp. raspberry syrup
2 tsp. maraschino liqueur
1 tsp. simple syrup

Glass: cocktail

Garnish: thin slice of lemon

Method: Shake with ice to chill; strain into chilled glass. Garnish.

London Dry Gin

The hallmark style of gin, defined by its crisp smack of juniper and the brisk background of botanicals, all built upon a base of neutral grain spirit. While London dry may be the style most often intended when we speak of gin, it's actually a more recent addition to the spirit's ranks, having originated in the 1820s and rising to prominence in the 1880s, a takeover that accelerated with the debut of the dry Martini around the turn of the last century. London dry is *the* gin for a Gin & Tonic and is a dependable go-to in a classic Martini, and has a flexible flavor that's at home in everything from a carefree Pink Lady (page 69) or Ramos Fizz (page 150 to such stiff-upper-lip mixtures as a Negroni (page 117) or a Gimlet (page 32). London dry is not a fossilized style: Venerable brands such as Tanqueray and Beefeater remain mainstays, but newer brands such as No. 3 Gin and Sipsmith prove there's still spirit in London dry's seasoned game. See the Liquor Cabinet (page 177) for more recommended brands.

Plymouth Gin

Named for the English city in which it must, by law, be distilled, this style of gin is today represented by a single brand, also conveniently named Plymouth. Dry and crisp, Plymouth gin bears many similarities to the more ubiquitous London dry, but the aroma and flavor have less prominent of a juniper presence, with a perfumed airiness and a savory earthiness picking up the slack. Plymouth is perfect in a Martini and most other drinks in which the gin's flavor takes center stage, and it functions well in any

GIN *(continued)*

CLARIDGE COCKTAIL

1 oz. gin
1 oz. dry vermouth
¼ oz. apricot liqueur
¼ oz. Cointreau

Glass: cocktail

Method: Stir with ice to chill; strain into chilled glass.

SLEEPY HOLLOW

2 oz. gin
½ oz. lemon juice
¼ oz. apricot liqueur
¼ oz. simple syrup
1 sprig fresh mint

Glass: cocktail

Method: Shake with ice to chill; double-strain into chilled glass.

cocktail that typically uses London dry. Keep an eye out for the 114-proof Plymouth Navy Strength, a muscular gin that gives up none of its delicate nature. And while not, strictly speaking, a Plymouth gin, Ford's Gin is similar in character, and in deliciousness.

Old Tom Gin

A crazy-popular style of gin near the end of the 19th century, Old Tom was all but extinct by the end of the 20th. The cocktail renaissance's quest to recover once-lost ingredients prompted Old Tom's recent return, and today this companionable style of spirit has a presence on many back bars. Constructed much like a London dry, Old Tom usually has juniper's forwardness but a different balance of background botanicals, and its defining character—a gentle sweetness—makes it a preferred style in a small subset of the cocktail world. The Martinez (page 114) is a good way to experience Old Tom's particular charms, as is a Tom Collins (page 62) or an Ephemeral (page 37), from Portland, Oregon bartender Dave Shenaut. See the Liquor Cabinet (page 177) for recommended brands.

Contemporary Gin

As the 20th century gave way to the 21st, distillers increasingly began tinkering again with gin, creating what's now a hodgepodge of spirits that's sometimes referred to as New Western gin, but is perhaps more conveniently thought of by the more generic term Contemporary gin. Whatever you wish to call the category, this fast-growing part of the gin world encompasses everything from the cucumber-and-rose-petal brightness of Hendrick's Gin from Scotland to the lavender-laced aromatics of Aviation Gin from Portland, Oregon. Often eschewing juniper's boldness for the lighter flavors of citrus and flowers (or the depths of roots and spice), this broad category of gin can be thought of in cocktail terms as "all, or none, of the above"—some work extraordinarily well in certain recipes, and not at all in others. Proceed with caution, but do proceed—there's a lot of flavorful goodness to be found.

Genever

It may seem unfair to list gin's ancestral Adam as the last on this list, but just as gin has evolved from Old Tom and London dry to the flood of Contemporary gins, genever has remained largely in stasis, and is a mystery or an afterthought in most American bars. For shame—genever (aka Holland gin) still enjoys a degree of fame in its native Netherlands and Belgium, and was a formative ingredient in the cocktail's earliest years. Made using a base of malt wine—rich and heavy, where London dry gin is crisp and dry—genever shares a juniper forwardness, but its character is more fragrant and funky, like unaged whiskey boosted with a little Hanseatic jazz. Mix a Martini with genever and you'll be suprised; but try it in an Improved Holland Gin Cocktail (page 108) or Holland Gin Daisy (below), and you'll get a glimpse of how the excitement for this cocktail thing first came about.

EPHEMERAL

1½ oz. Old Tom gin
1 oz. blanc vermouth
2 tsp. elderflower liqueur
3 dashes celery bitters

Glass: cocktail

Garnish: grapefruit twist

Method: Stir with ice to chill; strain into chilled glass. Garnish.

Dave Shenaut, Portland, Oregon

HOLLAND GIN DAISY

1½ oz. genever
¾ oz. lemon juice
¾ oz. curaçao
2 tsp. club soda

Glass: cocktail

Garnish: lemon twist

Method: Shake with ice to chill; strain into chilled glass. Garnish.

GABY DES LYS

2 oz. gin
½ oz. orgeat
2 dashes absinthe
2 dashes Angostura bitters

Glass: cocktail

Method: Shake with ice to chill; strain into chilled glass.

Adapted by Jennifer Colliau, San Francisco

A TASTE APART

HONEY

Cocktail hints from the hive.

Introducing the honey pot to the cocktail shaker can inspire Winnie the Pooh flashbacks in some, but I, for one, welcome the arrival of the drinks cart in my own personal Hundred Acre Wood.

Perhaps fearing the infantilizing of their evening soother, skeptics may view the use of honey in a drink as strictly kid's stuff. Such naysayers (pooh-poohers?) should be avoided during cocktail hour, because while honey does have the intense sweetness that first dazzled our childhood tastebuds, it also has a rugged boldness of flavor that meshes magically with those found in the spirits realm.

Prohibition-era tipplers sanded the rough edges off bad gin by mixing it with lemon juice and honey to make the Bee's Knees, and other early and mid-20th century drinks made trips to the honeycomb de rigueur—as evinced by the Scotch whisky-laced De Rigueur, which appeared in 1927's *Here's How*, and by its American kin, the Brown Derby, named for the Los Angeles restaurants popular in the mid-20th century. Honey's flower-driven flavor power also caught the eye of drinks scribe Charles H. Baker, Jr., who utilized it in the rum-based Bumble Bee; try the improved version shown here, by San Francisco bartender Erik Adkins.

Using honey in a cocktail requires less caution than that required to squeeze it from a bee: just be sure to measure carefully (as always), and give the shaker an extra few swirls or stirs before adding ice to ensure the viscous sugar dissolves. Even better: make a bottle of honey syrup (see page 186) and stow it in the fridge; it'll help make your cocktail party the most happening thing in Pooh Corner.

BROWN DERBY

2 oz. bourbon
1 oz. grapefruit juice
1/2 oz. honey syrup

Glass: cocktail

Method: Shake with ice to chill; strain into chilled glass.

Variation: Swap blended Scotch whisky for the bourbon, and you've got a **De Rigueur**.

BUMBLE BEE

1½ oz. mild Jamaican rum
½ oz. bold Jamaican rum
¾ oz. lime juice
¾ oz. honey syrup
½ oz. egg white

Glass: cocktail

Garnish: Angostura bitters, orange twist

Method: Combine ingredients in shaker and dry shake without ice until foamy; add ice and shake well to chill. Strain into chilled glass; dot surface with Angostura bitters; squeeze orange twist over drink and discard.

Adapted by Erik Adkins, San Francisco

LAST WORD

A long-lost oddball becomes a global superstar.

For a once-obscure cocktail, the Last Word sure gets around.

At the turn of the millennium, the Last Word was absent from pretty much every bar menu in the world. But shortly after Seattle's Zig Zag Café added Murray Stenson to its bartender roster in 2001, Stenson went rummaging through his library of midcentury bar manuals in search of menu ideas that would help Zig Zag stand out from the Cosmo-pouring crowd.

Assuming nobody had served the Last Word in 50 years, Murray Stenson put it on Zig Zag's menu and stood back to see what would happen.

Long a fan of the French herbal liqueur Chartreuse, Stenson noticed a promising recipe in the pages of *Bottoms Up*, Ted Saucier's 1951 book of drink recipes (and risque illustrations), the drink details compiled from hotels and restaurants across the country. According to Saucier, the Last Word recipe traced to the Detroit Athletic Club, and was introduced to them by vaudeville performer Frank Fogarty. Assuming (probably correctly) that nobody had served the Last Word in 50 years, Stenson put it on Zig Zag's list, and stood back to see what would happen.

Today, the Last Word graces bar menus from Sydney to Amsterdam to Spokane. The drink has offshoots and variations (including those on page 158), which you can order from virtually any craft-cocktail bar worldwide, including the bars in Edinburgh, Scotland; Christchurch, New Zealand; San Antonio, Texas; Ann Arbor, Michigan; and Livermore, California that have taken the Last Word as their namesake.

Four ingredients, in equal parts, and impressively delicious—how did we get along without this for so many years?

LAST WORD

3/4 oz. gin
3/4 oz. lime juice
3/4 oz. green Chartreuse
3/4 oz. maraschino liqueur

Glass: cocktail

Method: Shake with ice to chill; strain into chilled glass.

HANKY PANKY

Gin and vermouth tame the bitter beast.

HANKY PANKY

2 oz. gin
1 oz. sweet vermouth
¼ oz. Fernet-Branca

Glass: cocktail
Garnish: orange twist
Method: Stir ingredients with ice to chill; strain into chilled glass. Garnish.

Fernet-Branca can be a beneficent bully. An Italian liqueur crafted as a digestive in the mid-19th century, Fernet-Branca is made with botanicals including saffron and rhubarb, cardamom and chamomile. In concert, these ingredients perform a feat of gastro-wizardry, adeptly dispelling the digestive maladies that come from overindulgence.

That's the beneficent part—and the bully? Fernet-Branca's elbow-throwing onslaught of eucalyptus-laced bitterness can be so extreme that at first encounter, it may be wise to establish a safe word.

The Hanky Panky appeals to this petulant bear's soft side. Originating in London in the early 20th century, the Hanky Panky was first crafted by Ada Coleman at the Savoy Hotel's American Bar. Matching Fernet-Branca's brusque boldness with the more delicate botanical tones of gin and sweet vermouth, the drink matches and softens the liqueur's assertive tones. In this medium, Fernet-Branca still isn't quite cuddly—but it's definitely fun to be around.

CREOLE CONTENTMENT

Madeira and brandy prove the best of friends.

CREOLE CONTENTMENT

1½ oz. brandy
1 oz. madeira
½ oz. maraschino liqueur
1 dash orange bitters

Glass: cocktail
Garnish: cherry
Method: Stir ingredients with ice; strain into chilled glass. Garnish.

The history of the cocktail abounds with individuals whose influence hasn't been truly felt until the modern day. Prime example: Charles H. Baker, Jr., a journalist, globetrotter, and bon vivant fully deserving of legend, whose mid-20th century writings on food and drink risked extinction until the craft-cocktail renaissance revived his once-flagging legacy.

Baker deserves his own entry here—you'll find it on page 51—but here's a taste of something he introduced: the Creole Contentment. As Baker wrote in his *Gentleman's Companion* from 1939, his introduction to this drink came by way of an Episcopal bishop from Washington, though it purportedly originated in New Orleans—a city also deserving of its own entry (see page 90).

SHERRY COBBLER

A 19th century favorite is ready for its 21st century close-up.

In 1888, "Where Did You Get That Hat?" was setting crowds on fire after its debut at Miner's Eighth Avenue Theatre, Levi P. Morton was elected Vice President of the United States, and—according to barman Harry Johnson in that year's edition of his *Bartenders' Manual*—the Sherry Cobbler was "without doubt the most popular beverage in the country."

Ask a musician today to hum a few bars of the onetime hit, or a politician for his thoughts on Morton's legacy, and you'll likely draw a blank stare. But ask a craft-cocktail bartender for a Sherry Cobbler, and you'll probably be greeted with a short lesson on the beauty of sherry, as well as one hell of a drink.

One of the simplest drinks to come out of the 19th century, the Cobbler is nothing more than a glass of sweetened wine, served over pebble-size crushed ice (likely the "cobble" in the Cobbler) and prettied up with citrus slices and fresh berries. Sherry was the reigning king of the Cobbler, but French reds, German whites and even dessert wines and Champagne were fair game (as were whiskey or brandy, but really, the Cobbler is wine's prime turf).

A firm handshake compared to a cocktail's hearty backslap, the Cobbler deserves its return not only because of its low-octane agreeability, but because of its approachability of flavor. Today's craft bartenders have already caught on—Bellocq, which opened in New Orleans in 2011, built its menu around the basic Cobbler—and it's just as welcome at home. Aim for a drier style of sherry—I like amontillado or oloroso in mine—but you can skew sweet with a Pedro Ximenez; just remember to pull back on the added sugar. And don't skimp on the berries—such simple drinks appreciate the extra adornment.

SHERRY COBBLER

4 oz. sherry
1 Tbsp. sugar, to taste
2 slices orange

Glass: Collins

Garnish: mint sprig, lemon wheel, berries in season

Method: Shake ingredients (including orange slices) with ice to chill; double-strain into Collins glass filled with crushed ice. Garnish.

Variations: Pretty much any fortified wine (or unfortified, for that matter) will work in a Cobbler—just tweak the sugar accordingly.

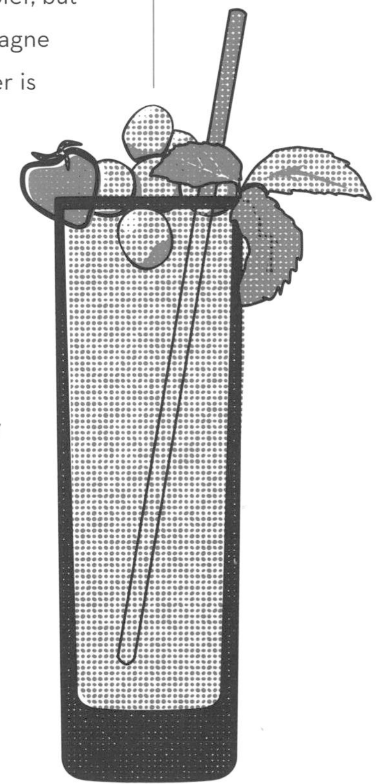

BLOOD AND SAND

Spoiler alert: the recipe includes neither.

BLOOD AND SAND

1 oz. blended Scotch whisky
1 oz. orange juice
¾ oz. sweet vermouth
¾ oz. Cherry Heering

Glass: cocktail

Garnish: cherry

Method: Shake ingredients with ice to chill; strain into chilled glass. Garnish.

Tips: Give the whisky's power a jolt by bumping the Scotch to 1½ oz. and dropping everything else to ¾ oz., or keep the above proportions and instead swap a blended malt like Great King Street or a single malt like Highland Park 12 for the blended Scotch. You can also add a teaspoon of lemon juice to give it a little more pep, or substitute blood-orange juice for the OJ. And if you put a slice of orange in the shaker before mixing, it'll give the cocktail an added—and welcome—dimension.

Some legacies deserve permanence, while others could use a little cleanup.

On the permanence side there's Rudolf Valentino, the actor who, in 1922, starred as an ill-fated matador in *Blood and Sand*. In 1926, just a few years before the advent of talkies would destroy the careers of many of his co-stars, Valentino shared that *Blood and Sand* was his favorite of his films; a few days later, he was dead from peritonitis, leaving only the legacy of a dashingly handsome star who would never age, and whose voice would never be heard.

The Blood and Sand cocktail, however, has a less-illustrious legacy. Its print debut was in 1930 as an equal-parts recipe in the *Savoy Cocktail Book*, but following its revival during the cocktail renaissance, the Blood and Sand began to suffer from its own imperfections. Fact of the matter, the Savoy's Blood and Sand just isn't all that great. Oh, it can be nice when made well, but "nice" isn't the same thing as "holy hell, that's scrumptious."

But craft bartenders like to tinker, and many have taken a crack at the Blood and Sand's formula. Some boost the whisky's profile by increasing its volume in the drink as well as by utilizing smokier, burlier styles. Others tweak the orange juice's insipid contribution, either swapping in the juice of blood oranges or adding lemon to the mix; and others just chuck three of the ingredients down the sink and drink the whisky on its own without all the fanfare.

Nothing against straight Scotch, but the Blood and Sand's legacy is one worth preserving. Tip one to Valentino, and don't view the recipe specs with anything resembling rigidity.

HOTEL NACIONAL SPECIAL

A Cuba-born mixture ripe for reinvention.

Like aspiring actors and athletes, some cocktails require a little coaching to reach their full potential.

Consider the Hotel Nacional Special. Introduced to the world in the 1930s by Wil P. Taylor, manager of Havana's Hotel Nacional, and memorably conveyed via the florid prose of Charles H. Baker, Jr. (see page 51), the Hotel Nacional Special is a Cuban-esque blend of rum and lime, given fleshy lusciousness with the flavors of apricot and pineapple.

The signature drink of Havana's Hotel Nacional de Cuba, cleaned up and polished for the palates of today.

Just one problem: As with many of the recipes he related, Baker's formula for the Hotel Nacional Special torques toward lameness. Enter the coaches: San Francisco bartender Erik Adkins and his colleague Jennifer Colliau. A fan of Baker's works, Adkins revamped many of the writer's recipes for Bay Area restaurants and bars including Slanted Door and (the sadly departed) Heaven's Dog. Using the splendid pineapple gomme syrup from Colliau's Small Hand Foods, Adkins translated Baker's promising-though-misguided formula into something much more palatable.

Palatable? Hell, I'd drink a tanker of them if I could.

The Hotel Nacional Special has made the rounds in recent years, with various takes on the original. One inspired riff is the Nacional, from Portland, Oregon bartender Jeffrey Morgenthaler. As he did with the drink's name, Morgenthaler slightly abbreviates and simplifies the recipe, swapping pineapple's sunny brightness for the fruity pop of peach bitters. It works.

HOTEL NACIONAL SPECIAL

1½ oz. aged rum
¾ oz. lime juice
¾ oz. pineapple gomme syrup
½ oz. apricot liqueur

Glass: cocktail

Garnish: thin slice of lime

Method: Shake with ice to chill, strain into chilled glass.

Tips: An aged Puerto Rican rum such as Bacardi 8 works well here, as does Banks 7 Golden Age.

Adapted by Erik Adkins, San Francisco

NACIONAL

1½ oz. white rum
1 oz. lime juice
¾ oz. apricot liqueur
¾ oz. simple syrup
2 dashes peach bitters

Glass: cocktail

Garnish: lime wheel

Method: Shake with ice to chill; strain into chilled glass.

Jeffrey Morgenthaler, Portland, Oregon

COCKTAIL STYLE

DRINKS OF GOD

Cocktails with a dab of divinity.

CHAMPS ELYSEES

1½ oz. brandy
½ oz. green Chartreuse
¾ oz. lemon juice
½ oz. simple syrup
2 dashes Angostura bitters

Glass: cocktail

Method: Shake with ice to chill; strain into chilled glass.

PAGO PAGO

1½ oz. amber Puerto Rican rum
½ oz. lime juice
½ oz. green Chartreuse
¼ oz. white crème de cacao
3 cubes fresh pineapple

Glass: cocktail

Method: Shake all ingredients with ice to crush pineapple and to chill drink; double-strain into chilled glass.

Adapted by Jeff Berry

With their sleeve tattoos, late-night habits, and, often, a gleeful predilection for sin of all stripes, most craft bartenders are hardly the ecclesiastical type. But while bartenders at Sunday-morning service may be as scarce as Vodka Tonics at Bourbon & Branch, liqueurs that first flowed inside monastery walls are among the things that can turn a drinker's eyes heavenward.

Just as monastic Belgian brothers developed (and in some cases, still make) some of the most flavorful beers in creation, monks in France long ago crafted some of the most distinctive liqueurs to populate the back bar. While these liqueurs may have originated as tonics or medicinals—much like other botanical-rich mixtures such as vermouth and quinquinas—generations of bartenders have reached for these vivid-tasting liqueurs to give their cocktails a little boost of blessedness.

> ***These liqueurs may have originated as tonics or medicinals, but bartenders have long reached for these bottles to give cocktails a boost of blessedness.***

Chartreuse—a liqueur that loaned its name to a color—traces its origins to the early 17th century, when Carthusian monks began making an *elixir de longue vie*, or elixir of long life, at their monastery in Massif de la Chartreuse in southeastern France. The recipe continued to evolve until the mid-18th century, when the monks perfected a blend of more than 130 botanicals—the precise ingredients are still a close-kept secret, but the list likely includes basil, mint, and hyssop—in a spirit base that, even when sweetened, still weighs in at a clock-cleaning 110 proof (yellow Chartreuse, a gentler 80-proof version sweetened with honey, debuted in 1838). In addition to the yellow and green styles which are aged 3 to 5 years, there are VEP versions of each in circulation, with the liqueur spending 10 to 15 years in oak. Though the day-to-day business practices are handled by a separate company, the Carthusian monks still own the liqueur and oversee the production process.

The history of Bénédictine dates back even earlier, to 1510, when Dom Bernardo Vincelli purportedly crafted the Cognac-based mixture in the Abbey of Fécamp. The recipe was thought lost during the French Revolution, but production of the liqueur resumed in 1863. Like Chartreuse, Bénédictine has a vivid and elaborate flavor, but where Chartreuse veers herbaceous and vegetal, Bénédictine looms moody and soft, flavored with 27 plants and spices (again, the precise list is kept proprietary, and the producers even maintain a museum of knockoffs and imitations) including coriander, saffron, and vanilla.

With such depth of range and intricately structured flavors, these liqueurs give otherwise two-dimensional cocktails a 3-D edge. Chartreuse laces classics including the Bijou (page 60) and the Last Word (page 39), as well as contemporary cocktails like the Coin Toss, from New York bartender Phil Ward, and the elegant Chartreuse Swizzle, from Marcovaldo Dionysos (page 126). New Orleans bartenders have shown particular fondness for Bénédictine, using it in drinks such as the Vieux Carre (page 93) and Cocktail à la Louisiane (page 91), and it also has an affinity for Scotch whisky, as tasted in the Bobby Burns (page 46).

It's perfectly appropriate to be thankful when handed a good cocktail. But when sipping a mix flavored with one of these monk-developed liqueurs, it's not out of place to genuflect and reply, "thank god for that."

DIAMONDBACK

1½ oz. rye whiskey
¾ oz. applejack
½ oz. yellow Chartreuse

Glass: rocks

Method: Stir with ice to chill; strain into glass filled with ice.

COIN TOSS

2 oz. full-bodied amber rum
¾ oz. Carpano Antica Formula vermouth
¼ oz. yellow Chartreuse
¼ oz. Bénédictine
2 dashes Peychaud's bitters

Glass: cocktail

Method: Stir ingredients with ice to chill; strain into chilled glass.

Variation: The Coin Toss may also be made with rye whiskey, applejack, brandy, or blended Scotch in place of the rum.

Philip Ward, New York City

ROB ROY & BOBBY BURNS

(Bagpipes optional.)

ROB ROY

2 oz. Scotch whisky
1 oz. sweet vermouth
2 dashes orange bitters

Glass: cocktail

Garnish: orange twist

Method: Stir with ice to chill; strain into chilled glass. Garnish.

Variation: Peychaud's bitters instead of orange. Try it.

BOBBY BURNS

2 oz. Scotch whisky
3/4 oz. sweet vermouth
1/4 oz. Bénédictine
2 dashes Angostura bitters

Glass: cocktail

Garnish: orange twist

Method: Stir with ice to chill; strain into chilled glass. Garnish.

Variation: Drink like David Embury, and swap Drambuie for the Bénédictine.

It's an annoying tendency—to me, anyway—that cocktails made with Scotch or Irish whiskies must often be hung with a moniker somehow related (often awkwardly) with the spirit's home country. The Blarney Stone, the Shamrock, the Paddy? All based on Irish whiskey, and all about as authentically Celtic as chicken vindaloo. And the Highland, the Thistle, the Glasgow—see what I mean?

The Rob Roy and the Bobby Burns may fit the nomenclature pattern—dressed up with names that boast their Scottish connection as delicately as do the gaudy plaid tam o'shanters displayed outside souvenir shops on Edinburgh's Royal Mile—but in the glass they're solid cocktails, with plenty worth experiencing.

The Rob Roy is the older of the duo, coming out of the closing years of the 19th century and created to honor (or to capitalize upon) an operetta of the day roughly based upon the story of Robert Roy MacGregor. Simply a Manhattan that swaps Scotch whisky for the Manhattan's rye or bourbon, the Rob Roy has its own difficult-to-define charm. Mildly smoky, if you go that way with your whisky (and you should—a brawnier blend like Black Grouse, or even a lightly peated single malt like Highland Park work well here), the Rob Roy can wear its Scotch-whisky flavor proudly, without too many other ingredients mucking up its majesty.

Several decades after its debut, the Rob Roy spawned the Bobby Burns—a spittin' image son of a cocktail that has its mother's eyes, appearing via a few dashes of Bénédictine (though David Embury's 1949 *The Art of Mixing Drinks* suggests substituting Drambuie). The liqueur softens the drink's edges a tad, and it gives the Bobby Burns a wider conversational repertoire.

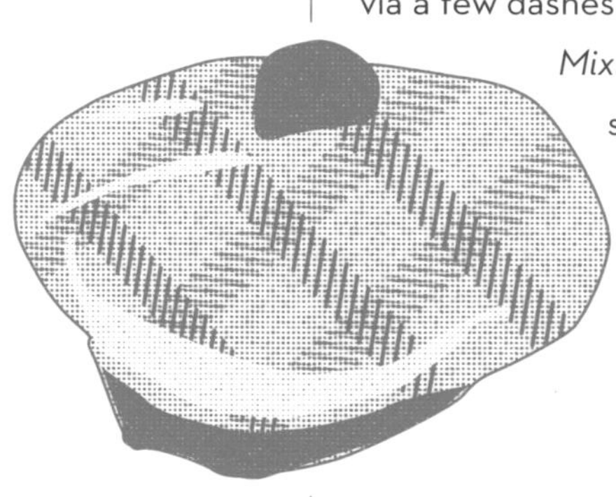

PICON PUNCH

There are worse ways to spend a summer afternoon.

First, the bad news: If you live in North America, making a true-to-form Picon Punch is gonna take some work, and maybe an international plane ticket.

Now, the good: There's no reason to sweat the small details. If you're comfortable with soft misdemeanors—like crossing the street against the light, or preferring the *Star Wars* sequels to the originals—you'll have no problem enjoying a not-entirely-according-to-Hoyle Picon Punch.

Beloved by Basque shepherds and the signature drink of Bakersfield, California (complicated story), the Picon Punch uses as its base an ingredient not currently imported: the bittersweet French aperitif Amer Picon. No problem—workarounds exist (see page 181). Between the bubbles, brandy's soft thrum, and the bittersweet bite of the liqueur, the Picon Punch proves a most agreeable summer companion.

It's tall, it's refreshing, it's mildly bitter. Serve with a straw and a sunny August afternoon.

PICON PUNCH

2 oz. Amer Picon (or substitute)
1 tsp. grenadine
Chilled club soda
½ oz. brandy

Glass: highball

Method: Mix first two ingredients in an ice-filled highball glass and fill almost to top with club soda; stir. Float brandy on top of drink.

LUCIEN GAUDIN

For those times that require a cocktail named for an Olympic fencing champ.

There are two things to know about this drink. First, the name: Lucien Gaudin was a French fencer, and apparently a damn good one. He medaled at the Olympics in 1924 and 1928, with four golds and two silvers in both foil and épée (whatever that is), and he also had French and international champion titles under his belt.

Second, the cocktail: I have no idea of what the connection (if any) between Gaudin and the drink may be, or if he ever even knew of its existence. The drink does likely flow from Europe—this recipe appeared in a French book in 1929, and Campari was scarce stateside until decades after the war—and its gin-and-Campari pairing marks a clear relationship to the Negroni.

But the drink is its own creature, and before dinner, a welcome diversion from the norm. *En garde. . .*

LUCIEN GAUDIN

1 oz. gin
½ oz. Campari
½ oz. Cointreau
½ oz. dry vermouth

Glass: cocktail

Garnish: orange twist

Method: Stir well to chill; strain into chilled glass. Garnish.

COCKTAIL ESSENTIALS

APPLEJACK & CALVADOS

Adam & Eve may have been onto something.

APPLEJACK RABBIT

1½ oz. applejack
¼ oz. orange juice
¼ oz. lemon juice
¼ oz. maple syrup

Glass: cocktail

Method: Shake with ice to chill; strain into chilled glass.

DIKI DIKI

1½ oz. Calvados
¾ oz. grapefruit juice
½ oz. Swedish punsch

Glass: cocktail

Method: Shake with ice to chill; strain into chilled glass.

The world doesn't always cooperate when you're in the mood for a drink of whiskey or a glass of gin. Our New World ancestors knew the situation well: back in the days before steamships and railroads (not to mention FedEx, and daily nonstops from LAX to CDG), if you wanted a swallow of something with some action to it, you usually had little choice but to go locavore.

Apples were among the first crops cultivated in the American colonies, and for generations, apple orchards were a key cultural touchstone—markers of permanence and civilization where before there were none. But few early apples were destined for pies or the teacher's desk. Until the late 19th century, most apples grown in the U.S. were squeezed for their juice, which—in an era before refrigeration and pasteurization—easily and quickly fermented into cider, a mainstay of the early American diet. In addition to being a safe alternative to often-sketchy water and a valuable source of nutrients, cider could convey a buzz ranging from nonexistent to noble.

From Normandy to New Jersey, distillers have long squeezed a spirituous bang from the apple.

But where there's a buzz, you'll find folks looking for a bang; enter applejack. The most rustic (and desperate) of distillers skipped the still altogether, instead freezing a container of hard cider by leaving it outside in winter, then skimming the alcoholic slush from the watery ice. But distilling technology also came into play, most notably with the arrival in New Jersey of William Laird in 1698. Laird began distilling brandy from New Jersey's then-abundant apple orchards, and in 1780 his descendants established the distillery that bears the family name. Today, the Laird family still operates the distillery, producing an estimable apple brandy and an applejack (made since the 1970s by softening the brandy's boldness with neutral spirits) under the Laird's label.

American apple brandy appears in most cocktail manuals (including this one) as "applejack," and in some as "apple whiskey," owing to the spirit's similarity in flavor and its brown, barrel-aged hue, as well as to its function in cocktails: swap apple brandy for some or all of the whiskey in a cocktail such as a Manhattan or an Old Fashioned, and you've still got one hell of a drink. Laird's Applejack still works fine in many drinks, but reach for an all-apple brandy (Laird's 100-proof gets a big thumbs-up) if you have the option.

Of course, American distillers were simply rediscovering what had long been known in Normandy. There, distillers produce Calvados, a sometimes fiery and often fine style of spirit that likewise has versatility in the shaker. Unlike American apple brandy, which is typically made with familiar styles of "table" apples and is often aged much like bourbon, French Calvados is made from varieties of tart or bitter cider apples (and often bears a touch of pear), and is aged in Limousin oak casks in a similar fashion as other French brandies. See the Liquor Cabinet (page 177) for recommended brands.

SYNCOPATION

1 oz. brandy

½ oz. Calvados

½ oz. Cointreau

½ oz. lemon juice

1 dash Angostura bitters

Glass: cocktail

Method: Shake with ice to chill; strain into chilled glass.

NEWARK

2 oz. applejack (Laird's bonded apple brandy works best)

1 oz. sweet vermouth

¼ oz. Fernet-Branca

¼ oz. maraschino liqueur

Glass: cocktail

Method: Stir with ice to chill; strain into chilled glass.

John Deragon and Jim Meehan, New York City

WIDOW'S KISS

Best served with a chair, a fire, and a furrowed brow.

WIDOW'S KISS

1½ oz. Calvados
¾ oz. yellow Chartreuse
¾ oz. Bénédictine
2 dashes Angostura bitters

Glass: cocktail

Garnish: cherry

Method: Stir well to chill; strain into chilled glass. Garnish.

Variation: The liqueurs can be pushy. Feel free to prune them back to ¼ oz. each, and to nudge the Calvados to 2 oz. And Laird's 100-proof apple brandy also works swimmingly in place of the Calvados.

Some drinks are bright and frisky, others bold and burly. And still others sing sad, beautiful ballads and are bedecked with decaying flowers, and continue to whisper at the edge of your attention even when it's wandered elsewhere.

Drinks historian Ted Haigh, under his alter ego of Dr. Cocktail, has called the Widow's Kiss a "cocktail of fall turning toward winter," and certainly this drink bears the leaves-in-the-wind character of time quickly passing and important things left unsaid and undone. But the Widow's Kiss isn't silent in its melancholy—rather, it's a conversational sort of drink, the kind of liquid companion who unwinds stories about a perfect night in Dublin long ago with two sisters from Reykjavik and a bartender who got off work early, and of how the night unfolded in such a way that all involved are still talking about it even decades after dawn arrived and everyone departed their separate ways.

The drink hails from the final years of the 19th century, and was created by George Kappeler, who introduced it in print in his *Modern American Drinks* from 1895. A German immigrant, Kappeler was head bartender at New York's Holland House hotel, and the Widow's Kiss—like others from Kappeler and his bartending countrymen including Harry Johnson, Leo Engel, and "The Only William" Schmidt—bears a richness of character and a bewildering baroque nature, the product of using two vividly flavored French liqueurs upon a base of French apple brandy.

This is not a drink for long July evenings, or for festive holiday gatherings. But between October and February, when daylight has all but given up against the lingering darkness, the Widow's Kiss is patiently waiting with another long story to share.

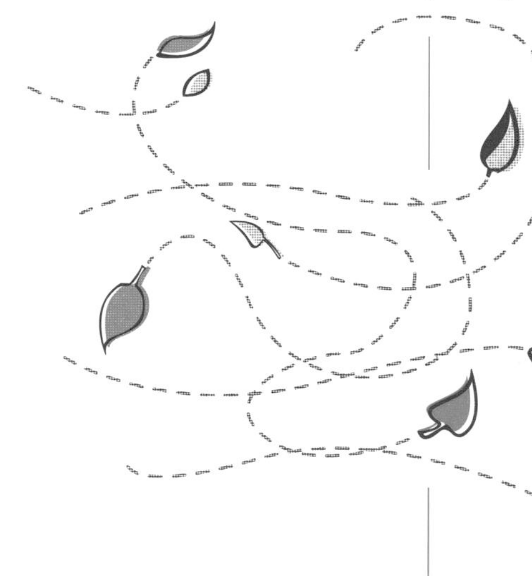

A NOT-QUITE-PERFECT GENTLEMAN

The libational legacy of Charles H. Baker, Jr.

"Watch this one when out under the moon in a desert overnight camp, riding camels out across the vast dunes, or strolling in the moonlight around the Sphinx with some congenial young woman companion."

The moonlight; the Sphinx; the desert night; and an agreeable companion—a typical cast of characters in a passage by mid-20th century journalist and roving bon vivant Charles H. Baker, Jr. That Baker wove drinks into these narratives—the "this one" in the above paragraph, a bizarre but not-without-its-charms mixture of gin, apricot brandy, and absinthe, dubbed the Sahara Glowing Heart Cocktail—seems almost beside the point when such tales take the reader from Mindinao and North Africa to the waters off Cuba and the sawtoothed spine of the Andes.

But Baker's drinks, and his writing, have proven a powerful force in the cocktail renaissance, and cocktails sourced from his books—1939's *The Gentleman's Companion: Around the World with Jigger, Beaker & Flask* and the follow-up 1951 *The South American Gentleman's Companion*—include today's craft-cocktail standards such as Remember the Maine and the Hotel Nacional Special (page 43).

Baker's recipes typically suffer one major drawback—the drinks quite often suck—but the tinkering of bartenders such as Erik Adkins (who crafted a Baker-themed bar menu for San Francisco's now-shuttered Heaven's Dog in 2009) and the biographical research of St. John Frizell, a writer and owner of Fort Defiance restaurant and bar in Brooklyn, have given Baker's recipes and reputation a helpful burnish.

The cocktails related by Baker often need some help, but his stories don't. With a Gin Fizz Tropical (page 80) in one hand and Baker's florid tales of excursions in Argentina and Tangier in the other, all that's required is an open imagination and a taste for a little adventure.

REMEMBER THE MAINE

2 oz. rye whiskey
3/4 oz. sweet vermouth
2 tsp. Cherry Heering
1/2 tsp. absinthe

Glass: cocktail

Garnish: cherry

Method: Stir with ice to chill; strain into chilled glass. Garnish.

PISCO APRICOT TROPICAL

1 1/2 oz. pisco
3/4 oz. lime juice
3/4 oz. pineapple gomme syrup
1/2 oz. apricot liqueur
2 dashes Angostura bitters

Glass: cocktail

Garnish: lime twist

Method: Shake with ice to chill; strain into chilled glass. Garnish.

Adapted by Erik Adkins, San Francisco

COCKTAIL STYLE

THE JULEP & THE SMASH

Essential drinks established upon the magnificence of mint.

MINT JULEP

2-3 oz. decent bourbon (the cheap stuff has no place here)
8-10 leaves fresh mint
1-2 tsp. sugar or simple syrup (to taste)

Glass: julep cup or highball

Method: Mix sugar with a little water in the bottom of a glass (or use simple syrup). Add mint leaves and gently bruise using a muddler or wooden spoon, lightly swabbing the inside of the glass with the mint oil without grinding the leaves into paste. Add bourbon and stir to mix. Fill glass with crushed, pebble-size ice, and stir with bar spoon until mixture is cold and frost appears on the sides of the glass. Add more ice to keep the glass full to the brim, and garnish with a large sprig or two of mint; serve with a short straw.

Variations: Substitute rye whiskey—or brandy, or genever, or absinthe, or Champagne—for the bourbon. Or, get fancy—to make a **Prescription Julep,** use 1½ oz. rye whiskey and ½ oz. brandy, or make a **Georgia Mint Julep** by using 1 oz. each of brandy and aged peach brandy. For extra hoopla, dash a teaspoon of fragrant Jamaican rum atop one of the whiskey- or brandy-based versions.

"Then comes the zenith of man's pleasure. Then comes the julep—the mint julep. Who has not tasted one has lived in vain. The honey of Hymettus brought no such solace to the soul; the nectar of the gods is tame beside it. It is the very dream of drinks, the vision of sweet quaffings."

Such did Kentucky-born journalist and humorist Irvin S. Cobb relate as part of an elaborately stem-winding series of observations and anecdotes in his *Own Recipe Book* from 1939. Cobb understandably had an enthusiasm for the Mint Julep—in this particular case, because he was paid to (the book was commissioned by Frankfort Distilleries)—but even without the mercenary motivation, his reverence for the Julep is both warranted, and widely shared.

The Mint Julep is among the most approachable of antiques. Dating back more than two centuries, and with the most basic of formulae, the Julep has delighted drinkers ranging from Cobb to Henry Clay to a visiting Charles Dickens, who in his letters recounted a night spent sipping a birdbath-size Julep in the company of Washington Irving in 1842.

Dickens and Irving tapped this mighty Julep in Baltimore—surprising territory, perhaps, to find the Julep, given the enduring tussle between Kentucky and Virginia regarding the drink's true home, and its popular connection with the genteel environs of rural planters rather than the dirt and bustle of an urban seaport. But for much of the 19th century—until the Civil War blew everything to hell—the Julep was likely the most popular drink in America, enjoyed as enthusiastically in Chicago and New York as in Richmond and Louisville.

Of course, our ancestors took a more flexible view of the Julep than do dogmatic drinkers such as Cobb. Bourbon has ruled the Julep cup for more than a century, but drinkers of the past were less picky. Rye whiskey makes for an admirable Julep, as does Cognac (which preceded bourbon on the Julep throne), and a mixture of the two (as cocktail historian David Wondrich related when he uncovered the Prescription Julep) is absolutely magical. Aged peach brandy also appeared in many antebellum Juleps, typically in concert with brandy; and the rich aromatics of Jamaican rum even graces a Julep, when dashed or spooned atop the preparation. And while that rumbling you hear is Cobb spinning in his grave, a malty Holland gin (or genever) makes for a memorable Julep, as does absinthe, and swapping the hard stuff for a good dose of Champagne is a fine way to spend an afternoon.

For much of the 19th century—until the Civil War blew everything to hell—the julep was likely the most popular drink in America, enjoyed as enthusiastically in Chicago and New York as in Richmond and Louisville.

But all the reverence surrounding the Julep can be overwhelming—and that's possibly why the Smash was invented. As Jerry Thomas noted in his 1862 *Bar-Tender's Guide*, the Smash is "simply a Julep on a small plan". Without the noble baggage of the Julep, the Smash is free to be its own creature, and is easily knocked together without need for superfluous ceremony.

Sugar, mint, and liquor may seem feeble foundations for a civilization—but on such concoctions a young republic was nursed. Sip a few, and taste history.

BRANDY SMASH

2 oz. brandy
1 tsp. simple syrup
8-10 mint leaves

Glass: rocks

Garnish: fresh mint sprig

Method: Add simple syrup and mint leaves to glass and gently bruise mint with a muddler. Add brandy and stir to combine; fill glass with crushed ice and stir again to chill and mix. Garnish.

Variations: Whiskey works as a substitute, of course, as does a nice, gentle aged rum, as does most anything else you're in the mood for.

BLACK JACK

Drawing on the talents of the original energy drink.

BLACK JACK (original)

½ oz. cold coffee
½ oz. brandy
½ oz. kirschwasser

Glass: cocktail

Garnish: sugared rim

Method: Rub cut lemon peel around the rim of the glass and dip glass lip in superfine sugar. Shake drink with ice; strain into the prepared glass.

BLACK JACK (Meehan)

1½ oz. Cognac
½ oz. kirschwasser
½ oz. cold-brew coffee
¼ oz. rich Demerara syrup

Glass: cocktail

Garnish: 3 cherries on a pick

Method: Shake with ice; strain into chilled glass. Garnish.

Adapted by Jim Meehan, New York City

BLACK JACK (Shoemaker)

1¼ oz. pisco
¾ oz. cold-brew coffee
½ oz. kirschwasser
¼ oz. rich Demerara syrup
1 dash aromatic bitters

Glass: cocktail

Method: Stir with ice to chill; strain into chilled glass.

Adapted by Daniel Shoemaker, Portland, Oregon

The Black Jack's timeline traces back more than a century to Jacques Straub's *Drinks*, published in 1914. But if the cocktail renaissance has taught us anything (other than that the appeal of the faux-speakeasy can quickly wear thin, and that some vintage drinks expired for good reason), it's that sometimes a contemporary approach can take a promising-yet-lackluster combo and give it a thoroughly come-hither makeover.

PDT mastermind Jim Meehan deserves a hat-tip for this deliciously drinkable riff on Cognac, coffee, and kirschwasser, the dry and funky cherry brandy. Be sure to use a quality cold-brewed coffee—Stumptown's bottled version is excellent, or it's dirt-simple to make cold brew on your own (page 188).

At around the same time that Meehan was tinkering with Straub's early formula in New York, Daniel Shoemaker was doing much the same thing out west. The owner of Teardrop Lounge in Portland, Oregon, and one of the more skilled practitioners of the cocktail arts, Shoemaker mirrored Meehan's move with cold-brew coffee, but selected as his base spirit the delicate flavor of Peruvian pisco.

So which of these three versions—Straub's, Meehan's, or Shoemaker's—pulls most convincingly at the palate? Try 'em all and see.

A TASTE APART

SLOE GIN

A sweet-tart toast to a reinvigorated English spirit.

There's a time in each of our drinking lives when an Alabama Slammer makes sense. Having long ago passed from misguided youth to slightly-less-misguided adulthood, I've found the time for such drinks—overly sweetened, with the vague fruity taste of mawkishly bad sloe gin—is behind me.

But let's not toss out the proverbial baby with the bad-liquor bathwater. Though long represented in the U.S. by bottom-shelf brands, sloe gin has a longer, more prestigious history in its British homeland. Classically made by steeping sloe berries—the small, plum-like fruit of the blackthorn bush—in gin, and then sweetening the mixture, sloe gin has, at its best (as encountered in brands such as Plymouth and Hayman's), a tart brightness and a bouncy complexity that works excellently in cocktails such as the Savoy Tango or the Charlie Chaplin (page 74), from 1931's *Old Waldorf Bar Days*.

SAVOY TANGO

1½ oz. sloe gin
1½ oz. applejack

Glass: cocktail

Method: Stir with ice to chill; strain into chilled glass.

AMER PICON

What to do when an ingredient goes AWOL.

The cocktail rebound has revived the manufacture or import of a slew of spirits and liqueurs, but among those yet to make the leap is the venerable French liqueur Amer Picon.

Created in 1837 by Gaetan Picon, and still ubiquitous in much of France, Amer Picon has a deep and luscious character redolent of orange peel, and a crisp, satisfying bitterness contributed by cinchona. Among the first bitter liqueurs to find its way into the mixing glass—the Brooklyn, which appeared in print in 1908, is among the drinks that call upon its talents—Amer Picon is now unavailable in the U.S. Not that it would make a huge difference if it were; the product was reformulated years ago.

I've kept the "Amer Picon" reference in recipes, but workarounds exist. Check the Liquor Cabinet (page 177) for alternatives—because there's no need to miss out on some of the mighty drinks that originally called for Amer Picon.

A TASTE APART

CHAMPAGNE

Bubbles make everything better.

CHAMPAGNE COCKTAIL

1 sugar cube
3-4 dashes Angostura bitters
Chilled Champagne

Glass: coupe or champagne flute

Garnish: lemon twist

Method: Place sugar cube on a saucer and soak with bitters; add to glass of chilled Champagne (careful—the drink will foam); garnish.

AIRMAIL

1½ oz. amber rum
¾ oz. lime juice
1 oz. honey syrup
1 oz. chilled Champagne

Glass: cocktail

Garnish: Angostura bitters

Method: Shake first three ingredients with ice to chill. Strain into chilled glass, and top with Champagne. Dash bitters atop drink's foam as garnish.

One could argue that with Champagne around, cocktails are superfluous.

One could also be wrong.

Champagne is bottled first kisses—each bubble an unsullied dream. And while excellent, blow-the-rent-money Champagne should only be mixed with good company, most sparkling wine—whether the signature sparkler from Champagne, or one of its noteworthy relatives—is perfectly at home with a little spirited accompaniment.

Punches bedazzled with bottles of Champagne freely flowed into gullets (wealthy ones, anyway) during the Age of Exploration, and the Champagne Cocktail is among the earliest drinks to bear the "cocktail" tag, appearing in Jerry Thomas' 1862 *Bar-Tender's Guide*. But in that drink, Champagne is the star of the show; bartenders from the 19th to the 21st centuries continue to revel in the ways a splash of bubbles can class up a cocktail glass.

Consider: the French 75 (page 33) is your basic Gin Sour laced with French decadence; a Boothby (page 110) reveals the late-19th century bartender's trick of fancying up a familiar cocktail with an accessory splash of royal mouthwash; and the Airmail is a step-and-a-half removed from a familiar Daiquiri.

Don't be reckless, though. Aim for decent-quality wine, or else you're ruining good gin or whiskey (but not too high-natured, as the reverse also applies). And definitely go for *brut*, or dry sparkling wine; you may need to check the sweetness level of your drink (the acidity in the wine begs for added sugar), but it'll keep the cocktail brisk and happy—first kisses while out on the town.

TWENTIETH CENTURY

An Art Deco cocktail barrels into the Internet age.

Twenty hours. Nowadays, that's about how long it takes to fly from Seattle to Singapore, if the gods of air travel are feeling benevolent (and your layover is in Narita, rather than Nairobi).

But in 1902, 20 hours was what it took to get from New York's Grand Central Station to Chicago's LaSalle Street Station via the 20th Century Limited, the swankiest rail marvel in America. Muckety-mucks from Theodore Roosevelt to Diamond Jim Brady to J.P. Morgan were among the passengers on the Art Deco-styled train over the years, and while such high-rollers can now ride their private Gulfstream between the two cities with just enough time to watch *Snakes on a Plane*, the general public has yet to see an airliner that can match the class, comfort, and spectacle of this railroad relic.

The 20th Century Limited was designed in an Art Deco theme, its suave blues and grays offset by the specially made red carpet that was rolled out at station stops.

A train as cushy as this requires a namesake cocktail, and by the time the *Café Royal Cocktail Book* was published in 1937, it had one. The drink didn't catch on—not much, anyway (it's absent from most other midcentury cocktail guides), until the cocktail resurgence put the Twentieth Century back in circulation.

Gin, lemon and chocolate is an unexpected combination, but somehow—with the moderating influence of Lillet—it just works. Works? Hell, it *sings*—so much so that the Twentieth Century has spawned a handful of contemporary offshoots, including the tequila-sparked Twenty-First Century from PDT whiz kid Jim Meehan in New York, and the smoky, whisky-fired 30th Century Man from Seattle bartender Nathan Weber.

All aboard!

TWENTIETH CENTURY

1½ oz. gin

¾ oz. lemon juice

¾ oz. Lillet blanc

¾ oz. white crème de cacao

Glass: cocktail

Garnish: lemon twist

Method: Shake with ice to chill; strain into chilled glass. Garnish.

TWENTY-FIRST CENTURY

1½ oz. blanco tequila

¾ oz. lemon juice

¾ oz. white crème de cacao

¼ oz. absinthe

Glass: cocktail

Garnish: lemon twist

Method: Shake first three ingredients with ice; rinse chilled glass with absinthe to coat; discard the excess and strain mixture into glass. Garnish.

Jim Meehan, New York City

30th CENTURY MAN

¾ oz. Islay single-malt Scotch whisky (Ardbeg recommended)

¾ oz. lemon juice

¾ oz. white crème de cacao

¾ oz. Cointreau

2 dashes absinthe

Glass: cocktail

Garnish: cherry

Method: Shake first four ingredients with ice; strain into glass rinsed with absinthe, as above. Garnish.

Nathan Weber, Seattle

A TASTE APART

LOST AND FOUND

Flavors that came back from the beyond.

ATTENTION

2 oz. gin
¼ oz. dry vermouth
¼ oz. crème de violette
¼ oz. absinthe
2 dashes orange bitters

Glass: cocktail

Garnish: lemon twist

Method: Stir with ice to chill; strain into chilled glass. Garnish.

AVIATION

2 oz. gin
¾ oz. lemon juice
½ oz. maraschino liqueur
¼ oz. crème de violette or Crème Yvette
1 tsp. simple syrup

Glass: cocktail

Garnish: cherry

Method: Shake with ice to chill; strain into chilled glass. Garnish.

A side effect of the cocktail resurgence is the peculiar pursuit of liquor-store spelunking—cocktail enthusiasts, well-versed in the works of Harry Johnson and Hugo Ensslin, venturing into off-the-beaten-path liquor stores to delve into the dusty shelves in search of forgotten bottles of spirits and liqueurs long since lost to the American market.

Finds happen, even today, though estate sales and auctions are probably now better sources of once-forgotten spirits. And while there are still a few items that remain missing from the mixology toolkit—yes, Amer Picon, we're talking about you—other essential ingredients from past eras of particular cocktail creativity are now back in circulation. In addition to absinthe (page 83), here are a few once-lost ingredients that have since been found.

Crème de Violette

With its exuberantly purple color and the flavor and aroma of French violet pastilles, this floral liqueur—along with its kin, crème de rose—played a small but notable role in late-19th/early-20th century mixology. During the great violette drought, circa 2006—well, it was great to me, anyway—I once went searching through liquor stores in Provence in pursuit of this elusive liqueur, and later had a colleague mule bottles from Japan when U.S. supplies were nonexistent. Today, there's violette to be had in volume, with excellent brands such as Rothman & Winter and Tempus Fugit, along with the vanilla-brushed relative, Crème Yvette. Violette has a certain perfumy quality that some find off-putting, like a too-close embrace with your great aunt—but violette's qualities come into play in classics such as the Aviation and the Attention (also known by the evocative name Arsenic and Old Lace).

Pimento Dram

This rum-based Jamaican allspice liqueur ("pimento" is island parlance for the allspice berry) took a peculiar turn through midcentury mixology, appearing in such fetching drinks as the Lion's Tail, and in a small host of rum-oriented mixtures that travel under tiki's broad umbrella. Rothman & Winter's St. Elizabeth Allspice Dram is the go-to brand here, but as with crème de violette, watch your measurements—a little goes a *loooong* way, but what a way that can be.

Swedish Punsch

Funky and alluring, and with a character spanning continents, Swedish Punsch is an odd yet enticing product long absent from American glasses. Based on Batavia arrack—a sort of proto-rum from Indonesia that earned a certain degree of fame for its role in early seafarer's punchbowls—Swedish Punsch also has characteristics of citrus and tea. Kronan Swedish Punsch—from Haus Alpenz, the same importer of the once-lost liqueurs under the Rothman & Winter line—lends its peculiar perfume to drinks such as the Doctor Cocktail, as well as the Calvados-based Diki Diki, which you'll find on page 48.

LION'S TAIL

2 oz. bourbon
½ oz. lime juice
½ oz. allspice liqueur
1 tsp. simple syrup
1 dash Angostura bitters

Glass: cocktail

Garnish: lime wheel

Method: Shake with ice to chill; strain into chilled glass. Garnish.

DOCTOR COCKTAIL

2 oz. Jamaican rum
¾ oz. lime juice
¾ oz. Swedish punsch

Glass: cocktail

Garnish: lime twist

Method: Shake with ice to chill; strain into chilled glass. Garnish.

BIJOU & SAN MARTIN

A boisterous party of botanicals from the turn of the last century.

BIJOU

1 oz. gin
1 oz. green Chartreuse
1 oz. sweet vermouth
1 dash orange bitters

Glass: cocktail

Garnish: lemon twist

Method: Stir with ice to chill; strain into chilled glass. Garnish.

SAN MARTIN

1½ oz. gin
1½ oz. sweet vermouth
1 tsp. yellow Chartreuse

Glass: cocktail

Garnish: lemon twist

Method: Stir with ice to chill; strain into chilled glass. Garnish.

The cocktail started out as a fairly simple creation: a spot of liquor dabbed with sugar and salted with bitters before being softened with water or ice. But by the end of the 19th century, as civilization hurtled pell-mell toward modernity, the cocktail became a sometimes loud and complicated affair. Sure, there was the simplicity of the Old Fashioned to turn to, but bartenders such as Harry Johnson and William Schmidt were embracing ever-more-vibrant cocktails that boasted a cacophony of flavors—only to have the whole thing snuffed out by 1920, when Prohibition unplugged the jukebox and turned up the lights.

For pure glitter and gay '90s abandon, consider a drink from Johnson's *Bartender's Guide*: the Bijou. Johnson's recipe calls for three ingredients in equal measure, plus a fourth for accent—but look at the ingredients. Gin, Italian *rosso* vermouth, the French herbal liqueur Chartreuse and the bright notes of orange bitters: each component brings its own party of botanical elements to the mix, as if the four dinner guests you've invited over for an intimate Saturday meal each stopped for a drink on the way, and invited everyone in the respective bars along for the ride.

But in such seemingly tumultuous chaos, beauty can be found. Should you find the noise too much, there are easily accessible remedies—simply twiddle the formula, upping the gin by half an ounce and ratcheting the other ingredients back by the same measure, or opt for the Bijou's close cousin as Plan B: the San Martin, an early-20th century cocktail (and apparently one of many by that same name) that held certain fame in South America. It's the same approach, but with the expressiveness dialed back a few notches, for when you really were just looking for a quiet conversation with favorite friends.

CAMERON'S KICK

Who's Cameron? Who knows—but this is the best cocktail you're not yet drinking.

Remember that old saw about how if you took one million monkeys and gave each of them a typewriter, they'd eventually come up with the works of Shakespeare? Well, edit "typewriter" to read "cocktail shaker" and stick the monkeys in a reasonably stocked bar, and the banana-addled mixologists would come up with a Cameron's Kick in about the same time it'd take those simian scribes to work their way around to *Titus Andronicus*.

The Cameron's Kick is notable for two things: its air of implausibility, and its undeniable deliciousness. (For others that strike a similar vein, see the Last Word, page 39, and the Twentieth Century, page 57.) With two Old World whiskies in equal measure as the base, matched against a dose of lemon juice and—of all things—the tiki-esque tones of orgeat in the sweetness role, the Cameron's Kick seems like something that no bartender—not a sober one, anyway—would put together on anything other than a lark or a dare, and it's a mix that, on paper, just shouldn't work.

But somehow, it does—and oh, how it does.

One of a flood of recipes that flows from Harry MacElhone's *Harry's ABC of Mixing Cocktails* from 1922, the Cameron's Kick has a parentage that remains a mystery. Was it the creation of a bartender blessed with divine inspiration, or one bestowed with too much free time? Was it a foul-up that resulted in something fair, or a freestyle riff that managed to not crash? Or was it, possibly, the crowd-sourced product of a gazillion ringed lemurs splashing things about in a spectacularly mismanaged bar? Nah, that one would leave a memorable story in its wake, not to mention a paper trail...and for all its tasty benefits, the Cameron's Kick doesn't have much of either.

CAMERON'S KICK

1 oz. blended Scotch whisky
1 oz. Irish whiskey
1/2 oz. lemon juice
1/2 oz. orgeat

Glass: cocktail
Garnish: orange twist
Method: Shake with ice to chill; strain into chilled glass. Garnish.

TOM COLLINS

Your kids' lemonade stand should have it so good.

TOM COLLINS

2 oz. gin
¾ oz. lemon juice
¾ oz. simple syrup
Chilled club soda

Glass: Collins

Garnish: lemon wheel

Method: Shake first three ingredients with ice to chill; strain into ice-filled glass. Top with chilled soda; garnish.

Tip: This one's a great stage for trying out different gins—London dry, Old Tom, genever, whatever.

Historical records prove that summer indeed existed before the advent of the Collins—but how our forebears weathered the season without this essential assuager is still largely a mystery.

In some ways, the Collins is the most obvious of recipes—step one, make fizzy lemonade; step two, add booze—but its simplicity is seductive. According to drinks historian David Wondrich, the Collins evolved out of basic gin punches served in London in the 1830s; by 1876, it was appearing in American bar manuals as the Tom Collins, made with Old Tom gin.

Other versions of the Collins exist. One may occasionally encounter a Whiskey Collins (sometimes called a John Collins, which gets brain-achingly confusing as you dig into Collins history), Rum Collins, and Tequila Collins sauntering through the glass—but at the core of the Collins charm, and the key to its utility as a summer refresher, is the classic Tom Collins, made with dry gin.

But wait—didn't I just say a Tom Collins is traditionally made with Old Tom gin? Yes, but...these things get complicated, and the Collins is a shining example. Grab a bottle of Old Tom gin, and you've got a bang-up Tom Collins. But substitute Plymouth gin, or a London dry like Beefeater, or your favorite Contemporary gin like Hendrick's or Martin Miller's or the stuff you like that's distilled by those guys down the street, and what do you have? A bang-up Tom Collins.

You see, even as the Collins story and identity has elements of complexity, its simplicity forgives all. There's a lesson in there, somewhere—one best mulled over while sipping a second round.

COCKTAIL ESSENTIALS

APERITIFS

Lower-octane libations that deliver a flavorful wallop.

Hard-punching heavyweights like Ali, Frazier, and Foreman became legends in the ring—but in the bar, as in boxing, skilled welterweights can help keep everything in perspective.

Aperitifs are the Boom Boom Mancinis of mixology—lighter on their alcoholic feet, but still packing a formidable flavor. Aperitifs such as vermouth, Americanos, and an array of closely allied quinquinas and chinati deliver intricately tuned bumps of piquancy, and function as delicate countorweights to the hammer-punches of whiskey and gin. While there are some aperitif liqueurs, most aperitifs are crafted from wine or mistelle (partially fermented grape juice) that's had its alcohol level slightly boosted by the addition of brandy or another distilled spirit (much like fortified wines such as sherry or port), and that's also been flavored and enhanced, or "aromatized," with spices, herbs, and other botanical ingredients. These products may have lost ground, and prestige, during the cocktail's darker days in the late 20th century, but the cocktail renaissance has sparked a similar blossoming of aperitifs, with venerable European styles joined by newfangled domestic upstarts in cocktails across the country.

As far as cocktails are concerned, vermouth is the aperitif regent: full-flavored yet nuanced, vermouth is the perfect companion to spirits across the spectrum. Vermouth's ancestry dates to the Middle Ages, when wine was laced with wormwood—*vermud*, in Old High German—to produce a medicinal vermifuge, and spices and other botanicals were added to deflect wormwood's intense palate-punching bitterness. Commercial production of rich, dark *rosso* vermouth started in Turin in the late 18th century and within a few decades, French producers were adding their own spin on vermouth in the Mediterranean city of Marseillan—where Noilly Prat continues to make its distinctive oxidized vermouth—and the alpine region of Chambery, where a more delicate, floral style of vermouth emerged.

Vermouth may have led the charge, but it was the scout for the coming aperitif army. Military excursions by the French into North Africa sparked the development of Dubonnet, an aromatized wine doctored with

APPETIZER À L'ITALIENNE

2 oz. sweet vermouth
1 oz. Fernet-Branca
1 dash absinthe
2 dashes simple syrup

Glass: cocktail

Garnish: lemon twist

Method: Stir with ice to chill; strain into chilled glass. Garnish.

Tip: Use a bold-flavored vermouth such as Carpano Antica Formula or Punt e Mes.

APERITIFS *(continued)*

CHRYSANTHEMUM

2 oz. dry vermouth
1 oz. Bénédictine
1 tsp. absinthe

Glass: cocktail

Garnish: orange twist

Method: Stir with ice to chill, strain into chilled glass. Garnish.

BONAL & RYE

2 oz. rye whiskey
1 oz. Bonal Gentiane-Quina
½ oz. Cointreau
2 dashes orange bitters
1 dash Angostura bitters

Glass: cocktail

Garnish: orange twist

Method: Stir with ice, strain into chilled glass. Garnish.

Todd Smith, San Francisco

Peruvian cinchona bark (from which quinine is derived) to produce an antimalarial tonic, and likewise enhanced with other botanicals to help mask cinchona's bracing bitterness. Other quinquinas soon followed, such as Lillet, Byrrh, and St. Raphael, and malaria-plagued parts of Italy echoed with the development of cinchona-spiked wines such as Barolo Chinato, and more elaborate cinchona-laced *aperitivi*. The French also introduced the earthy bitterness of gentian root into aperitifs, producing flavorful tonics such as Suze and Salers, a move reflected in Italy in the class of gentian-laced Americanos.

> ***Long a part of Europe's culinary culture, aperitifs caught the eye of American drinkers when the wines appeared in the context of cocktails.***

These aperitifs joined the expanding class of wines and spirits that were originally administered for medicinal purposes, but were soon embraced by the self-medicating as flavorful diversions. In addition to a bitterness that can range from a sharp thunderclap to a low rumble, these wines often have a bright acidity and an ethereal blend of flavors that, all together, help spark a healthy appetite, and arguably aid digestion, without the palate-deadening properties that higher-alcohol preprandials carry as baggage.

Around the same time these aperitifs were evolving and becoming integral elements in European life, Americans were tinkering with the idea of the cocktail. Inevitably, in your-chocolate's-in-my-peanut-butter fashion, the two notions collided. While vermouth was imported into the U.S. as early as the mid-1800s, this mingling didn't happen in earnest until the 1880s, when bartenders began mixing it with most anything that came within reach. The lightly adorned Vermouth Cocktail was an early favorite, as were vermouth-based concoctions such as the Bamboo Cocktail (see page 86) and, later, the Chrysanthemum. But vermouth also helped dampen the boozy bang of whiskey and gin, producing a cocktail that still had the stiffness of an actual drink, but that was a trifle more civilized. It was also more flavorful: while the simple ancestral cocktails can be lovely things, they can be viewed as simple Daguerreotypes compared to the Kodachrome properties that aperitifs bring to the equation.

Today, vermouths and aperitifs are essential components of any home bar. A good, basic Italian rosso—or sweet, red vermouth, such as those from Martini & Rossi or Cocchi Vermouth di Torino—is a basic staple, as is a French dry such as those from Dolin or Noilly Prat. Blanc or bianco vermouths—Dolin is the outstanding winner here—add a useful tool to the aperitif arsenal, as do other wines such as Lillet blanc and Byrrh, and the quinquina-gentian hybrids, Bonal Gentiane-Quina and Cocchi Aperitivo Americano. And while Old World producers still rule the aperitif roost, recent years have seen the advent of such New World vermouths as those from Vya, which hew closer to traditional styles, as well as newfangled takes on the aperitif by Oregon-based Imbue, Sutton Cellars from San Francisco, and the innovative vermouths from New York-based Atsby and Uncouth Vermouth. These vermouths often stray from traditional style—and some even eschew wormwood, a deal-breaker for European regulators and some aperitif sticklers—but they bring another flavor component to the cocktail equation, which can be a very good thing indeed.

CORONATION

1 oz. dry vermouth
1 oz. sweet vermouth
1 oz. applejack
1 dash apricot liqueur

Glass: cocktail

Method: Stir with ice to chill; strain into chilled glass.

QUINQUINA COCKTAIL

1 oz. brandy
¾ oz. Bonal Gentiane-Quina
½ oz. apricot liqueur
2 dashes absinthe

Glass: cocktail

Garnish: lemon twist

Method: Stir with ice to chill; strain into chilled glass. Garnish.

Adapted by Chantal Tseng, Washington, D.C.

MILK PUNCH

A cow walks into a bar...

MILK PUNCH

1 oz. brandy
1 oz. dark rum
¼ oz. simple syrup
4 oz. whole milk

Glass: goblet or rocks

Garnish: fresh-grated nutmeg

Method: Shake with ice to chill. Strain into glass filled with crushed ice. Garnish.

Variation: Swap bourbon for the brandy. Or the rum. Or both.

There are some things in life I'm content to never experience: the pain of childbirth; the trauma of combat; and the after-effects of an epic bender built around bottomless glasses of Milk Punch.

But while Milk Punch should never be over-experienced, it must definitely be experienced by any even halfway-curious drinker. A product of mixology's Mesozoic era, this soft, lightly sweet convergence of dairy and distillery fills a particularly welcome position in the cocktail pantheon: it's gentle and innocent enough to be served at Sunday brunch, but it's also got a boozy side robust enough to dispel the ghosts of Saturday night.

Much like its contemporary and close kin, Egg Nog, Milk Punch also has a flexibility of composition that leaves room to flavorfully roam. Early incarnations of the drink call for a base split more-or-less evenly between brandy and rum—a combination of flavors that must be considered a prized heirloom from our ancestors. Bourbon soon moved into the picture, though, replacing one or both of its predecessors, and this version is the one most likely found today when encountering Milk Punch in the wild (and while the drink was once ubiquitous at American bars—the ones open in the morning, anyway—today its habitat is largely in New Orleans, though cocktail-articulate restaurants across the country are rediscovering its appeal as a brunch drink).

Whichever arrangement of base spirit you choose, keep a couple of basic rules in mind: the Milk Punch needs a little lusciousness to share the vice with the booze, so whole milk is preferred; and as tasty as they might be, keep your intake to one or two. Considering the gustatory disturbance that may accompany a liquor-and-lactose binge, you'll be better off switching to gin.

JAPANESE COCKTAIL

A museum-piece 19th century cocktail that's lost none of its swagger.

Cocktails aren't designed to last. Most originate in the twinkle of a bartender's eye, spawned by a flirtation between notion and experience, and emerge from the cocktail shaker with a lifespan that even a fruit fly would consider brutish and short. But some drinks manage to linger—and a lucky handful even grasp what passes in this world for immortality.

This cocktail was likely named for the first Japanese delegation to visit the United States, in 1860—at least one member of which purportedly frequented Jerry Thomas' New York bar.

The Japanese Cocktail is older than all but a few of its cocktail peers; not only is it authentically pre-Prohibition, but it likely predates the Civil War. It also has what could be considered the purest of cocktail pedigrees: The recipe first appeared in Jerry Thomas' landmark *Bar-Tender's Guide* from 1862, but unlike the other drinks in that volume, the Japanese Cocktail is likely a Thomas original. Possibly named as a nod to the first official visit to the United States by a Japanese delegation, in 1860, the Japanese Cocktail has a graceful flavor that evokes an era of spats and diamond tie-pins, while still dancing lively enough in the glass to engage modern drinkers.

Of course, heritage isn't enough to keep the Japanese Cocktail afloat, and it benefits from the fact of being immensely delicious. The heady fruitiness of brandy is matched with the ethereal nuttiness of orgeat, and the mellow earthiness of Boker's Bitters pushes the drink across the border that divides merely excellent from sublime. The swath of lemon zest is an integral ingredient: without its citrusy brightness, the drink is missing a dimension. That would be a shame; this rare bird from centuries past deserves to be admired with full plumage.

JAPANESE COCKTAIL

2 oz. brandy
½ oz. orgeat
2 dashes Boker's bitters

Glass: cocktail

Garnish: wide lemon twist

Method: Stir with ice to chill; strain into chilled glass. Squeeze lemon twist over drink and use as garnish.

Tips: Easy with the orgeat—brands vary in sweetness, so you may want to tweak the amount to taste. Angostura bitters may be substituted for Boker's, but the Boker's are excellent, and worth seeking out.

A TASTE APART

ORGEAT

Going nuts for the flowery sweetness of almonds.

ARMY & NAVY

2 oz. gin
¾ oz. lemon juice
½ oz. orgeat
2 dashes Angostura bitters

Glass: cocktail

Method: Shake with ice to chill; strain into chilled glass.

SUPREME

2 oz. applejack
½ oz. lime juice
¼ oz. orgeat
1 dash grenadine

Glass: cocktail

Method: Shake with ice to chill; strain into chilled glass.

Variation: Skip the grenadine and you have a **Harvest Moon.**

Though its name has been known to tongue-tie countless bartenders and home mixologists, orgeat (pronounced *OR-zha*) is a style of syrup essential for any craft-cocktail bar.

Akin to Mexican horchata, orgeat has a milky appearance and the rich, nuanced flavor of almonds. But it'd be a mistake to think of orgeat as simply "almond syrup"—because the taste of good orgeat has greater complexity than your average, everyday almonds ever achieve.

True, the common domesticated almond forms the base of such orgeat (though most cheaper commercial versions today are made with almond flavoring). But that familiar rich sweetness was traditionally balanced with bitter almonds, which added (as the name suggests) a slight twinge of bitterness, along with the heady floral notes that made orgeat so alluring—a fragrance that is enhanced with the addition of orange-flower water. Unfortunately, unprocessed bitter almonds contain compounds that are toxic in high quantities. But as San Francisco bartender (and Small Hand Foods founder) Jennifer Colliau discovered, the stones of fruits such as apricots and peaches contain compounds that contribute the same flavor, and Colliau now adds small amounts of apricot kernels to her recipe for superlative orgeat.

The small-batch orgeats from Small Hand Foods and B.G. Reynolds are excellent, though their fresh, natural flavor comes at the price of perishability—after opening the bottle, keep the orgeat refrigerated and use it quickly (not that you'll need prompting once you've tasted it). If you're looking for a bottle to keep in the cupboard for those times when a sudden Mai Tai urge strikes, the French producer Giffard makes a very good option.

CLOVER CLUB & PINK LADY

Never underestimate a pink drink.

"The Clover Club drinker is traditionally a gentleman of the pre-Prohibition school," wrote Jack Townsend and Tom Moore McBride in their 1951 *The Bartender's Book*. Townsend and McBride went on to note that the drinker of this once-dusty classic may never have been a member of the tony Clover Club, or knocked one back in the echelons of Philadelphia's Bellevue-Stratford Hotel, where club members—lawyers, literary figures, and run-of-the-mill captains of industry—gathered. "But he belongs with that set," they attest.

The Clover Club cocktail seemed unlikely to have a recovery in the early years of the cocktail renaissance; raw egg white and grenadine made for an unexciting combo. But then bartenders started playing with fresh raspberry syrup in lieu of grenadine, and bartending doyenne Julie Reiner borrowed the drink's name when opening her craft bar in Brooklyn in 2008, and the Clover Club's recovery was well under way.

And the Pink Lady, the Clover Club's close cousin? It was never a drink for high rollers, Townsend and McBride wrote—instead, it was for a different sort of drinker. "She's that nice little girl who works in files, who's always so courteous but always seems so timid. She's the one who sort of reminds you of your aunt, the quiet one." *Oof*. But while the Pink Lady's innocuous-sounding name and gentle pink hue seem to promise no mischief, making it the midcentury analog of the Cosmopolitan, the Pink Lady packs a brick in its purse, owing to the added dose of applejack that boosts not only its potency, but its flavor.

As formidable as a Studebaker, the Clover Club is now in full comeback mode, while it's rare you come across a Pink Lady on a bar menu, despite its feisty-as-a-firecracker character. Shame, that.

CLOVER CLUB

1½ oz. gin
¾ oz. lemon juice
½ oz. raspberry syrup
¼ oz. egg white

Glass: cocktail

Garnish: raspberry

Method: Dry-shake ingredients without ice to foam egg white, then add ice and shake again to chill. Strain into chilled glass; garnish.

Variation: No raspberry syrup? No problem. Muddle 4 raspberries with ½ oz. simple syrup, drop the lemon to ½ oz., and add ½ oz. dry vermouth along with the gin and egg white.

PINK LADY

1½ oz. gin
½ oz. applejack
¾ oz. lemon juice
½ oz. grenadine
¼ oz. egg white

Glass: cocktail

Method: Dry-shake ingredients without ice to foam egg white, then add ice and shake again to chill. Strain into chilled glass.

WHISKEY SOUR

Simplicity is sometimes exactly what life demands.

WHISKEY SOUR

2 oz. rye whiskey or bourbon
¾ oz. lemon juice
½ oz. simple syrup
¼ oz. egg white (optional)

Glass: sour, cocktail, or rocks

Garnish: cherry and lemon wheel

Method: Shake with ice to chill; strain into chilled sour or cocktail glass, or strain into ice-filled rocks glass. Garnish.

Variation: Float ½ oz. of dry red wine atop the finished drink to make a **New York Sour**.

The Whiskey Sour is a liquid Everyman—it's Archie Bunker, Willie Loman, Arthur Dent, and Walter Mitty, all in a single glass. But if a simple sour seems to have the no-frills panache of a Denver omelet, think again: this most basic of cocktails used to be the Diamond Jim Brady of the mixology set.

Once upon a time, cocktails were like charcoal sketches: rough and basic, still capable of beauty, but perhaps a bit coarse and unfinished for some tastes. Splash in some citrus, though, and you've got some color—the sketch's stark contrasts now skew gay and lively, but you've still got the basic booze and sugar elements as before.

Nineteenth-century sours gave the old-fashioned cocktail a fresh perspective, and put some pep in the old drink's step. But the basic sour was just the start: before long, bartenders were swapping out the sugar for liqueur, or taking the sour's sharp snap and loosening it up in a long drink like a Collins.

The Gin Sour spawned variations ranging from the Clover Club to the Last Word, the Brandy Sour begat the Sidecar, and the Rum Sour eventually took a new, familiar name (see the Daiquiri, page 102). But while the Whiskey Sour has its offspring—the New York Sour notable among them—the drink retains the power of the paterfamilias. Bourbon gives the drink boldness, and rye whiskey a little edge; an Irish whiskey sour has its moments, as perhaps does the Scotch sour, though those moments are fewer and further between. You have plenty of options for riffing on the familiar; but sometimes the situation calls for keeping things simple. Serve it up or on the rocks, or in a paper cup, garnished with a sunny afternoon, a tennis ball, and a dog to chase after it in the yard.

DRINKS OF EMPIRE

Cocktails that flowed from England's global sprawl.

The cocktail is as distinctly an American creation as the Chicago Cubs, *Star Wars*, and Watergate. But just as baseball, Hollywood films, and political dumbfuckery have become wildly popular international exports, the cocktail has also found ardent fans—and picked up enduring influence—far from home.

The British were early enthusiasts of matching liquor with any ingredient that happened within arm's reach, and drinks such as Grog (kind of an ancestral Daiquiri, kind of) and the Gimlet have their roots in the British Navy. The soldiers and administrators of the British Raj similarly left indelible marks on the cocktail, via two enduring refreshers: the Gin & Tonic, and the Pegu Club (for a third, knock together a Burrah Peg—simply a brandy or Scotch and soda).

Like French quinquinas (see page 63), quinine-spiked tonic water originated with medicinal purposes in mind, to combat malaria in the sub-equatorial regions to which Her Majesty's interests had spread; bitter as a bastard, tonic water has a bite that can be tempered with a splash (or ample glug) of gin. Administrators and officers in Rangoon adopted a different approach to the afternoon gin, mixing it with lime, curaçao, and bitters in the cool of the Pegu Club. Today, the Gin & Tonic is the avenue down which countless summer afternoons are whiled away, and the Pegu Club name adorns one of New York's most influential cocktail bars.

The U.K.'s grip on the globe has largely loosened over the past century. But with a bottle of gin and some limes in hand, Brittania still rules the cocktail hour, if not necessarily the waves.

GIN & TONIC

2 oz. London dry gin (Tanqueray excels in the G&T)

½ lime

4-6 oz. chilled tonic water, to taste

Glass: Collins

Garnish: lime wedge

Method: Squeeze juice from lime-half into glass and add gin; fill with ice, and top with tonic to taste. Garnish.

PEGU CLUB

2 oz. gin

¾ oz. lime juice

¾ oz. curaçao

2 dashes Angostura bitters

1 dash orange bitters

Glass: cocktail

Garnish: lime wheel

Method: Shake with ice to chill; strain into chilled glass. Garnish.

EL PRESIDENTE

How to drink like a head of state.

EL PRESIDENTE

1½ oz. white rum
1½ oz. blanc vermouth
1 tsp. curaçao
½ tsp. grenadine

Glass: cocktail

Garnish: orange twist, cherry (optional)

Method: Stir with ice to chill; strain into chilled glass. Twist orange peel over drink and use as garnish, or not.

Based on its name alone, you might expect El Presidente to carry with it a touch of brutality—maybe a whiff of cigar smoke and hair oil along with a metallic taste of gunpowder, frequent companions of the banana-republic strongmen so prevalent at the time of this drink's early-20th century creation.

But this Havana-born palate-soother is as friendly as can be, which earned the drink top status in the Caribbean—and the U.S.—in the 1920s and '30s. Recipes for this drink calling for dry vermouth were long in circulation; those were wrong, as cocktail historian David Wondrich recently discovered, and when mixed with the softer, sweeter blanc vermouth, El Presidente reveals the richness of its personality.

Smooth and subtle, El Presidente deserves the tag hung upon it by society correspondent Basil Woon: the "aristocrat of cocktails," a drink that's a suave El Jefe without the compromising character of cordite.

A TASTE APART

GRENADINE

Pomegranates add a little blush to the bar.

Contrary to misguided notions of bibulous machismo, "pink" and "fruity" weren't always mixological taboos. Raspberry syrup long lent its bright flavor and garnet color to a range of bold mixtures, a stage it eventually ceded to the pomegranate-based grenadine.

Its name derived from the French diminutive for pomegranates, grenadine was used by bartenders to doctor drinks with color and sweetness for much of the early 20th century. Its flavor more red-fruit rugged than the bouncy brightness of raspberries, grenadine gradually lost its pomegranate connection as food chemists moved into the midcentury bar.

But in our HFCS-averse age, bartenders and cocktail aficionados have turned back to grenadine's true nature, making their own versions (see recipe, page 187) in order to craft cocktails such as the Jack Rose in their full, nothing-to-laugh-about pinkish glory.

JACK ROSE

2 oz. applejack
3/4 oz. lemon juice
1/2 oz. grenadine

Glass: cocktail

Method: Shake with ice to chill; strain into chilled glass.

CURAÇAO & TRIPLE SEC

Citrus-laced cocktail essentials.

Lemons and limes are the cocktail's closest citrus companions, but orange liqueurs are also a big part of the party.

Curaçao—traditionally based on brandy or rum, and flavored with the dried peels of bitter oranges (originally grown on the Caribbean island of Curaçao, hence the name)—is a rich and complex cordial that's been a part of the bar pretty much from the beginning. Curaçao works particularly well with aged spirits like whiskey and rum. See the Liquor Cabinet (page 177) for recommended brands.

For drinks where "dry and crisp" is preferred to "deep and round," triple sec is the answer. Its citrusy snap and gentle sweetness work perfectly with the bright flavors found in gin and tequila.

I've called for Cointreau in recipes in this book, but there are other good triple sec options in the Liquor Cabinet on page 177.

A TASTE APART

APRICOT

Deploying summer's sweetness in cocktails poured year-round.

CHARLIE CHAPLIN

1 oz. sloe gin
1 oz. apricot liqueur
1 oz. lime juice

Glass: cocktail

Garnish: thin lime wedge

Method: Shake with ice to chill; strain into chilled glass. Garnish.

SELF STARTER

1½ oz. gin
¾ oz. Lillet blanc
¼ oz. apricot liqueur
1 tsp. absinthe

Glass: cocktail

Method: Stir first three ingredients with ice to chill; strain into chilled glass that's been rinsed with absinthe.

Whichever biblical scholar first speculated it was an apple that the serpent put into Eve's hand was overlooking a fundamental truth of fruit: the apricot possesses the more seductive power in the orchard.

Prunus armeniaca, the common apricot, has a bright appeal that, admittedly, can pale when compared to its voluptuous stone-fruit kin, the peach. But the apricot is Mary Ann to the peach's Ginger: more wholesome, perhaps, but with its own unquestionable charm.

For whatever reason, the apricot has also lent itself particularly well to the artistry of the distiller. Apricot brandy—the clear eau de vie distilled directly from fermented fruit—has a bracing headiness that's made it an historical favorite in central Europe, and apricot-accented liqueurs (erroneously called "apricot brandy" in some recipes) have long laced cocktails with traces of libational lushness.

Similarly appealing fruits that lend themselves well to cocktails include pineapples and raspberries (see page 89). But the apricot brings its own sun-ripened shine to a drink, especially when costarring with a flavorful foil such as sloe gin in the Charlie Chaplin (a sepia-toned survivor of 1931's *Old Waldorf Bar Days*); as a complement to gin and Lillet in the Self Starter, from 1930's *Savoy Cocktail Book*; or in a vivacious dance with Peruvian pisco in Charles H. Baker's Pisco Apricot Tropical (see page 51).

FLORIDITA COCKTAIL

A little love for the black sheep of the extended Daiquiri family.

Pity the Floridita, also known as La Florida Cocktail. Not only is its familiar name a diminutive, said in the honey-sweet way you'd address your kindergartener's playmates, but of all the rum-bolstered glory that came out of the Havana bar La Florida—see the Daiquiri section (page 102) for more on this bar's place of honor—the Floridita has been neglected even as the fortunes of the Daiquiri, its close relative, have soared.

It's no wonder, though, that this drink has faded—it's a mixture of mixological no-no's. Vermouth shaken with rum and citrus? Barbaric, in some circles. With crème de cacao? Shame on your mother. And with grenadine? Please, stop—the nuns are fainting.

But despite its sins, the Floridita has an appeal that bears a visit, or three. A Hail Mary over the cocktail shaker would not be out of place.

FLORIDITA COCKTAIL

1½ oz. white rum
½ oz. lime juice
½ oz. sweet vermouth
1 dash grenadine
1 dash white crème de cacao

Glass: cocktail
Garnish: lime wheel
Method: Shake with ice to chill; strain into chilled glass. Garnish.

DON'T GIVE UP THE SHIP

Because the world needs more drink names rooted in the War of 1812.

Captain James Lawrence had more than a dozen American cities and counties named after him, and his last command has served as everything from an unofficial motto for the U.S. Navy to the title of a 1959 Jerry Lewis comedy. Of course, Lawrence died violently and young, proving that such a legacy can come at a steep price.

June 1, 1813. Boston Harbor, then blockaded by the British Royal Navy. Under Lawrence's command, the USS *Chesapeake* sails into Massachusetts Bay and encounters the HMS *Shannon*. The *Shannon* challenges; the *Chesapeake* accepts. An intense 11 minutes of cannon fire and close-quarter combat with muskets and sabers results in more than 100 casualties, the mortally wounded Lawrence among them. His final command notwithstanding, the *Chesapeake* falls to the enemy.

What does this have to do with the cocktail? Not a damn thing, beyond the name. Good story, though, and a good drink—which is as perfect a match as anyone needs.

DON'T GIVE UP THE SHIP

1½ oz. gin
1½ oz. Dubonnet
1 tsp. curaçao
1 tsp. Fernet-Branca

Glass: cocktail
Method: Stir with ice to chill; strain into chilled glass.

SIDECAR

A debonair drink approaches the century mark.

SIDECAR

2 oz. brandy
3/4 oz. Cointreau
1/2 oz. lemon juice

Glass: cocktail

Garnish: sugared rim (optional)

Method: To make sugared rim, moisten lip of empty glass with the cut edge of a lemon and dip the moistened edge in a saucer filled with superfine sugar; shake off excess sugar before serving. Shake with ice to chill; strain into chilled glass.

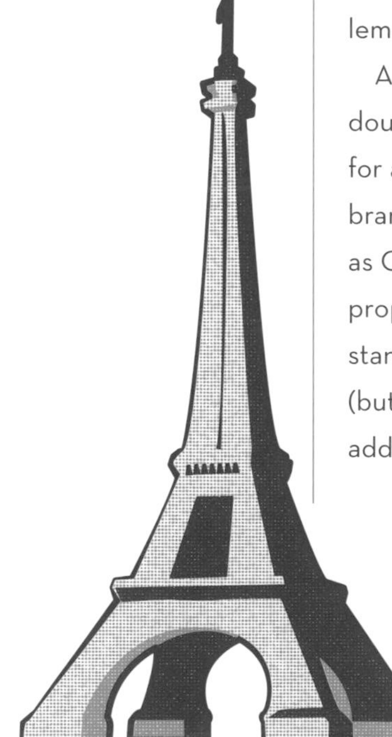

If there's one thing the history of mixology has taught us, it's that there's no shortage of ways to ruin good liquor. But finding cocktails that perfectly play a select cast of ingredients against each other, creating a whole that's oh-so-much more than the sum of its parts? Rare currency, to be sure.

Behold the Sidecar, bona fide cocktail royalty. Yes, it's ridiculously simple to make—three familiar ingredients, available in most any decent bar, simply shaken together and served while still exuberant from the cocktail shaker—but in this modest frog of a recipe hides a prince of a drink.

The Sidecar (or Side Car, as our ancestors preferred) was a hot commodity in 1920s Paris and London. Both cities have laid claim to the drink's creation (there's also a too-convenient-to-be-true creation myth involving an American Army officer and a motorcycle), and while it's likely that this dispute may never be definitively settled, the drink bears the hallmarks of a perfect post-WWI hybrid. A backbone of French brandy serves as a foundation for the crisp, bright flavor of Cointreau, with fresh lemon serving as intermediary to keep the flavors balanced.

All cocktails should be made with the best possible ingredients, but this is doubly so for the Sidecar to preserve its place on the cocktail throne. Aim for a VSOP or better Cognac, or a rugged Armagnac or notable American brandy (see page 179 for more details), and a premium orange liqueur such as Cointreau, Giffard Triple Sec, or Combier Liqueur d'Orange. Ingredient proportions have changed over the years from equal parts of each to a standard 2:1:1 ratio; the version here, I think, best balances the drink's flavor (but, as always, tinker to your own taste). The sugared rim is a more recent addition, and is optional—deploy as the situation dictates.

COCKTAIL ESSENTIALS

BRANDY

This liquor regent is a garrulous booze-of-the-people in the cocktail glass.

Whiskey is useful for when your spine needs straightening, and gin for when your upper lip needs stiffening. And brandy? It promises boldness, while leaving you weak in the knees.

Brandy is a time-honored fortifier for life's many moments when resolve is needed, but it also carries the aura of passion and indulgence. Distilled anywhere fruit ripens and desire exists, brandy is most at home in France—a place well acquainted with passion and indulgence—where the best amber-hued Cognacs and Armagnacs represent the pinnacle of the spirituous experience.

Brandy may technically be made from any type of fruit, but the spirit is most abundantly (and memorably) distilled from grapes that have been fermented into wine. It's from this grape-based wine that some of the earliest medieval distillers in Belgium and Holland first drew drops of potent *brandeiwijn*, or "burnt wine," as they tinkered at their alembics. The raw spirit was undoubtedly harsh, but its character was such a paradigm-shifter for these early experimenters that the clear distillate was christened with the holy-sounding term *eau de vie*—water of life. (The "water of life" handle travels well; not only is "eau de vie" still used as a term for unaged brandies across the fruit spectrum, but it also appears in localized forms as *aquavit*, the signature spirit from Scandinavia, and as *uisquebaugh*, the Gaelic term that gave rise to "whisky.")

> *Brandy is a time-honored fortifier for life's many moments when resolve is needed, but it also carries the aura of passion and indulgence.*

Young brandy is clear and aromatic, an exuberant puppy of a spirit that nevertheless needs the enrichment of character that comes with maturity. European distillers clued into the benefits of aging brandy in oak casks early on, and today the maturation and blending of brandy is a form of fine artistry. The rules and guidelines surrounding brandy (bureaucracy-bound

BOMBAY COCKTAIL

1½ oz. brandy
¾ oz. sweet vermouth
¾ oz. dry vermouth
¼ oz. curaçao
2 dashes orange bitters
2 dashes absinthe

Glass: cocktail

Garnish: lemon twist

Method: Stir with ice to chill; strain into chilled glass. Garnish.

Adapted by Thad Vogler, San Francisco

COCKTAIL ESSENTIALS

BRANDY *(continued)*

BRANDY SCAFFA

1¼ oz. brandy
¾ oz. green Chartreuse
½ oz. maraschino liqueur
3 dashes Boker's bitters

Glass: rocks

Method: Build ingredients in an empty rocks glass. A scaffa is served room-temperature, so skip the ice and the stirring.

Adapted by Daniel Shoemaker, Portland, Oregon

BURNT FUSELAGE

1 oz. brandy
1 oz. curaçao
1 oz. dry vermouth

Glass: cocktail

Garnish: lemon zest

Method: Stir with ice to chill, strain into chilled glass. Garnish.

Cognac in particular) are both myriad and maddening, but there are a few basic principles to keep in mind when stocking the liquor cabinet.

Blends that lean to the younger side—often labeled VS for Cognac—can be more rugged and less refined, and are best saved for bold-flavored punches. For cocktail purposes, a VSOP Cognac or comparable is a better bet; the youngest brandies in the blend will have greater maturity (four years and beyond), and the result will be a cocktail with more depth and nuance. XO Cognacs and other older brandies are best sipped on their own—with spirits in the blend sometimes reaching back a generation or more, they've earned your undivided attention—but can also contribute to a blowout celebratory cocktail. Above all, skip the spirituous plonk; cheap brandy has a garish, smeared-lipstick quality that tastes like broken promises. French brandies in general offer better options, though Spanish brandies are worth exploring, and the California brandies from some craft distillers are sublime; see the Liquor Cabinet (page 177) for suggestions.

Brandy was possibly the first style of spirit to trickle from a still, and brandy is also a good candidate for the role of the world's first mixing spirit. Brandy-fueled punches kept the British navy afloat during the peak

centuries of exploration and colonization, and New World bartenders frequently reached for the spirit during the cocktail's 19th century gestation. Brandy Cocktails, Fixes, and Smashes populate many of mixology's earliest records, aged apple brandies appear in cocktails both vintage and contemporary (see page 48), and other styles of fruit eau de vie—from the musky, cherry-based kirschwasser to poire William, an ethereal spirit distilled from ripe pears—appear in drinks such as the Rose from 1920s Paris.

A cocktail-bound brandy should have a fragrance that's bright and endearing, ranging from fruit to flowers to spice, or somewhere in between, and a flavor that's at once deep and evocative, and lively and complex. Brandy's rich nuances work well with similarly styled ingredients: fruit and winter spice are beloved by brandy's flavors (and citrus—either fresh, or in liqueurs such as curaçao—is a particular paramour), as are aromatic ingredients such as vermouth, orgeat, and herbal liqueurs such as Bénédictine and Chartreuse. Aggressive or bitter flavors, however, must be used with caution, as an intemperate hand with amaro or the like can trample brandy's delicate daisies into a muck of forgettable flavor.

RITZ COCKTAIL

¾ oz. Cognac
½ oz. Cointreau
¼ oz. lemon juice
¼ oz. maraschino liqueur
2-3 oz. chilled Champagne

Glass: cocktail

Garnish: orange twist

Method: Shake first four ingredients with ice to chill; strain into chilled glass. Top with chilled Champagne; garnish.

Dale DeGroff, New York City

ROSE

2 oz. blanc vermouth
1 oz. kirschwasser
1 tsp. raspberry syrup

Glass: cocktail

Garnish: cherry

Method: Stir with ice to chill; strain into chilled glass. Garnish.

COCKTAIL STYLE

THE FLIP & THE FIZZ

A brief interlude on eggs and bubbles.

GIN FIZZ TROPICAL

2 oz. gin (Plymouth recommended)
1 oz. lime juice
½ oz. orgeat
½ oz. pineapple gomme syrup
½ oz. fresh, organic egg white
1 oz. chilled club soda

Glass: fizz

Garnish: thin lime wheel threaded with a mint tip

Method: Dry shake everything except soda; shake well with ice; double-strain into glass; top with soda.

Adapted by Erik Adkins, San Francisco

As contemporary bartenders and cocktail historians have wildcatted mixology's past, a few exploratory wells have tapped deep reservoirs of boozy bounty.

The Flip was one of the mainstays of mixology's earliest epoch. A variety of ingredients found their way into Flips during Colonial days and the early years of the infant republic—the Flip's family tree includes everything from ale and rum to cream and molasses—but a common element was a raw egg, beaten or shaken into the mixture, which was sometimes seared into a froth with a red-hot poker before being swallowed by a tavern's lip-smacking patron. In the years before central heating and Polarfleece, such hot flips did double duty, assuaging dim tempers (and occasionally exacerbating them) while upholstering one's insides with a sort of internal sweater.

Fizzes date to a somewhat later period, and had their heyday during the closing decades of the 19th century (and the dawn of the one following). These sparkling drinks (sometimes, but not always, prepared with an egg white, egg yolk, or the whole damn thing) owed much to the growing commercial availability of carbonated water, which took a simple mixture such as a basic Gin Sour and pumped it full of vitality. For drinkers in the late 1800s, this effervescence proved irresistible, especially during the day's early hours, when the fog and fuzz from the long night before begged for a little clearing, and the bubbly bounce of a Gin Fizz seemed the best medicine for this particular ailment. Soon enough, there were multitudes of Fizzes in circulation—perhaps the most extravagant of which, the Ramos Fizz (page 150), still walks among us in New Orleans and in craft-cocktail bars around the world.

Unlike close relatives like the Collins (page 62) and the Rickey (page 87), the Fizz is served sans ice. While those long refreshers are designed to be lingered over throughout a summer afternoon, the Fizz is a short tonic, meant to be tossed back while it's still giddy, before heat and time make it as flabby and unappealing as the hungover toper before whom it sits.

The Flip and the Fizz seem somewhat unlikely to have a revival—raw eggs have a squick factor that turns off many modern drinkers, and drinks designed for morning consumption now trend toward the timid or the salad-like—but each has crept back into some degree of circulation during the current renaissance. Cases in point: the modern love of drinks such as the Gin Fizz Tropical, an oldie from Charles H. Baker, Jr.'s *The Gentleman's Companion* that was recently revamped by San Francisco bartender Erik Adkins; the Apricot Flip from John Deragon, former barman at PDT in New York; and a Flip made by shaking a whole egg with pretty much any amaro—Averna, Cynar, what have you—results in a surprisingly worthwhile diversion.

APRICOT FLIP

2 oz. brandy
¾ oz. apricot liqueur
½ oz. simple syrup
1 whole, organic egg

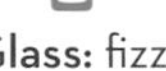

Glass: fizz

Garnish: fresh-grated nutmeg

Method: Dry-shake all ingredients to mix; shake well with ice to chill. Double-strain into chilled glass; garnish.

John Deragon, New York City

GIN FIZZ

2 oz. gin
¾ oz. lemon juice
1 tsp. superfine sugar
Chilled club soda

Glass: fizz

Method: Shake gin and lemon together with ice; strain into chilled glass and add 2-3 oz. chilled soda. Sprinkle sugar atop drink and stir in to spark the effervescence.

Variation: Chuck ½ oz. of egg white into the shaker to transform your Gin Fizz into a **Silver Fizz**.

Tips: Old Tom gin works best, or use Plymouth or London dry. The fizz is also worthwhile when made with brandy, aged rum, or whiskey.

COLLEEN BAWN

¾ oz. rye whiskey
¾ oz. yellow Chartreuse
¾ oz. Bénédictine
1 whole, organic egg
1 tsp. simple syrup

Glass: coupe

Garnish: fresh-grated nutmeg and cinnamon

Method: Dry-shake all ingredients until mixed; shake well with ice. Double-strain into chilled glass; garnish.

Adapted by Murray Stenson, Seattle

MORNING GLORY

An essential part of a balanced (boozy) breakfast.

MORNING GLORY

1 oz. rye whiskey
1 oz. brandy
1 tsp. simple syrup
½ tsp. curaçao
2 dashes bitters (Boker's preferred, or use Angostura)
1 dash absinthe
1 oz. chilled club soda

Glass: fizz

Garnish: lemon twist

Method: Combine all ingredients except soda in a mixing glass and fill with ice; stir until chilled, and strain into chilled glass. Add club soda and give a quick stir; garnish.

Tip: After adding the club soda, sprinkle a pinch of superfine sugar into the drink and stir to produce a foamier fizz.

Variation: Swap Champagne for the club soda, and embrace the ensuing chaos.

Ever since the first Mesopotamian winemaker or Babylonian brewer awoke after a Bronze Age rager, mankind has sought ways to offset the grim, grey aftermath of a bright and giddy night before.

The Morning Glory is everything the Mimosa wants to be, but isn't: a delicious drink for the morning hours, with a knack for sweeping cobwebs from the mind and malice from the soul. Designed with the late 19th century's most efficient and popular painkillers—whiskey, brandy and absinthe, with a dash of bitters for added medicinal benefit—the Morning Glory has both the punch and the reach of your standard cocktail. Softened with a smidge of club soda, the drink more readily quells a tempestuous stomach while delivering enough alcoholic aid to sand the edges off a temple-thudding headache.

So desperate was the need among our forebears for an effective A.M. remedy that the "Morning Glory" label has been hung on an array of drinks—and that's not including the brigade of corpse-revivers, brace-ups, fog-cutters and other extended relations. This version (which appeared in the posthumous 1887 edition of Jerry Thomas' *Bar-tender's Guide*) joins other worthy drinks such as the Morning Glory Fizz—a delicious nervine of Scotch whisky, lemon, absinthe, egg white, and seltzer that popped up in the late 1800s and pinballed around in popularity for decades thereafter—as well as more questionable Morning Glory compounds such as those of whole eggs and crème de menthe, or vodka with cream and chocolate liqueur.

This brings us back, thank god, to this mixture of rye whiskey and brandy. Should you approach the Morning Glory during an evening's entertainment, it's permissible to throw caution to the wind and replace the club soda with Champagne, creating the full Gilded Age spats-and-boutonnière effect of a civilized sport who's still up for a little dirt and danger. But fair warning for the next morning: you may need a little help to rejoin the living.

A TASTE APART

ABSINTHE

Ignore the myths and mysteries—this storied spirit can stand on its own merits.

For much of the 20th century and into the 21st, absinthe was often discussed with the sort of earnest, furtive whisper that's saved for acquiring high-grade hashish or exchanging questionably legal insider stock tips. Even today, less than a decade after the once-forbidden (in the U.S. and much of Europe, anyway) spirit emerged from legal limbo, openly advocating absinthe can spark degrees of skepticism and wariness similar to those that greet passing references to fetish porn or the admission of a fondness for Dubstep.

Absinthe has long had the reputation as a dashing, bibulous bastard, both in its native France and Switzerland as well as the U.S. Notoriously potent—it regularly ranks above 110 proof—and with a ghostly, ethereal aroma and flavor, absinthe was a *fin de siècle* scapegoat for a range of alcoholic ills. Banned in the U.S. (a warm-up act for Prohibition) in 1912, absinthe reemerged in 2007 as a legally produced and obtainable spirit.

Traditionally consumed with only the addition of water and sugar, absinthe became an integral part of American cocktail culture in the mid-1800s. Fragrant with anise, mint, and hyssop, and with a cascading chorus of flavors that lends a Baroque complexity to cocktails, absinthe was dispensed in drops and dashes in such cocktail stars as the Sazerac (see page 95), and it's easy to see why: the spirit's springy fragrance and resonating depth add a bloomers-in-the-air Can Can quality to even staid and respectable cocktails when deployed with sufficient discretion—say, a dash or two.

ABSINTHE COCKTAIL

1 oz. absinthe

½ tsp. anisette

1 dash bitters

2 oz. chilled water or club soda

Glass: cocktail

Method: Shake with ice to chill; strain into chilled glass.

Tips: Anis del Mono, from Spain, is a wise choice for anisette. Angostura bitters is traditional here, but Peychaud's lend a more suitable flavor, along with an alluring pinkish hue.

ABSINTHE DRIP

1 oz. absinthe

1-2 sugar cubes or 1-2 tsp. simple syrup (optional)

2-3 oz. chilled water (not optional, to taste)

Glass: Pontarlier absinthe glass or wine glass

Special tools: absinthe spoon (optional)

Traditional method: Pour absinthe into glass. Perch absinthe spoon across top of glass and place sugar cube on its surface; slowly drizzle chilled water through the sugar cube to dissolve until preferred dilution is reached; stir with absinthe spoon and serve.

Easy method: Pour absinthe into glass; add desired amount of simple syrup. Add chilled water, to taste; stir and serve.

SOUTH SIDE

Summer's swelter doesn't stand a chance.

SOUTH SIDE

2 oz. gin
3/4 oz. lemon juice
1/2 oz. simple syrup (to taste)
8-10 leaves fresh mint

Glass: cocktail

Garnish: mint leaf

Method: Shake with ice to chill; double-strain into chilled glass. Garnish.

Variations: Skip the cocktail glass and strain into either a fizz glass (no ice) or an ice-filled Collins glass and top with an ounce or two of chilled club soda for a **South Side Fizz**—or make it a **South Side Royale** by adding a splash of chilled Champagne to the basic South Side, or in place of soda in the Collins variation.

EAST SIDE

2 oz. gin
1 oz. lime juice
3/4 oz. simple syrup
8-10 leaves fresh mint
2 slices cucumber

Glass: cocktail

Garnish: thin slice cucumber

Method: Muddle cucumber in cocktail shaker and add remaining ingredients. Shake with ice to chill; double-strain into chilled glass. Float garnish atop drink.

The South Side is Tom Wolfe in cocktail incarnate: crisp and droll, and dapper in a perpetual-summer kind of way. Perhaps this seems apt because the South Side—occasionally spelled as a single word (don't ask me who decides these things)—has such an extensive history in the hands of the Hamptons' linen-suit-and-seersucker set, and a particularly longstanding legacy at New York's tony 21 Club, but this mixture of gin, lemon, and mint also comes about its breezy appeal all on its own.

It may be a fixture at the 21 Club and a Hamptons essential, but the South Side is welcome anywhere the sun shines and summer's heat seems relentless.

Several theories regarding the South Side's provenance have been floated over the years, some more plausible than others, but bickering over the drink's patrimony is antithetical to the South Side's relaxed charm. Suffice it to say that the drink's simple mixture—nothing more than a Gin Sour into which a sprig of mint has strayed—has satisfied generations of summer quaffers since its circa 1920s debut (its recipe appeared in print in 1922's *Harry's ABC of Mixing Cocktails*).

No doubt part of its savoir faire is due to the drink's flexibility: While perfectly appropriate served shaken and strained into a cocktail glass, the South Side also easily cozies up to a splash of soda in an ice-filled Collins glass, or to an adeptly applied slug of Champagne. Bright, crisp, and refreshing, the South Side is comfortable everywhere.

The venerable South Side is also ripe for contemporary exploration. The East Side, which circulated among New York's craft-cocktail bars in the mid-2000s before finding a special welcome on the mixology circuit in Los Angeles, takes the classic, swaps lime for lemon, and introduces the additional cooling power of cucumber.

PERIODISTA

Boston may be onto something.

The Periodista is the Red Sox of cocktails: bewilderingly beloved in Boston, with an appeal that's been slow to spread beyond the 617 area code.

The Periodista has all the hallmarks of a classic Cuban cocktail—rum, *check*; lime, *check*; fruit-liqueur embellishments, *check*—but while there are Internet rumors linking the drink to Havana circa 1962, the Periodista's true provenance is likely lost in the rum-fog of time. More recently, this fetching mix of flavors has surfaced as a favorite cocktail in Boston, and is recommended as a rediscovered (or, depending on your point of view, a newly minted) classic by such esteemed barmen as Jackson Cannon, who lists Eastern Standard and the Hawthorne on his resumé. Coming from the creator of such scrumptious drinks as the Honey Fitz (see page 142), this recommendation is good enough for me.

PERIODISTA

1½ oz. rum (see below)
½ oz. lime juice
¼ oz. Cointreau
¼ oz. apricot liqueur
1 tsp. simple syrup

Glass: cocktail

Garnish: lime wheel

Technique: Shake with ice to chill; strain into chilled glass. Garnish.

Tips: While the Periodista is not without appeal when made with a crisp, light rum, darker, aged rums are favored in this drink; recommended brands include the mellow Appleton Estate Signature Blend, the buttery Banks 7 Golden Age, or the funky and muscular Smith & Cross.

JOURNALIST

A veteran of the Hearst era gets a second wind in the age of HuffPo.

The Journalist dates to typewriter-and-public-telephone days, to that now-antique era when journalism seemed like a growth industry and when practitioners of the craft might view a bold, gin-fueled drink such as this as a suitable warmup for a day's work.

But things have changed. Today's newspapers are largely ink-and-paper cries for help; a freelancer feeding frenzy has replaced raucous newsrooms filled with salaried reporters; and 140-character snippets have supplanted the hard-news lede as the mode through which the day's events are related.

Does this sound a little sour and bitter? Then it's just like the Journalist, a modified Martini that appeared in 1930, in Harry Craddock's *Savoy Cocktail Book*. There may no longer be much of a future in the profession, but with this fortifier in front of you, the world still shows possibility.

JOURNALIST

2 oz. gin
½ oz. dry vermouth
½ oz. sweet vermouth
2 dashes lemon juice
2 dashes curaçao
1 dash Angostura bitters

Glass: cocktail

Method: Stir with ice to chill; strain into chilled glass.

A TASTE APART

SHERRY

Spain's signature wine makes friends behind the bar.

BAMBOO COCKTAIL

1½ oz. dry vermouth
1½ oz. dry sherry (use fino or amontillado)
2 dashes orange bitters
2 drops Angostura bitters

Glass: cocktail

Garnish: lemon twist

Method: Stir with ice; strain into chilled glass. Garnish.

Variation: Substitute sweet vermouth for dry, and lose the bitters, to make an **Adonis**.

LA PERLA

1½ oz. reposado tequila
1½ oz. manzanilla sherry
¾ oz. pear liqueur

Glass: cocktail

Garnish: lemon twist

Method: Stir with ice to chill; strain into chilled glass. Garnish.

Jacques Bezuidenhout, San Francisco

The 21st-century cocktail renaissance is a story of many comebacks—rye whiskey, vermouth, and a good chunk of the cocktails in this chapter fit that category—but among the beverages that boomeranged from "where are they now" territory to mixology's measure of au courant, sherry ranks near the very top of the list.

Sherry is the fortified wine from the Spanish region of Jerez, matured in a signature solera process that blends wines of various ages to make sherries with dizzying depths of flavor. Though sweeter cream sherries and bland, dry cooking sherries were the most visible versions in the U.S. in the late 20th century, the wine has an impressive range, from crisp, dry finos and manzanillas to nutty (yet still dry) amontillados and olorosos to the rich Pedro Ximenez (PX) sherries, which can have a lustrous resonance akin to port.

Before sherry stumbled into its ignoble late-20th century role of the drink of doddering grandmothers, its sexiness quotient on par with that of a tea cozy, the wine was an integral part of the formative years of mixed drinks. Sherry served as a basic building block of Egg Nogs, cups, and cocktails; perhaps its greatest star turn was in the Sherry Cobbler (see page 41). In the late 1800s, sherry's charm was such that it appeared in drinks of advanced deliciousness such as the Bamboo Cocktail, a drink with a popularity that ranged from Yokohama to the sleekest bars in Manhattan. More recently, the wine has been embraced by bartenders such as Derek Brown and Chantal Tseng, who opened the sherry-focused Mockingbird Hill in Washington, D.C. in 2013, and San Francisco bar consultant Jacques Bezuidenhout, whose pairing of sherry with tequila in La Perla created a cocktail for the ages.

RICKEY

How to survive a summer in Washington, D.C. (or, for that matter, anywhere).

We each have our own personal heat-misery index: the point each summer at which we begin to forlornly pine for January. In places where the mercury and the humidity both hang near the century mark during the depths of July and August, serious cooling action is a necessity, and in that interminably sweaty era before the advent of air conditioning, a good deal of those heat-countering measures came in a glass.

Behold this enduring heat-buster from Washington, D.C., circa mid-1880s: the Rickey. Named for Democratic lobbyist and Confederate veteran "Colonel" Joe Rickey—who requested its manufacture in bars ranging from St. Louis to New York to, most significantly, a Congressional watering hole called Shoomaker's in the nation's capital (where Rickey was the owner as well as a regular, and where the drink was likely created for him by bartender George A. Williamson)—the Rickey is on par with the Gin & Tonic and the Mint Julep as the most effective summer-heat assuagers known to mankind.

Key to the Rickey's charm is its simplicity. Water comprises half the drink's components—in one form, carbonated, and in the other, frozen—and the third member of the quartet is the juice squeezed from half a lime (use a whole lime, if it's tiny). And for the star of the show? Most spins on the Rickey utilize gin for the drink's backbone, which forms an unerringly satisfying concoction akin to a Gin & Tonic without tonic's bittersweet bite. But Joe Rickey's original Rickey used whiskey—bourbon or rye, your call—and in that direction lies paradise.

Gin or whiskey, go in the direction of your own choosing, but keep one principle in mind: Rickey called for no sugar in his eponymous drink, believing sweetener counterproductive to the drink's cooling mission. That point's arguable, but his taste was spot on: save the sugar and liqueurs for other drinks in your summer repertoire, and let the Rickey sail unsweetened.

RICKEY

2 oz. gin or bourbon
½ lime (use a whole lime if small)
Chilled club soda

Glass: Collins

Garnish: Squeezed lime shell

Method: Fill glass with ice (cubes work, but crushed is better) and add lime juice and spirits. Top with chilled soda; stir and garnish. Serve with a straw.

EAST INDIA COCKTAIL

Brandy's a bold base for this most delectable of boozy fruit cups.

EAST INDIA COCKTAIL

2 oz. brandy
1 tsp. curaçao
1 tsp. pineapple gomme syrup
2 dashes maraschino liqueur
2-3 dashes Boker's bitters (or substitute Peychaud's or Angostura)

Glass: cocktail

Garnish: lemon twist, cherry

Method: Stir with ice to chill; strain into chilled glass. Garnish.

Variation: Substitute raspberry syrup for the pineapple gomme and enjoy a slightly different style of dazzle.

Every creative form has moments that divide what came before from what will henceforth be: from Filippo Brunelleschi's Middle Ages revelation of linear perspective that put the wheels of Renaissance art in motion, to John Lennon's twang of feedback on *I Feel Fine*—the precursor to thousands of shrieking Stratocaster solos. There are many milestones in mixology, but among the more deliciously notable is the seismic shift in choice of sweeteners that took cocktails into the realms of Fancy and Improved (for more, see page 108), and transformed black-and-white drinks into vivid Cinerama-esque cocktails.

The East India Cocktail is a prolonged riff on the Brandy Cocktail, with such minor alterations added upon one another that, together, they create a distinctively different—and mighty dashing—sort of creature. Recipes for the East India began circulating sometime before 1882, when a version appeared in Harry Johnson's *New and Improved Bartender's Manual*; by 1900, its formula had been refined and improved into what you see here.

Built upon an elegant base of brandy—against which are filigreed the flavors of pineapple, bitter orange, maraschino, and that indefinable note from the bitters—the East India Cocktail is one of the more luscious drinks in the cocktail catalog. At some point, cocktail guides began substituting raspberry syrup for the pineapple (a highly recommended variation), or pineapple juice for the pineapple gomme (not as great of an idea, but still not too shabby).

A TASTE APART

PINEAPPLE & RASPBERRY

Fruit your cocktails are sweet on.

In the late 19th century, putting pineapple or raspberry into a drink as modifying flavors was akin to casting Marilyn Monroe or Cary Grant in a film's minor role: the small role didn't diminish the brightness of the talent, but rather it bathed everything in the surroundings in a much more attractive glow.

It helps that pineapples and raspberries have a natural voluptuousness of flavor, and that the character of each is both accentuated and well-preserved when the fruit is used to flavor syrup. Pineapple (via its genus sobriquet, Ananas) and raspberry were among the handful of fruits deployed into syrup form in 1862's *A Manual for the Manufacture of Cordials, Liquors, Fancy Syrups, &c., &c.*, Christian Schultz's less-familiar companion to Jerry Thomas' *How to Mix Drinks* (other syrups include those made with cherries and red currants, along with the almond-rich orgeat and capillaire, made with maidenhead fern). Delectable on their own, both fruits have a special affinity for brandy; the bright, bramble flavor of raspberry also has a special friend in gin, as in the Clover Club cocktail (see page 69), and the bosomy richness of pineapple is particularly desirable when paired with the tropical sparkle of rum, tequila, or mezcal. And American whiskey has memorable marriages with pineapple, as in the Prince of Wales cocktail, adapted here from David Wondrich's *Imbibe!*; and with raspberry in the Blinker, reintroduced to the world via Ted "Dr. Cocktail" Haigh's *Vintage Spirits and Forgotten Cocktails*.

As with any other ingredient that finds its way into a cocktail shaker, care needs to be taken regarding quality. Whole, fresh fruits are vastly superior to canned or bottled (frozen may suffice in a pinch), and for syrups, either make your own at home using the best fruit you can find (recipes are listed on page 186), or use a preferred version such as those from Small Hand Foods in San Francisco.

PRINCE OF WALES

1½ oz. rye whiskey
¼ oz. simple syrup
¼ tsp. maraschino liqueur
1 chunk fresh pineapple
1 dash Angostura bitters
1 oz. chilled Champagne

Glass: cocktail

Garnish: lemon twist

Method: Combine everything except Champagne in a cocktail shaker and shake with ice until chilled; double-strain into chilled glass and top with Champagne. Garnish.

BLINKER

2 oz. rye whiskey
1 oz. grapefruit juice
¼ oz. raspberry syrup

Glass: cocktail

Garnish: lemon twist

Method: Shake with ice to chill; strain into chilled glass. Garnish.

COCKTAIL STYLE

NEW ORLEANS

A few words about the Crescent City, the spiritual home to the cocktail.

ABSINTHE FRAPPE

1½ oz. absinthe
½ oz. simple syrup
2 oz. chilled club soda

Glass: goblet

Garnish: 2 dashes Peychaud's bitters

Method: Shake absinthe and simple syrup with ice to chill. Fill goblet with crushed ice and add soda, followed by the strained cocktail. Garnish by adding bitters to top of drink.

Variations: A few leaves of fresh mint muddled into the shaker at the start makes for a very agreeable touch.

New Orleans is the Jerusalem, the Mecca, the bodhi tree of mixology. The Crescent City may not be the actual birthplace of the cocktail—though that claim still finds itself sallied about with regularity—but what New Orleans may lack in historical precedence, it makes up for with inspiration and influence.

Not to mention enthusiasm. Our thirsty ancestors may have first cobbled together mixtures of booze, sugar, and bitters elsewhere—New York and the Northeast assert a more convincing claim—but it took a laissez-faire place like New Orleans to transform the act of self-lubrication into a refined art.

Exhibit A: the Sazerac (page 95). Break this NOLA standard down to its basic components, and it's nothing more than a souped-up Old Fashioned (or, more accurately, an improved Whiskey Cocktail—page 106). But rather than follow the established practice of dabbling everything together in the mixing glass, the creator of the Sazerac took a more labor-intensive direction: while the essential elements—sugar, liquor, and bitters (as with many New Orleans-based drinks, the local Peychaud's variety is called for)—are first mixed in the standard fashion, the drink finishes with a flourish, with the serving glass rinsed with absinthe (a city staple since 1837, and star of the hometown favorite Absinthe Frappe) before the drink is strained into it.

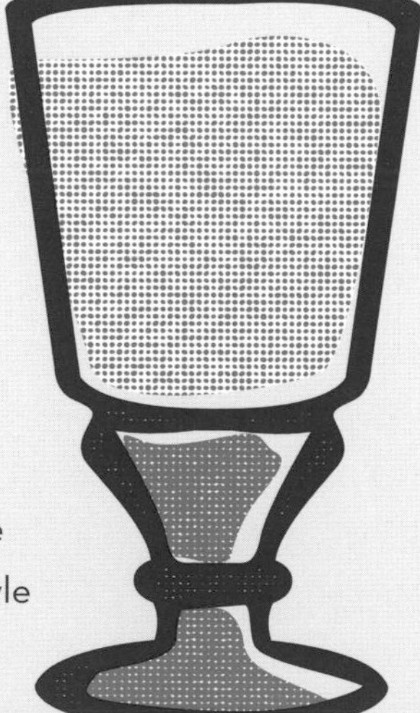

The come-hither pink of Peychaud's and the lascivious whiff of absinthe may, at first blush, suggest the Sazerac and its Crescent City kin are nothing more than particularly licentious local riffs on wider-established norms. But such flourishes and diversions are partially what define classic New Orleans-style cocktails and make the concoctions not only distinctive, but earn them a place on Louisiana's groaning table alongside culinary classics such as oysters Rockefeller and crawfish étoufée.

As it has for Creole cuisine and the style of music that sprang from Storyville, New Orleans has taken these local liquid oddities and gone global. The Sazerac may be a signature NOLA cocktail, but it's mixed from Sydney to Seattle, and the Ramos Fizz (page 150) and the Vieux Carre (page 93)—first crafted by Walter Bergeron at the Hotel Monteleone in the 1930s—are likewise familiar fixtures on craft-cocktail menus worldwide.

Other places may lay a stronger claim to being the birthplace of the cocktail, but what it may lack in historical precedent, New Orleans makes up for in inspiration and influence—not to mention enthusiasm.

But the city is also home to rare birds that don't often travel far from their NOLA nests, or that are found largely in fossilized form, passed around between far-flung collectors but infrequently encountered in the wild. The raspberry-rich Roffignac (page 92) is one such creature, named for a French count who fled the Revolution and later served as mayor in the 1820s; the Cocktail à la Louisiane—a rich and seductively sweet mixture that was the house cocktail at the Restaurant de la Louisiane—is another. And during the time when absinthe was scarce in the U.S. due to bans both domestic and foreign, New Orleans nurtured an enduring taste for its ethereal anise flavor via imported substitutes such as the Spanish anisette Ojen (deployed most memorably in an Ojen Frappe), and homegrown alternatives such as Milky Way and Herbsaint.

But while some New Orleans-based drinks may seem like liquid relics preserved in whiskey-hued amber, the city itself is a morphing organism, and the recent spate of cocktail evolution is transforming the city's bars and

COCKTAIL À LA LOUISIANE

3/4 oz. rye whiskey
3/4 oz. sweet vermouth
3/4 oz. Bénédictine
2 dashes absinthe
2 dashes Peychaud's bitters

Glass: cocktail

Garnish: cherry

Method: Stir with ice to chill; strain into chilled glass. Garnish.

CREOLE

1 oz. rye whiskey
1 oz. sweet vermouth
2 dashes Bénédictine
2 dashes Amer Picon

Glass: cocktail

Garnish: lemon twist

Method: Stir with ice to chill; strain into chilled glass. Garnish.

COCKTAIL STYLE

NEW ORLEANS *(continued)*

> **ROFFIGNAC**
>
> 1 oz. brandy
> 3/4 oz. rye whiskey
> 3/4 oz. raspberry syrup
> 1 tsp. red-wine vinegar
> 2 oz. chilled club soda
>
> **Glass:** highball
>
> **Garnish:** raspberry, lemon wheel
>
> **Method:** Shake everything except club soda with ice to chill; add soda to shaker and strain drink into glass filled with fresh ice. Garnish.
>
> *Adapted by Chris Hannah, New Orleans*

restaurants, and its cocktails both old and new. While the city's formative drinks decades were influenced by characters ranging from Antoine Amédée Peychaud to Henry Charles Ramos, today's New Orleans has likewise given rise to some of the most powerful mixology minds in the country. Figures such as Chris McMillian and Paul Gustings have revived the reputation of time-burnished standards, and local bartender-entrepreneurs including Neal Bodenheimer, Kirk Estopinal, and Nick Detrich have reawakened NOLA's mixology memory at a growing empire of bars including Cure, Bellocq, and Cane & Table that are placing the city's contemporary cocktail credentials in the same culinary spotlight shared by local chefs like Donald Link and John Besh.

And some of the most memorable cocktails to be found in New Orleans are served at one of the city's more venerable establishments, Arnaud's French 75 bar, only a half-block from the bead-flinging frenzy of Bourbon Street. With his shaved head and formal white jacket, bartender Chris Hannah has embarked on a mission to reestablish NOLA as the Holy Land for cocktail true believers. Hannah's explorations of the city's drinking past uncovered the "aha" secret behind the Roffignac's former glory (a dab of vinegar to spark the drink's bright flavor), and his original drinks are often nods to the city's bibulous heritage while planting themselves resolutely in the Facebook-age present. Consider Hannah's Bywater, named for the city's Caribbean-accented neighborhood; rich with the island tastes of rum and falernum, and lent French finery via Chartreuse and Amer Picon, the Bywater is a New Orleans drink at its core, but fully at home in today's cocktail renaissance.

Between such trailblazing bars and local events such as the annual Tales of the Cocktail conference, which every summer turns the city into a playground for thousands of bartenders from around the world, New Orleans has credentials supporting its status as the Holy See of cocktails. The drinks coming across the bar at places such as the French 75, SoBou, Broussard's, Cure, Bellocq, and Cane & Table (and a recent feather in the city's cocktail cap, Beachbum Berry's Latitude 29) may bear little resemblance to sacramental wine, but for a city like New Orleans, it's pretty damn close.

VIEUX CARRE

¾ oz. rye whiskey
¾ oz. brandy
¾ oz. sweet vermouth
1 tsp. Bénédictine
1 dash Angostura bitters
1 dash Peychaud's bitters

Glass: rocks

Garnish: lemon twist

Method: Stir with ice to chill, strain into glass filled with fresh ice. Garnish.

BYWATER

1¾ oz. amber rum (Cruzan Single Barrel recommended)
¾ oz. Amer Picon
½ oz. green Chartreuse
¼ oz. falernum
2 dashes Peychaud's bitters

Glass: cocktail

Garnish: orange twist

Method: Stir with ice to chill; strain into chilled glass. Garnish.

Chris Hannah, New Orleans

SEELBACH COCKTAIL

Bourbon fuels a bona fide Kentucky classic.

SEELBACH COCKTAIL

1 oz. bourbon
½ oz. Cointreau
7 dashes Angostura bitters
7 dashes Peychaud's bitters
2-3 oz. chilled Champagne

Glass: coupe or champagne flute
Garnish: lemon twist
Method: Stir first four ingredients with ice to chill; strain into chilled glass. Top with Champagne. Garnish.

The Great Gatsby is unclear as to whether Daisy Buchanan had an affinity for bourbon. F. Scott Fitzgerald clearly did, however, and he chose one of the most glamorous places in bourbon country—the Seelbach Hotel in Louisville—as inspiration for the fictitious hotel that hosted Daisy's wedding.

Still one of the most elegant places in town to grab a drink, the Seelbach has a house cocktail that, appropriately enough, is based on bourbon—and, given the hotel's prestige, it's also appropriately bolstered with Champagne. The bourbon is softened with a trace of orange liqueur, but then this softness is rendered ridiculous by the addition of fourteen—*fourteen!*—dashes of bitters. But Champagne absolves all transgressions, or at least erases the memory of them, and the muscular Seelbach Cocktail can be exceptional at that.

LIBERAL

A whiskey-rich cocktail with bipartisan appeal.

LIBERAL

2 oz. rye whiskey
½ oz. sweet vermouth
¼ oz. Amer Picon (or substitute)
2 dashes orange bitters

Glass: cocktail
Garnish: lemon twist
Method: Stir with ice to chill, strain into chilled glass. Garnish.

Whether you use the word as a self-descriptor or fling it as an epithet, don't approach (or avoid) the Liberal solely because of its name. Instead, grab one because of its hot-damn deliciousness.

An early incarnation appeared in George Kappeler's *Modern American Drinks* in 1895, but it quickly evolved into more-or-less the version posted here by 1914, when it appeared in Jacques Straub's *Drinks*.

A member of the extended Manhattan family, the Liberal is also notable for its use of Amer Picon. This French bitter liqueur is scarce stateside but workarounds exist (see page 181), and its use in the Liberal was an early precursor to the flood of richly embittered, amaro-laden cocktails of today.

It takes a little effort to mix a Liberal, but do take the trouble—it's so good, it'll make a bleeding heart out of you regardless of your political stripe.

SAZERAC

The king of New Orleans cocktails.

There are some in this world—mainly centered around New Orleans—who would assert that by all normally understood rules of primogeniture, the Sazerac is the undisputed king of cocktails. But lines of succession are rarely unsullied, and when you're talking about a mixture that sprang from the bullshit-fertile fields of the barroom, both rules and normality are open to interpretation.

But there are several immutable truths about the Sazerac. First, it did originate in the liquor-loving bars of New Orleans, a place where—even during the cocktail's darkest decades—the Sazerac reigned supreme, garnished if not with a crown, then with the air of certainty that it's the *ne plus ultra* of lip moisteners.

The second truth, however, is less prestigious: the Sazerac is a pretender to the throne. Contrary to what Crescent City boosters ranging from *Famous New Orleans Drinks and How to Mix 'Em* author Stanley Clisby Arthur to today's Bourbon Street bartenders may assert, the Sazerac is not the first and original cocktail. Though the Sazerac's format may have been familiar during the cocktail's early days, the name wasn't bandied about (in print, anyway) until the turn of the 20th century. It may have been liquid royalty in NOLA, but elsewhere, as Bartender's Union of New York president Jack Townsend and Tom Moore McBride noted in their *The Bartender's Book* in 1951, "the Sazarac [sic]-Zazarac-Schmazarac is just a variant of an Old Fashioned with trimmings."

But let's not ignore the third truth of the Sazerac: it's goddamned delicious. It started out as a Cognac-based cocktail, then switched to rye whiskey at some point; I usually follow bartending oracle Dale DeGroff and split between the two, sometimes leaning harder on the Cognac. Pretender or not, the Sazerac is still a king of the cocktail hour.

SAZERAC

2 oz. rye whiskey
1 tsp. simple syrup
2 dashes Peychaud's bitters
1/2 tsp. absinthe

Glass: rocks

Garnish: lemon twist

Method: Add the absinthe to a chilled rocks glass and rotate the glass to "rinse," or coat the bottom and sides of the glass, with absinthe; discard excess. Stir whiskey, syrup, and bitters with ice; strain into absinthe-rinsed glass. Twist lemon peel over drink and discard.

Variation: Try Cognac in place of rye, or mix them half-and-half like Dale DeGroff; 1 1/2 oz. Cognac and 1/2 oz. rye is also excellent.

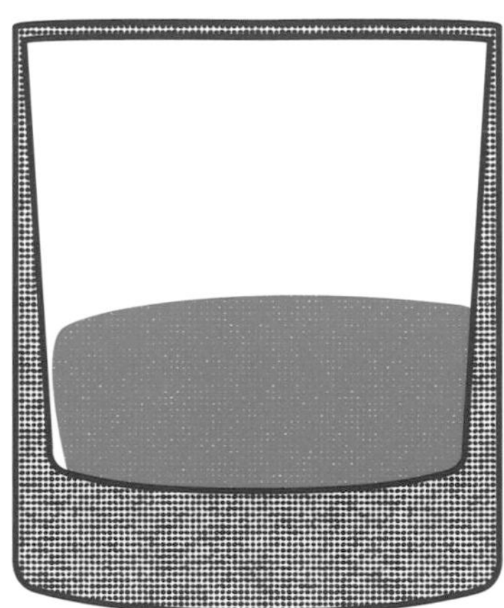

COCKTAIL ESSENTIALS

WHISKEY

What beer wants to be when it grows up.

DIXIE COCKTAIL

2 oz. bourbon
1 tsp. gomme syrup (or simple syrup)
1 tsp. curaçao
1 dash Angostura bitters
3-4 dashes crème de menthe

Glass: rocks

Garnish: lemon twist

Method: Stir with ice to chill; strain into glass filled with fresh ice. Garnish.

Adapted by Erik Adkins, San Francisco

It's an aphorism of spirits that whiskey is simply distilled beer—and it's another truism that beer in pretty much any form is amazing. Whiskey often needs nothing more than a glass and maybe a little water or ice as ideal accompaniments, but the spirit is also a backbone of mixology. And whiskey is increasingly a global drink, having long ago spread from its native Ireland to Scotland, and then to the New World before progressing more recently to distilleries in Asia and Australia. A whiskey's place of origin is a matter of more than simple geography: different whiskies bring different characteristics to a cocktail shaker. Check the Liquor Cabinet (page 177) for recommended brands.

Bourbon

Perhaps the most familiar style of whiskey to American drinkers is bourbon, a spirit born in Kentucky and now distilled from the Seattle suburbs to the Florida coast. Built upon a base of corn (bourbon's recipe must be at least 51 percent corn), the spirit is made with a touch of malted barley, which aids fermentation, and flavor accents are typically added in the form of rye—which contributes a dry, spicy flavor—or wheat, which produces a softer, sweeter whiskey. Regardless of the recipe, all whiskies labeled "straight bourbon" (the stuff you want) are aged a minimum of two years in new, charred-oak barrels (though a minimum of four years is more typical, and bourbon hits its sweet spot between six and 12 years) and bottled without any coloring or flavoring.

Close your eyes and think of cornbread—got it? Alluring, mildly sweet, and maybe a little rustic—beguiling in a farmer's-daughter kind of way. That's what bourbon tastes like, which makes it perfect for drinks like the Old Fashioned (see page 106) and the Mint Julep (page 52), along with contemporary drinks such as the Kentucky Buck from San Diego bartender Erick Castro.

But that mellowness can be bourbon's mixological weakness: most cocktails require a drier whiskey, with a little more edge, in order to maintain a balanced flavor. That's when you need bourbon's historically northern cousin, which brings its elbow-throwing properties to the mixing glass to keep other ingredients from stepping out of line. In other words, these are situations where you need . . .

Rye Whiskey

Cornbread, meet rye bread—soft and sweet, meet dry and spicy. Rye may be a little more rangy than bourbon, but it's a hell of a lot of fun once you get acquainted.

Rye was once the king of American whiskies, and considering its bounce-back over the past decade, it has high hopes (if little chance) of reclaiming the crown. Straight rye whiskey is much like its bourbon kin: swap rye for corn as the foundation of the mash bill, and all other variables—the barrel, the bottling—remain constant.

But while bourbon's soft sweetness has made it the current sipping-whiskey favorite, rye's bucket-of-knuckles bang makes it better suited for most cocktails. Hit a cocktail with vermouth or liqueurs, and the flavor of most bourbons quickly folds, forming a mix that's soft and flabby; but swap bourbon for rye, and those sweeter ingredients encounter a little push-back, resulting in a cocktail with a pleasing balance and a powerful whiskey pop.

One thing, though: make sure you're using a straight American rye whiskey, such as Rittenhouse, Sazerac, or Old Overholt. Otherwise, you may find yourself stepping into unexpected territory, as comes with another whisky (note the missing "e") that sometimes travels under the nom-de-booze "rye."

KENTUCKY BUCK

2 oz. bourbon
¾ oz. lemon juice
½ oz. simple syrup
1 ripe strawberry
2 dashes Angostura bitters
Chilled ginger beer

Glass: Collins

Garnish: sliced strawberry, lemon wheel

Method: Muddle strawberry in a shaker with syrup and lemon; add bourbon, bitters and ice and shake to chill. Double-strain into ice-filled Collins glass; top with ginger beer.

Erick Castro, San Diego

COCKTAIL ESSENTIALS

WHISKEY *(continued)*

PAPER PLANE

¾ oz. bourbon
¾ oz. Aperol
¾ oz. lemon juice
¾ oz. Amaro Nonino

Glass: cocktail

Method: Shake with ice to chill; strain into chilled glass.

Sam Ross, New York City

RAPSCALLION

2¼ oz. Talisker (or a smoky Islay single-malt Scotch)
¾ oz. Pedro Ximenez (PX) sherry
1 tsp. absinthe

Glass: cocktail

Garnish: lemon twist

Method: Stir whisky and sherry with ice to chill. Rinse chilled cocktail glass with absinthe and discard excess. Strain cocktail into rinsed glass; twist lemon peel over drink and discard.

Adeline Shepard and Craig Harper, Copenhagen

Canadian Whisky

Oh, Canada. (*Sigh.*) Northern neighbor, your whisky situation presents quite a quandary.

Once upon a time, Canadian whisky was largely a rye-focused spirit, but that's long since stopped being the norm (though there are notable exceptions). Instead, an overwhelming majority of Canadian whisky is a blend of spirits, with neutral spirits and other ingredients making up a good chunk of many familiar Canadian brands. That's not inherently bad, but the mildness many brands have aimed for comes off in a way that many dedicated whisky fans consider boring (or worse).

But for every swing of the pendulum, there's a return, and there are early signals that Canadian whisky may be staging a comeback. Brands such as Forty Creek began burnishing Canadian's reputation years ago, and imports such as Whistle Pig have proven there's tasty stuff to be found above the 49th parallel. More recently, decent whiskies such as those from Alberta Distillers have begun flowing south of the border, and even some of the widely known brands are starting to realize there's a growing demand for better-tasting booze.

Still, most Canadian whisky sold in the U.S. is aimed to be mixed with nothing more exotic than a can of Sprite. The good stuff is increasingly available, but while you're on the lookout for mild styles of the spirit that still deliver some flavorful complexity, be sure to check out . . .

Irish Whiskey

Ireland is whiskey's ancestral home, and contemporary drinkers are increasingly bonkers for the stuff. Irish has all the mildness of the more prevalent Canadian spirit, but its character—usually produced by mixing pot-distilled whiskey from malted barley with lighter grain whiskey—has a lot more game to it. Familiar brands include Jameson and Bushmills, but keep an eye out for the single-pot-still whiskies from Red Breast and Green Spot, as well as for whiskies from up-and-coming Irish craft distillers like Teeling's.

There aren't a great many Irish whiskey cocktails in circulation, though thanks to transplanted Belfast bartenders Sean Muldoon and Jack McGarry at Dead Rabbit Grocery and Grog in New York, that's changing; Muldoon's interpretation of a classic Tipperary is immensely enjoyable, and drinks such as the Emerald—nothing more than an Irish whiskey Manhattan made with orange bitters—is a worthwhile diversion.

But this world tour of whiskey hasn't yet reached the land of bounty, the place that brought us . . .

Scotch Whisky

No "e", lots of attitude. Scotch is a complicated thing: you have mild, silky blends destined for an ocean of highballs (and a good all-around choice for cocktails), and you also have a vast universe of single malts ranging from the feathery light flavors of Lowland malts like Auchentoshan to big, brawling bastards like the smoky bantamweights from Islay: Laphroaig, Ardbeg, and their ilk. Though cocktails such as the Rob Roy have earned a place in mixology's hall of fame, Scotch rarely plays well with other ingredients. But there are exceptions—oh boy, are there exceptions. When the whisky finds an agreeable assortment of companions in a mixing glass, watch out—Scotch has a boldness of flavor that can be roguish and seductive all at the same time.

Japanese Whisky

A relative newcomer to the American bar, and well worth seeking out. Japanese whisky started out almost a century ago as a more-or-less clone of Scotch whisky, but it has since evolved and earned its own special identity. Grab it when you see it, and give it a spin on its own or in a Whiskey and Soda highball, the drink of choice on its home turf.

TORONTO COCKTAIL

2 oz. Canadian whisky or rye whiskey

¼ oz. Fernet-Branca

¼ oz. simple syrup

2 dashes Angostura bitters

Glass: cocktail

Garnish: orange twist

Method: Stir with ice to chill; strain into chilled glass. Twist orange peel over glass; use as garnish.

TIPPERARY

1½ oz. Irish whiskey

1 oz. sweet vermouth

½ oz. green Chartreuse

½ oz. chilled water

2 dashes orange bitters

1 tsp. rich simple syrup

Glass: cocktail

Method: Stir with ice to chill; strain into chilled glass.

Adapted by Sean Muldoon, New York City

CHAPTER 3

MUSES & BRIDGES

Five enduring classics and the drinks they've inspired

When I first visited the Northwest rain forests soon after relocating to Seattle, I was introduced to the concept of the "nurse log"—a massive, ancient Douglas fir or cedar that's fallen, and upon whose decaying form a number of (sometimes enormous) younger trees grow.

It's an imperfect analogy to compare the Manhattan or the Daiquiri to a nurse log—after all, drinks such as these not only weathered the ruin of Prohibition, but emerged after Repeal even stronger than before. But while neither the Negroni nor the Martini are the clear equivalents of decaying conifers forgotten in our past, such drinks do serve as fertile foundations for a steadily thickening canopy of variations and new interpretations.

Each of the drinks highlighted here originated a century or more ago. But today's bartenders and cocktail enthusiasts continue to appreciate their appeal—which is to say, they drink the hell out of them—and when the need for a new recipe arises, these drinks often serve as templates through which novel variations can take shape.

Of course, bartenders have known this for a long time, and some of the most memorable twists on the Daiquiri and the Manhattan have histories stretching back almost as long as those of the original drinks. But today's cocktail resurgence has brought new opportunities—and new ideas and ingredients. Here are the cocktails that managed to bridge yesterday's Golden Age of mixology with today's cocktail renaissance, and a few of the many twists and turns they've inspired along the way.

DAIQUIRI

Cuba's contribution to the global cocktail party.

Everyone from Pythagoras to the Pope has recognized there's something special about the number three. And while there's no shortage of significant cocktail trios, the Holy Trinity of mixology is the unity of rum, sugar, and lime.

Our punch-drinking ancestors in both the Old World and the New long recognized this bibulous truism, and in rum's ancestral Caribbean home, variations on the theme ring throughout the islands. As exotic-drinks scholar Jeff "Beachbum" Berry wrote in *Potions of the Caribbean*, by the time of the Daiquiri's debut around the turn of the last century, "recombining rum, lime and sugar into a new drink was like changing a tire and saying you invented the wheel." But while the Daiquiri may have had predecessors that passed along similar strands of genetic code, the drink both encapsulates the tradition and expands on the possibilities, and continues to be a font of tropical inspiration.

Long credited to Jennings Cox, an American mine superintendent stationed in Cuba, the Daiquiri became the island's signature cocktail—and a fashionable stateside favorite—in the decades following its 1896 origin. And why not? The basic Daiquiri has a simplicity of creation and a majestic balance that have helped its enduring relevance. Built upon a base of crisp Cuban rum—unlike the richer (and occasionally raunchier) rums from the English islands of Barbados and Jamaica, the rum from Cuba (and those from Puerto Rico, to which the Bacardi family fled during Castro's ascent) has a bright crispness of character that, when pinched with the tart tang of lime and softened with the smoothness of sugar, produces a drink that bears a perpetual smile.

It's also perpetually ready to party. Like its northern colleague the Manhattan (see page 109), the Daiquiri is a ready-made launch pad for improvisation. Bartenders realized this early on, and were riffing on the Daiquiri's dependable trio of ingredients almost from the start. The most renowned

DAIQUIRI

2 oz. white rum
¾ oz. lime juice
2 tsp. simple syrup, to taste

Glass: cocktail

Garnish: thin lime wedge

Method: Shake with ice to chill; strain into chilled glass. Garnish.

DAIQUIRI REDUX

FLORIDITA DAIQUIRI (aka Daiquiri #4)

2 oz. white rum
¾ oz. lime juice
1 tsp. maraschino liqueur
1 tsp. simple syrup

Glass: cocktail
Garnish: lime wheel
Method: Shake with ice to chill; strain into chilled glass. Garnish.

HEMINGWAY DAIQUIRI (aka Daiquiri #3)

2 oz. white rum
¾ oz. lime juice
¼ oz. grapefruit juice
¼ oz. maraschino liqueur
1 tsp. simple syrup (optional)

Glass: cocktail or goblet
Garnish: lime wheel
Method: Shake ingredients with ice to chill; strain into chilled cocktail glass, or strain into goblet filled with crushed ice. Garnish.

DAISY DE SANTIAGO

2 oz. white rum
1 oz. lime juice
½ oz. yellow Chartreuse
½ oz. simple syrup
1 oz. chilled soda water

Glass: goblet
Garnish: mint leaf
Method: Combine first four ingredients in glass and stir to combine. Add crushed ice and soda; stir to mix; garnish.

Adapted by Erik Adkins, San Francisco

maestro of the mixture was Spanish-born barman Constantino Ribalaigua Vert, who during the four decades he presided over the legendary Havana bar La Florida, mixed so many Daiquiris—reputedly 10 million—that he earned the title *El Rey de los Coteleros*: the Cocktail King. The Daiquiri was both Constante's paintbrush and his canvas, the simple foundation upon which (and the medium through which) he dazzled the thirsty hordes of American tourists who ventured south during the dry years of Prohibition, including Cuba's most notable expatriate (and Daiquiri hound), Ernest Hemingway.

Constante's tinkering with the Daiquiri was seemingly minor, but the effects were extraordinary and enduring. The basic drink could be lengthened and made more luxurious simply by swapping ice cubes for shaved ice (or, as technology evolved, by tossing the whole thing into a Waring blender). Orange juice and curaçao enlivened Constante's Daiquiri #2, and maraschino liqueur, when added to the basic formula and served as a frosty frappe (with grapefruit, for the Daiquiri #3, and without, for #4), lends a complexity and depth that's so overpoweringly alluring that Hemingway adopted his own mucked-up, Big Gulp-size variation on the formula as his oh-so-regular Floridita favorite.

By the 1960s, the Daiquiri was not only a favored cocktail in the Kennedy White House—the First Lady reportedly mixed them with frozen limeade—but it was also serving as the template through which the dueling tiki empires of Don the

Beachcomber and Trader Vic's waged battle (for more on these guys, see page 159). Donn Beach added the vanilla/violet tones of parfait amour and blended the drink to make a Royal Daiquiri, whereas Victor Bergeron—who had traveled to Havana to sit at Constante's bar for instruction—introduced orgeat and curaçao to what was essentially an aged-rum Daiquiri to create perhaps the most notable Daiquiri descendant, the Mai Tai (see page 159).

By the turn of the 21st century, however, the Daiquiri was in a slump. The finely tuned balance of ingredients and the promising *rat-tat-tat* of Constante's shakers had been supplanted by the hum of a horde of Daiquiri Dude and similar Slurpee-esque styles of drink machines. These devices discharged frozen ropes of lime-green goo (or equally suspect strawberry-pink or banana-ish yellow strands) into plastic go-cups for tourists to stab with straws as they stagger down Bourbon Street or the Vegas Strip. The Daiquiri seemed to be dead; the sun-soaked Caribbean swank once ruled by El Rey de los Coteleros had devolved into the crass-convenience lifestyle of *Jersey Shore*.

But when the cocktail renaissance came around, the Daiquiri soon joined the Manhattan and the Martini as one of the esteemed classics ripe for revival. Bartenders broke down the Daiquiri to its fundamentals, considering each component in relation to one another, then reassembled the drink, in some cases custom blending (or inspiring the creation of) rums designed to sing particularly harmoniously in this three-part choir. With Cuban-made Havana Club still locked out by an ongoing American embargo (though at the time of this writing, the situation seems about to change), and many major brands lacking the desired oomph, bartenders are turning to Daiquiri-primed rums such as Caña Brava, Banks 5 Island, and Plantation 3 Stars to craft cocktails with a bright, clean edge, but with an underlying glint of cheeky funk.

DAIQUIRI REDUX *(continued)*

BOUKMAN DAIQUIRI

1½ oz. white rum (Flor de Caña recommended)
½ oz. Cognac
¾ oz. lime juice
½ oz. cinnamon syrup (see page 185)

Glass: cocktail
Garnish: lime wedge
Method: Shake with ice to chill, strain into chilled glass. Garnish.

Alex Day, New York City

WINTER DAIQUIRI

1½ oz. aged rum (something mellow—Banks 7 Golden Age works great)
¾ oz. lime juice
½ oz. vanilla syrup (see page 185)
¼ oz. allspice liqueur
1 dash Angostura bitters

Glass: cocktail
Garnish: half lime wheel studded with cloves
Method: Shake with ice to chill, strain into chilled glass. Garnish.

Mindy Kucan, Portland, Oregon

DAIQUIRI REDUX *(continued)*

TRINIDAD HOOK

2 oz. overproof rum (preferably Trinidad—hence the name)
3/4 oz. lime juice
1 oz. passion-honey mixture (see below)
2 dashes Angostura bitters

Glass: cocktail
Garnish: long spiral-cut lime twist
Method: Shake with ice to chill; strain into chilled glass. Garnish.
Passion-honey mixture: Heat 2 oz. honey until liquid; stir in 2 oz. pure unsweetened passion fruit nectar. Let cool; keep refrigerated.

Martin Cate, San Francisco

NUCLEAR DAIQUIRI

3/4 oz. overproof white Jamaican rum (Wray & Nephew)
3/4 oz. lime juice
3/4 oz. green Chartreuse
2 tsp. falernum
1 tsp. simple syrup (optional)

Glass: cocktail
Method: Shake with ice to chill; strain into chilled glass.

Gregor de Gruyther, London

Older variations such as the Daiquiri #4 (which also travels as the Floridita Daiquiri) and the Daiquiri #3 (often referred to, largely erroneously, as the Hemingway Daiquiri) have gained a second wind, as have other venerable twists, such as Charles H. Baker, Jr.'s Chartreuse-soaked Daisy de Santiago (all on page 103). The ease of tweaking the Daiquiri's open-source code has also appealed to today's bartenders, who utilize a range of rums (and rum blends) to expand the Daiquiri's possibilities, and mix and mingle sweeteners and modifiers to push the simple cocktail in myriad directions.

Thus we have interpretations such as the cinnamon-warmed Boukman Daiquiri, crafted for Death & Co. by Alex Day; the rich vanilla notes of the Winter Daiquiri from Portland bartender Mindy Kucan for Northwest tiki bar Hale Pele; and the passion fruit-nudged Trinidad Hook from Martin Cate, owner of San Francisco rum wonderland Smuggler's Cove. True to form for a cocktail with friends around the globe, love for the Daiquiri has also inspired variations such as the Nuclear Daiquiri, a mixture with an H-bomb's potency, made with overproof Jamaican rum and green Chartreuse and created by Gregor de Gruyther at LAB bar in London.

But perhaps the Daiquiri's most positive and, one hopes, lingering effect is revealing itself as the cocktail renaissance matures. Daiquiri Time Out—a stop-and-smell-the-roses effort built around the Daiquiri's inherently relaxing qualities—takes the simple three-ingredient drink and makes it the fulcrum upon which calm and considered reflection may be balanced. Propounding the view that, even during life's most trying moments, there's always time for a Daiquiri, the DTO has spread worldwide as a distinctive kind of event—one with a drink at its core, perhaps, but with a brightness of intent that spreads far beyond the barroom.

OLD FASHIONED

The cocktail version of comfort food.

When the world feels too complicated, and the drudgery of daily life seems too much, it's time for an Old Fashioned.

Then again, an Old Fashioned is also entirely appropriate when everything seems just peachy. But with its simple, familiar preparation ritual and its name a blatant nod to bygone days, the Old Fashioned seems particularly well-suited to those times when a little comfort-drink soothing is just the ticket.

This is as it should be: the Old Fashioned is perhaps the most nurturing cocktail in the canon. At its core nothing more than a basic mix of sugar, bitters and (usually) whiskey, the Old Fashioned is the mixological equivalent of a coelacanth, a living fossil of a fish that was thought to have gone extinct by the end of the Cretaceous period yet still swims the oceans today. But while the coelacanth is desperately endangered, the Old Fashioned is anything but—from the indignities thrust upon it during the cocktail's late-20th century dark ages, the Old Fashioned has rebounded in both enthusiasm and numbers with a virile vengeance that even the most procreation-adept bunny would envy.

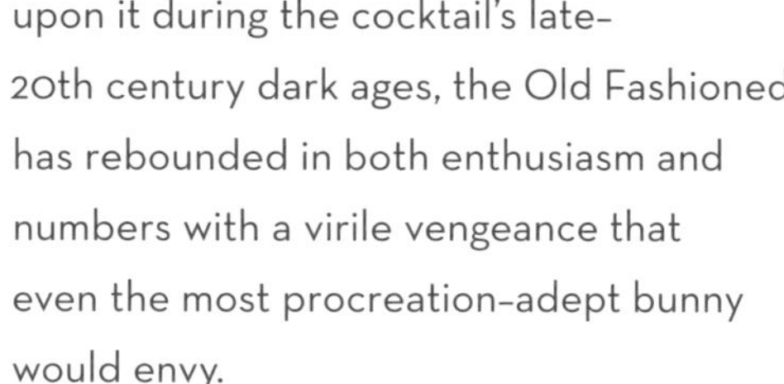

The Old Fashioned's deepest DNA stretches back to the circa-1800 birth of the cocktail (which, as defined in the *Balance & Columbian Repository* in 1806, was composed of a spirit, sugar, bitters and water), and for decades the Old Fashioned's ancestor circulated simply as a Whiskey Cocktail (or Brandy Cocktail, or Holland Gin Cocktail, or—you get the idea). But in the mid-19th century, bartenders began prodding at the basic formula (see "Fancy & Improved," on page 108), and what some saw as creative tinkering was interpreted by others as the unwanted meddling with a good thing. Eventually, by the century's

OLD FASHIONED

2 oz. bourbon or rye whiskey (or any spirit, really)

1 sugar cube or 1 tsp. superfine sugar or 2 tsp. simple syrup

2 dashes Angostura bitters (or any bitters, really)

Glass: rocks

Garnish: lemon twist

Method: Place sugar cube in glass and soak with bitters and a few drops of water; crush to paste with wooden muddler. You can use loose sugar instead, or simple syrup (skip the added water if the latter), but the ritual contributes to the experience. Add whiskey and stir to mix and dissolve sugar; add ice and stir again to chill. Garnish.

closing years—drinks journalist Robert Simonson says the "Old Fashioned" label turns up in 1888, and a recognizable recipe appears in George Kappeler's *Modern American Drinks* in 1895—those desiring a simple, old-style cocktail that hadn't been mucked with by a well-intentioned bartender came to refer to the drink as an "Old Fashioned," proving that even during the good-old days, people still had a hankering for the good-old days.

Of course, muckery happens, and by the second half of the 20th century, much of it was happening to the Old Fashioned. What started as the most simple and effortlessly elegant of mixtures turned into a slopped-out slob, unnecessarily embellished with fruit and club soda into a faded shadow of its former self. With mashed maraschino cherries streaking the glass like smeared lipstick and glugs of seltzer leaving the drink saggy and limp, all that was needed was the garnish of a smoldering Pall Mall to make the tragic picture complete.

But along with its classic compatriots the Martini, Daiquiri, and Manhattan, the Old Fashioned has been dusted off and cleaned up by bartenders in the current cocktail resurgence. Muddled bar fruit and superfluous soda were given the heave-ho, and the Old Fashioned returned to its once-accustomed fighting weight, stripped back to the essential basics of nothing more than whiskey, bitters, sugar, and ice, accessorized with a modest strip of citrus.

Usually, anyway. For while the Old Fashioned's recent sins were forgiven and its lustrous legacy restored, bartenders will still be bartenders. The descendant of the Whiskey Cocktail still seems to beg bartenders to add fancifications and improvements, just as its predecessor did 150 years ago. And though the Old Fashioned has taught us that this road can conceivably lead to ruin, today's bartenders have the benefits of hindsight, and are feeling free to tinker while still respecting the Old Fashioned's inherent beauty.

New York bartenders Richie Boccato and Michael McIlroy (then working at Little Branch, among other places) riffed on the standard by swapping half of the whiskey for American apple brandy, and adding the citrusy earthiness of orange bitters in place of Angostura's baking-spice spark, resulting in the American Trilogy. Fellow New Yorker Phil Ward, whose East Village bar Mayahuel has introduced countless drinkers to the wonders of agave, dispensed with the whiskey altogether, using reposado tequila and a dab of smoky mezcal for the base. And for Rob Roy in Seattle, Andrew Bohrer took the Old Fashioned in an Old World direction, building an autumnal drink upon the ethereal depths of French Calvados, and emboldening the mix with a touch of bitter, walnut-rich nocino (all on page 108).

Such interpretations (and there are many more—Robert Simonson wrote a full book about them, suitably titled *The Old-Fashioned*) would likely set our Fancy Whiskey Cocktail-averse ancestors' teeth on edge. That's okay—there are plenty of things worth getting dogmatic about, and drinks aren't among them. But for such a stylish character as the Old Fashioned,

having gone through disgrace and then being restored to glory gives the drink additional forbearance—it's fine being mixed in the manner you prefer.

FANCY & IMPROVED

Between the early 19th-century origins of the simple cocktail and its late 1800s reincarnation as the Old Fashioned, came the tinkering and twiddling that resulted in the now mostly forgotten class of Fancy and Improved Cocktails. These minor modifications to the established formula typically entailed nothing more than a barspoon here of curaçao or maraschino and maybe a dash of absinthe there—precursors to the more full-fledged creativity that kicked into a higher gear in the years after the Civil War. Few such manifestations have survived in the long run; the Improved Holland Gin Cocktail is one that's come back from the beyond. A *Jurassic Park*-style resuscitated drink that's essentially an Old Fashioned made with genever and lightly accented with liqueurs, the cocktail is a flavorful fossil from the days when the Transcontinental Railroad was the newest and hottest thing around.

OLD-FASHIONED MADE NEW

AMERICAN TRILOGY

1 oz. rye whiskey (100 proof preferred)
1 oz. American apple brandy (100 proof preferred)
1 cube Demerara sugar or 1 tsp. rich Demerara syrup
2 dashes orange bitters

Glass: rocks
Garnish: orange twist
Method: Follow same steps as for the Old Fashioned.

Richard Boccato and Michael McIlroy, New York City

OAXACA OLD FASHIONED

1½ oz. reposado tequila
½ oz. mezcal
1 tsp. agave nectar
2 dashes Angostura bitters

Glass: rocks
Garnish: flamed orange twist (page 27)
Method: Follow same steps as for the Old Fashioned.

Philip Ward, New York City

WALNUT OLD FASHIONED

2 oz. Calvados
¼ oz. rich Demerara syrup
¼ oz. nocino (walnut liqueur)
3 dashes Angostura bitters

Glass: rocks
Garnish: lemon twist
Method: Stir with ice; strain into ice-filled glass. Garnish.

Andrew Bohrer, Seattle

IMPROVED HOLLAND GIN COCKTAIL

2 oz. genever
1 tsp. rich Demerara syrup or gomme syrup
2 dashes maraschino liqueur or curaçao
1 dash absinthe
2 dashes Boker's bitters

Glass: rocks or cocktail
Garnish: lemon twist
Method: Stir with ice to chill; strain into chilled cocktail glass, or into ice-filled rocks glass. Garnish.

MANHATTAN

Can one drink conquer the world? Possibly, possibly...

If the Old Fashioned is a more-or-less direct descendant of the first proto-cocktail to crawl out of the primordial punch bowl, then the Manhattan represents an evolutionary advance from pelt-wearing bibulous Neanderthal to upright-walking, pinky ring and pocket square-accessorized sporting drink about town.

The Manhattan's elegance of flavor isn't its only gesture of civility; the cocktail itself marked a new stage of well-mannered drinking. Before the Manhattan's circa-1870s debut, the cocktail realm was ruled by muscular mixes that were predominantly composed of the base spirit (or, skewing in the other direction, by softer mixtures such as the Sherry Cobbler (page 41)—unquestionably delicious, but without the certain spark and flash of danger that more robust cocktails carry). But the Manhattan and its multitudinous kin bridged the gap between short-and-sharp and soft-and-slow (initially, anyway), with the then-novel combination swathing whiskey's iron fist in vermouth's velvet glove.

As often encountered early on (and as described in the posthumous 1887 edition of Jerry Thomas' bar guide), the Manhattan's major component wasn't whiskey, but vermouth. The aromatized wine comprised a full two-thirds of the drink's volume, its botanical vivacity fortified with a dose of whiskey. The hobnobbing duo was given a common element to bond over via a dash or two of bitters—the cardamom-centric Boker's in some versions, the winter-spice heavy Abbott's or Angostura in others, and in 1884, George Winter's bar manual even called for Peruvian bitters (presumably Amargo Chuncho, usually encountered in Pisco Sours); each has its merits. And as with the development of other cocktails, the early formula wasn't ironclad—as the Manhattan gradually found its footing, the whiskey often appeared in the company of dry vermouth rather than sweet red vermouth, and the proportions fluctuated as well.

Of course, the Whiskey Cocktail had other aspects added to it as it ventured into "Fancy" or "Improved" territory—barspoons and dashes of curaçao and absinthe, for example—

MANHATTAN

2 oz. rye whiskey
1 oz. sweet vermouth
2 dashes Angostura bitters

Glass: cocktail

Garnish: lemon twist or cherry

Method: Stir with ice to chill; strain into chilled glass. Garnish.

Note: Use bourbon if the cause moves you. This is a good drink to try out different bitters—Boker's and Abbott's are very good, as are Dale DeGroff's aromatic pimento bitters.

and in the 1880s, so did the Manhattan. During the 1890s and into the new century, the Manhattan gradually went topsy-turvy, often appearing as an equal-proportions mix of whiskey and vermouth (along with bitters and assorted accoutrements) before finally emerging as the whiskey-heavy cocktail more recognizable to today's drinkers. But even as the drink developed, some of the flourishes remained, many of them worthwhile: a Boothby (the Champagne-laced Manhattan recently embraced by San Francisco bartenders) has all the hail-fellow charm of the familiar cocktail at its base, but with the buoyant flashes of ebullience that frequently accompany Champagne on its rounds.

But one person's bubble-brightened Manhattan is another's totally new cocktail. As the Manhattan settled into its identity around the turn of the 20th century, variations on the theme emerged—all identifiable relatives, but as distinct from each other as siblings and cousins at a family reunion. There was the Martinez—for more on that part of the family tree, flip to page 113—and the Brooklyn, a Manhattan (in some cases, made with dry vermouth rather than sweet) dashed with touches of maraschino liqueur and Amer Picon. A close contemporary was the Star Cocktail (recorded by Harry Johnson in 1888), which followed the Manhattan's equal-parts formula but swapped in applejack for the whiskey; by 1914, this followed the now-customary 2-to-1 formula (in Jacques Straub's *Drinks*) and traveled as the Marconi (or, if you prefer, the Marconi Wireless, as Albert Stevens Crockett listed it in 1931's *Old Waldorf Bar Days*). An additional relative of the original is the Saratoga Cocktail (one of several traveling under that name, apparently), which pops up in 1887 and splits the base spirit between rye whiskey and brandy, creating a three-

MANHATTAN MOVES ON

REVERSE MANHATTAN

2 oz. sweet vermouth
1 oz. rye whiskey or bourbon
2 dashes bitters

Glass: cocktail
Garnish: lemon twist or cherry
Method: Stir with ice to chill, strain into chilled glass. Garnish.
Tips: A bold vermouth like Carpano Antica Formula works well here, as does a higher proof whiskey, such as the cask-strength Booker's bourbon. Angostura will get you there, but Boker's or Abbott's are worth finding for this drink, as are Dale DeGroff's aromatic pimento bitters.

BOOTHBY

2 oz rye whiskey or bourbon
1 oz. sweet vermouth
1 dash Angostura bitters
2 dashes orange bitters
1 oz. chilled Champagne

Glass: cocktail
Garnish: cherry
Method: Stir all ingredients but Champagne with ice to chill; strain into chilled glass, and top with Champagne. Garnish.

MARCONI WIRELESS

2 oz. applejack
1 oz. sweet vermouth
2 dashes orange bitters

Glass: cocktail
Garnish: lemon twist or cherry
Method: Stir with ice to chill; strain into chilled glass. Garnish.

MANHATTAN MOVES ON *(continued)*

BROOKLYN

2 oz. rye whiskey
3/4 oz. dry vermouth
1/4 oz. maraschino liqueur
1/4 oz. Amer Picon or substitute

Glass: cocktail
Garnish: orange twist
Method: Stir to chill; strain into chilled glass. Garnish.
Note: Some call for sweet vermouth; it's better that way.

SARATOGA COCKTAIL

1 oz. rye whiskey
1 oz. Cognac
1 oz. sweet vermouth
2 dashes Angostura bitters

Glass: cocktail
Garnish: lemon twist
Method: Stir with ice to chill; strain into chilled glass. Garnish.
Note: Boker's Bitters and Abbott's Bitters love this drink, too.

GREENPOINT

2 oz. rye whiskey
1/2 oz. sweet vermouth
1/2 oz. yellow Chartreuse
1 dash Angostura bitters
1 dash orange bitters

Glass: cocktail
Garnish: lemon twist
Method: Stir with ice to chill; strain into chilled glass. Garnish.

Michael McIlroy, New York City

ingredient, equal-parts cocktail (plus bitters, of course) that's just as damn delicious today as it was when Grover Cleveland inhabited the White House.

After Prohibition, the Manhattan eventually bounced back to take the top spot as the nation's most-preferred cocktail (according to survey results published in 1951 in Jack Townsend and Tom Moore McBride's *The Bartender's Book*), before eventually giving way to the Martini—and then to the slow, inexorable slide into Vodkatini territory, a realm from which we're still trying to extricate ourselves today.

But when the cocktail renaissance was first getting started, a few essential things happened. First, people revisited the Manhattan and recognized its inherent awesomeness; second, greater attention was paid to the drink's technique—ingredients were measured, fresh vermouth was introduced instead of the rank, oxidized remnants of a bottle that'd been kicking around the back bar since the Bicentennial; and third, rye whiskey was given another shot in the drink's starring role, which pushed not only cocktails but the American whiskey industry onto a fresh trajectory. Made with bourbon, the Manhattan ain't bad at all (especially if your bourbon carries a little muscle—such as a bottled-in-bond Old Grand Dad, or Knob Creek)—but with rye whiskey (especially one of the higher-proof ryes such as 100-proof Rittenhouse or 101-proof Wild Turkey), the Manhattan positively sings. The whiskey's spark of spice grips the softer botanicals of the vermouth in a firm handshake, and the balance is so engaging and reliably entertaining that it qualifies the drink as one of the greatest quaffs around.

As the Manhattan's excellence reemerged, bartenders began revisiting the practice of tinkering with the base formula, creating drinks still recognizably related but as firmly individualistic as the Brooklyn and the Saratoga. Some introduced Punt e Mes (the extra-bitter style of vermouth produced in Milan) and matched its rich bitterness with the softness of a liqueur; this produced drinks such as the Red Hook and the Slope (page 156), as well as the Chartreuse-laden Greenpoint from Michael McIlroy (formerly at New York's Milk & Honey, and now a partner in Attaboy), and the Newark (page 49) from PDT's Jim Meehan and John Deragon, a variation that includes New Jersey's apple brandy as well as the surly, burly flavor of Fernet-Branca.

With its extra-bitter nature, Punt e Mes could even be considered a two-in-one vermouth-and-bitters combo. That's essentially the approach followed by Boston (now San Francisco) bartender John Gertsen when making the Moto Guzzi, with the bombast of barrel-strength bourbon. Some Italian amari lend a similar characteristic, resulting in mixes such as the Averna-fortified Black Manhattan, from Todd Smith in San Francisco, and the Uptown Manhattan from another Bay Area bartender, Marcovaldo Dionysos. And in New York, Audrey Saunders helped get the whole Manhattan-riff thing rolling with her Little Italy, which adds the brusquely bitter Cynar.

The Manhattan has never been a drink particularly concerned with hard-and-fast rules, so these recent variations and interpretations should carry little shock. Instead, they show a familiar drink that's long in the tooth, but still capable of turning on the charm whenever the need arises.

MANHATTAN MOVES ON *(continued)*

LITTLE ITALY

2 oz. rye whiskey (preferably the 100-proof Rittenhouse)
3/4 oz. sweet vermouth
1/2 oz. Cynar

Glass: cocktail
Garnish: two cherries
Method: Stir with ice to chill; strain into chilled glass. Garnish with two cherries on a cocktail skewer.

Audrey Saunders, New York City

MOTO GUZZI

1 1/2 oz. cask-strength bourbon
1 1/2 oz. Punt e Mes

Glass: rocks
Method: Stir with ice to chill; strain into chilled glass.
Note: Booker's is the preferred bourbon for this drink.

John Gertsen, Boston

BLACK MANHATTAN

2 oz. rye whiskey or bourbon
1 oz. Averna
1 dash Angostura bitters
1 dash orange bitters

Glass: cocktail
Garnish: cherry
Method: Stir with ice to chill; strain into chilled glass. Garnish.

Todd Smith, San Francisco

UPTOWN MANHATTAN

2 oz. bourbon
3/4 oz. Amaro Nonino
2 dashes orange bitters
1 tsp. Cherry Heering

Glass: cocktail
Garnish: orange twist, cherry
Method: Stir with ice to chill; strain into chilled glass. Squeeze orange twist over drink. Garnish with cherry.

Marcovaldo Dionysos, San Francisco

MARTINI

Leave the dogma at the door—the Martini is flexible enough for all.

"We may understand how cults form with the martini as with all arts, how rituals develop, how superstitious or even sorcerous beliefs and practices betray a faith that is passionate and pure but runs easily to fanaticism. But though we understand these matters we must not be lenient toward them for they divide the fellowship."

—Bernard DeVoto, *The Hour*

Pretty rich, coming from DeVoto. In his 1948 essay that initially ran in *Harper's*, and that was later expanded into a short book, DeVoto castigates those who deify the Martini—and then proceeds to deify the damn Martini.

Still, DeVoto was speaking to a pressing cultural issue of the time (considering that the culture in question was that of the comfortable class in New York City and its spreading suburbs, and the time was the Martini-loving post-WWII period). The Martini is the most revered and ritualistic of cocktails, and fundamentalism and its corresponding condemnation of heresies both real and imagined have been part of the drink's subculture ever since the earliest days of the Cold War.

It wasn't always this way—the Martini used to just be a drink, one among many, and one that had a recipe and reputation that was anything but sacrosanct. Nobody's completely certain when and where the Martini came about—those who profess otherwise display the unquestioning suspension of disbelief common to small children on Christmas Eve—and its evolution from just another drink into a fetishistically dry-as-the-Sahara archetype took more than half a century.

Most (but not all) cocktail genealogists agree that it's likely the Manhattan begat the Martinez, and the Martinez begat the Martini. The Manhattan we've already covered; the Martinez pops up in the 1880s (in his 1884 bar manual, O.H. Byron describes it as "like a Manhattan, but with gin"), and in the posthumous 1887 edition of Jerry Thomas' bar manual, the recipe for the already popular Martinez is spelled out (page 114). The sweetness of Old Tom gin; soft, red Italian vermouth; a dollop of maraschino, and the cardamom and baking-spice touch of Boker's bitters: delicious,

MARTINI

1½ oz. dry gin
¾ oz. dry vermouth
1 dash orange bitters (optional, but desired)

Glass: cocktail

Garnish: lemon twist

Method: Stir with ice to chill; strain into chilled glass. Garnish.

but the kind of thing that would make DeVoto and his multitudinous kin of absolutists blanche.

More auspiciously, in 1888, New York bartender Harry Johnson documented the Bradford a' la Martini, with equal parts Old Tom gin and vermouth (unspecified, but likely the sweet, Italian variety), along with dashes of orange bitters (Johnson also listed a Martini Cocktail which swapped Boker's bitters and dashes of gum syrup for the orange bitters); and in 1895, the Old Tom/sweet vermouth combo was circulating as the Martini Cocktail, from George Kappeler at the Holland House in New York. If that still looks odd by contemporary standards, consider what was passing as a Martini Cocktail in France a year later, as recorded by Louis Fouquet: equal parts Italian vermouth and an unspecified style of gin, along with orange bitters, absinthe, curaçao, and the almond-esque nuttiness of crème de noyaux.

The dry Martini is "a mass madness, a cult, a frenzy, a body of folklore, a mystique, an expertise of a sort which may well earn this decade the name of the Numb (or Glazed) Fifties." —New York Times, 1952

But while there were close-but-no-cigar Martinis being mixed in the closing years of the 19th century, cocktails more recognizable to the modern Martini drinker were developing under different names: the Turf Cocktail, as recorded in the 1900 edition of Harry Johnson's bar guide, with Plymouth gin and French (that is, dry) vermouth—but with added dashes of orange bitters, maraschino, and absinthe. In 1888,

THE MARTINI IN MOTION

MARTINEZ

2 oz. sweet vermouth
1 oz. Old Tom gin
2 dashes gomme syrup nor simple syrup
2 dashes maraschino liqueur
1 dash Boker's bitters

Glass: cocktail
Garnish: lemon twist
Method: Stir with ice to chill; strain into chilled glass.

TUXEDO

2 oz. dry gin
1 oz. dry sherry
1 dash orange bitters

Glass: cocktail
Garnish: lemon twist
Method: Stir with ice to chill; strain into chilled glass.
Note: For a bone-dry drink, use a fino or manzanillo sherry; if a little more weight is desired, aim for an amontillado.

TURF CLUB

1 oz. Plymouth gin
1 oz. dry vermouth
2 dashes absinthe
2-3 dashes maraschino liqueur
2-3 dashes orange bitters

Glass: cocktail
Garnish: lemon twist
Method: Stir with ice to chill; strain into chilled glass.

Johnson had also recorded the recipe for the Marguerite, which similarly had the equal-parts combo of Plymouth gin and dry vermouth, along with dashes of orange bitters and anisette, served garnished with a cherry and lemon peel. Around 1897, however, the connection seemed to be coming clear: on December 4 of that year, the *Enterprise Tribune* in Centralia, Washington (of all places), noted the popularity of the Manhattan and the Martini—the latter prepared, it was detailed, with equal parts Plymouth gin and French vermouth, with a dash of orange bitters—and observed, "This is preferred by many to the combination of Italian vermouth and Tom gin." *Et voila* ... somewhere along the way, civilization advanced.

The first years of the 20th century cemented the dry gin (Plymouth was often specified) and dry vermouth mixture we've come to recognize as the Dry Martini (not that there was any such thing as a "Wet Martini" at the time—rather, the "dry" was called to distinguish the drink from the Sweet Martini, made with—you've got it—sweet vermouth), often with the addition of orange bitters to the mix. But there's one additional hitch (besides the bitters, that is) before we get to the Martini that a thousand steakhouses are serving right this moment: the ratio of these Martinis ranged anywhere from equal parts gin and vermouth to a more robust 2:1 ratio of gin to vermouth.

Robust? That's practically drowning in vermouth by the standards of the most fervent Martini true-believer, as typified by DeVoto (his preferred ratio was the impossible-to-mix 3.7 to 1, positively flooded with vermouth when compared to the Martinis detailed by his contemporary, the Westchester-based attorney, drinks dogmatist, and author David Embury, who required a 7 to 1 ratio).

Martini drinkers (and those who preferred its identical twin, the Gibson, which wears an onion garnish in lieu of an olive or lemon twist) didn't seem to be going to the barricades in defense of their desired proportions until the post-war years, when the quest for the driest (ergo, the booziest) Martini went hand-in-hand with suburban

THE MARTINI IN MOTION *(continued)*

KANGAROO COCKTAIL

2 oz. vodka
3/4 oz. dry vermouth

Glass: cocktail
Garnish: lemon twist
Method: Stir with ice to chill; strain into chilled glass. Garnish.

FITTY FITTY

1½ oz. dry gin
1½ oz. dry vermouth
1 dash orange bitters

Glass: cocktail
Garnish: lemon twist
Method: Stir with ice to chill; strain into chilled glass.
Note: Plymouth gin plays well with the soft strains of Dolin dry vermouth, whereas a juniper-forward London dry like Tanqueray appreciates the mild funk of Noilly Prat's dry vermouth.

Adapted by Audrey Saunders, New York City

sprawl and the kinds of buzzed businessmen and executives since depicted in *The Man in the Grey Flannel Suit* and *Mad Men*. In 1952, the *New York Times* described the Dry Martini as "a mass madness, a cult, a frenzy, a body of folklore, a mystique, an expertise of a sort which may well earn this decade the name of the Numb (or Glazed) Fifties," and quoted a bartender who criticized the craze for ever-drier mixes: "These guys who ask for the very dry martini are just chiselers. They only want more gin for the same money."

Quarreling over the ratio of gin-to-vermouth, though, was fiddling as the Martini burned—for around the same time this was happening, a stealth assault was taking place. Recipes for the Kangaroo Cocktail (page 115) appeared in books such as Crosby Gaige's *Standard Cocktail Guide* from 1948, and it looked pretty much like a Dry Martini with one big exception: the gin was missing. In its place? Vodka. By the late 1960s, vodka had moved into the prominent position; along with the gradual disappearance of vermouth, this meant Martini drinkers were increasingly slugging back glasses of nothing more than icy vodka. Maybe the Russians won the Cold War, after all.

Perhaps the Martini isn't truly a bridge drink—its minor variations have been the cause for so many dueling opinions, and the dogmatists remain so damn annoying, that many bartenders today give it a wide berth as a cocktail foundation. But on the positive side, the cocktail renaissance has also brought sanity to the mixture—not surprisingly, most notably from Pegu Club owner Audrey Saunders. Audrey made it suitable—scratch that; she made it *desirable*—to once again enjoy a Martini the way our less-dogmatic ancestors did, as an equal-proportion drink, dubbed the Fitty Fitty (page 115) (derived from the bitters-free Fifty Fifty in 1930's *Savoy Cocktail Book*). It's delicious; it's civilized; hell, it's amazing. Mix one and admire the Martini's inherent charm—and if you want to fling the heresy label about, go argue elsewhere.

ABOUT THAT OLIVE

The olive in the Martini is perhaps the quintessential cocktail garnish, preserved in neon and clip art for the ages. It's pretty—but it's also pointless. A good Martini merits a short spray of oil from a lemon zest, and nothing more, as a garnish—the drink neither desires nor deserves to be laden with tepid, salty olives (what globetrotting bar educator Angus Winchester refers to as "the testicles of the Devil"), that warm the drink and add an inescapable brininess. But let's leave it to DeVoto once more: "Nothing can be done with people who put olive in martinis, presumably because in some desolate childhood hour someone refused them a dill pickle and so they go through life lusting for the taste of brine."

NEGRONI

The drink that's introducing the world to the beauty of bitter.

Beauty and belligerence seldom mingle so sweetly as when they nestle together in a Negroni.

The Negroni is the most perfect of cocktails—and perfection is quite a claim, especially in the company of such standards as the Daiquiri and the Manhattan. But the Negroni strikes an enviable balance that's often aspired to but seldom encountered in the craft-cocktail wild; the drink has an almost unfuckuppable formula of equal parts strong, bitter, and sweet, and has a bibulous heritage rooted in the Old World while feeling absolutely at home in the New.

Of course, the Negroni can also be a bit of a bastard, an absolutely terrifying cocktail to Campari initiates for whom the drink could conceivably be considered a form of hazing. Mainstays like the Manhattan may have only the merest nod toward bitter, but the Negroni conveys its brusque bitterness to Negroni newcomers with all the delicacy and nuance of Moe Howard's eye-pokes at Larry and Curly.

As with many other objects of complicated beauty, the Negroni is a product of Italy. Its origin story is simple and believable, though not completely without dispute: around 1920 at the Bar Casoni (now the Caffé Giacosa) in Florence, head bartender Fosca Scarselli filled an order for a customer with a wildly unbelievable background. Camillo Negroni's resume included listings for both "Count" and "rodeo cowboy," the former acquired by fortune of his noble birth, and the latter via the years he spent slumming in the American West, roaming and gambling through the 1880s and '90s until returning to Firenze in 1905.

The count's customary drink was the Americano—an absurdly delicious mixture of Campari, sweet vermouth, and soda water that was enjoying an entirely deserved moment at the time. Part of the Americano's appeal was its heritage; the drink was derived from the Milano-Torino, a sturdy combo of sweet vermouth (that low-octane aperitif that sprang from the Piedmont city of Turin) and Campari, the bitter, garnet-hued spirit-based aperitif developed by Gaspare Campari in 1860 and produced in Milan.

NEGRONI

1 oz. gin
1 oz. sweet vermouth
1 oz. Campari

Glass: rocks or cocktail

Garnish: small orange wheel or orange twist

Method: Build drink in ice-filled rocks glass; stir to combine, and garnish with orange wheel. To serve straight-up, stir ingredients with ice and strain into chilled cocktail glass; garnish with orange twist.

The Milano-Torino is tasty, but can come across as a loud-talker of a drink; with soda water, however, it softens and brightens into the fully guzzle-worthy Americano. But on that particular day (booze legend says), the Count was seeking neither softness nor brightness—instead, he asked Scarselli to *irrobutire*, or fortify his Americano. Swapping the soda water for gin, Scarselli easily accomplished the mission and created the fuel for countless bartender benders in the century to come.

But while the Negroni became a signature drink at Florence establishments such as Caffe Rivoire—its longtime spiritual home—it was decades before the drink fully translated into the cocktail-culture mainstream. Part of the reason was the limited availability of Campari; while now commonplace in restaurant and hotel bars worldwide, the bitter red liqueur stayed relatively close to its Italian home until after the century's mid-point. The liqueur did creep into Continental cocktails from time to time—in 1927, Harry MacElhone's *Barflies and Cocktails* (a Prohibition-era cocktail book that sprang from MacElhone's New York Bar in still-wet Paris) featured a recipe for the Boulevardier, a Negroni-esque cocktail based on bourbon rather than gin. (It wasn't McElhone's first mix of whiskey and Campari—the Old Pal, which uses dry vermouth instead of sweet, appeared in his 1922 *ABC of Mixing Cocktails*.)

But the 1930s and '40s posed their own unique set of challenges to the spread of Italian-made products and drinks like the Negroni, and it wasn't until after the

VIVA LA NEGRONI

AMERICANO

1½ oz. sweet vermouth
1½ oz. Campari
2-3 oz. chilled soda water

Glass: highball
Garnish: orange wheel
Method: Combine first two ingredients in ice-filled glass; top with soda, stir to combine. Garnish.

BOULEVARDIER

1 oz. bourbon
1 oz. sweet vermouth
1 oz. Campari

Glass: rocks or cocktail
Garnish: orange twist
Method: Follow instructions for Negroni.

NEGRONI SBAGLIATO

1 oz. Campari
1 oz. sweet vermouth
1 oz. chilled Prosecco (or other dry sparkling wine)

Glass: rocks
Garnish: orange wheel
Method: Build in ice-filled glass; stir to combine. Garnish.

AGAVONI

1 oz. reposado tequila
1 oz. sweet vermouth
1 oz. Campari

Glass: rocks
Garnish: grapefruit twist
Method: Build in ice-filled glass, stir to combine. Garnish.
Tip: Substitute mezcal for tequila.

Bastian Heuser, Berlin

VIVA LA NEGRONI *(continued)*

CONTINENTAL
1½ oz. gin (Plymouth recommended)
¾ oz. Cynar
½ oz. blanc vermouth

Glass: cocktail
Garnish: lemon twist
Method: Stir with ice to chill; strain into chilled glass. Garnish.

Douglas Derrick, Portland, Oregon

CONTESSA
1 oz. gin
1 oz. Aperol
1 oz. dry vermouth

Glass: rocks
Garnish: orange twist
Method: Stir with ice to chill; strain into chilled glass. Garnish.

John Gertsen, Courtney Hennessy, and Ryan McGrale, Boston

WHITE NEGRONI
1 oz. gin
1 oz. Suze (or other gentian aperitif)
1 oz. Lillet blanc

Glass: cocktail
Garnish: lemon twist
Method: Stir with ice to chill; strain into chilled glass. Garnish.

Wayne Collins, London

KINGSTON NEGRONI
1 oz. overproof Jamaican rum (Smith & Cross)
1 oz. Carpano Antica Formula vermouth
1 oz. Campari

Glass: rocks
Garnish: orange twist
Method: Stir with ice to chill; strain into ice-filled glass. Garnish.

Joaquín Simó, New York City

Second World War that rosso vermouth and Campari freely mingled with English gin in the bars of America. In 1951, Ted Saucier's *Bottoms Up*—a collection of recipes from restaurants, hotels, and bars in America and Europe—included a recognizable recipe for the Negroni (though served with a lime twist) from the Restaurant Marguery in New York. It wasn't until almost 1960 that Campari advertisements in publications like the *New Yorker* included recipes for the Negroni (sometimes listed under the name "Campari Cocktail"), and the Americano (or a simple Campari and soda) remained at center stage, at least in terms of promotional efforts.

By the time today's cocktail renaissance reached full flower, the Negroni was no longer a shrinking violet. Today, the Negroni is perhaps unrivaled in the level to which it's been embraced, even fetishized, by craft bartenders and the cocktail devout.

But what is it about this drink, above so many others, that causes even the most jaded of palate to still go weak in the knees? One reason might be the Negroni's cascading levels of flavorful complexity, as three of the most multifaceted ingredients in the cocktail world—gin, vermouth, and Campari, each prepared with an apothecary's cabinet worth of botanicals—are thrown into a mixological cage-match competition, only to discover they're the best of friends. The Negroni's range stretches from the ethereal airiness of citrus and rhubarb to the earthiness of angelica and juniper, and the drink's lingering bottom note resonates with a multiplying series of bitter slaps. There's *amore* in the Negroni, but there's also a touch of rough play, and for those who've grown accustomed to the flavorful romps provided by so many other types of cocktail, the Negroni provides a welcome familiarity along with a ferocious pinch as a reminder to never stop taking the drink seriously.

The Negroni is also wonderfully well-suited to experimentation, its even match of ingredients and its ruggedness of flavor always game for diversions. The Boulevardier only hints at the possibilities, as does the Negroni Sbagliato (page 118), a twist on the drink supposedly devised by accident when a bartender at Bar Basso in Milan grabbed a bottle of Prosecco instead of gin. Accident or not, the Sbagliato is magnificent, as are some of the more recent Negroni diversions.

For his Chocolate Negroni, Naren Young, an Australian bartender now roosting in New York, made a seemingly simple twist on the basic cocktail by boosting its bitter quotient via Punt e Mes vermouth (which has an earthy quality not unlike that of good dark chocolate), and giving the drink's succulence an even-more-embraceable aspect through a couple of dashes of chocolate molé bitters and a spoonful of crème de cacao. Bartender Joaquín Simó, formerly of Death & Co. and more recently at Pouring Ribbons in the East Village, traded gin for the rough-and-tumble funk of Navy-strength Jamaican rum, producing the Kingston Negroni. And recognizing that the Negroni sometimes needs a hammock-drink touch, Giuseppe González translated the classic recipe into the icy Negroni Swizzle, the drink's sharpness softened with a dab of seltzer and its flavor deepened with a pinch of sea salt.

Campari is arguably the required constant in a Negroni—options abound for gin and vermouth, but Campari has no perfect analogue (though Gran Classico, a bitter liqueur from Tempus Fugit, comes pretty damn close). There are options, though, for tinkering with the Negroni formula

VIVA LA NEGRONI *(continued)*

CHOCOLATE NEGRONI

1 oz. Plymouth gin
3/4 oz. Punt e Mes
3/4 oz. Campari
1 tsp. white crème de cacao
2 dashes chocolate molé bitters

Glass: rocks
Garnish: orange twist
Method: Build ingredients in rocks glass and stir; add large ice cube and garnish.

Naren Young, New York City

NEGRONI SWIZZLE

1 oz. London dry gin
1 oz. sweet vermouth
1 oz. Campari
1 oz. chilled club soda
1 pinch sea salt

Glass: Collins
Garnish: orange wheel
Method: Combine ingredients in glass and fill with crushed ice. Swizzle with barspoon until frost forms on exterior of glass, adding more ice if needed. Finish by packing the glass with crushed ice and inserting a straw; garnish.

Giuseppe González, New York City

via other bitter-delivery vehicles: Boston bartenders John Gertsen (now in San Francisco), Courtney Hennessy, and Ryan McGrale opted for Campari's rhubarb-rich sibling, Aperol, when crafting the Contessa (page 119), the drink's brightness further amplified by substituting dry vermouth for the usual rosso. London bartender Wayne Collins opted for a more earthy direction for the White Negroni (page 119) using a French gentian aperitif in place of Campari (Collins used Suze, though Saler's and Aveze also work splendidly) and the citrusy Lillet blonde for the wine component. And in Portland, Oregon, bartender Douglas Derrick has applied his skills for several years to a series of monthly Negroni variations, showcasing the best at annual Negroni Socials.

The traditional Firenze style of presenting a Negroni is to serve the mixture over ice and garnish with a slice of orange, while American bartenders typically opt to serve the Negroni straight up with a sliver of the fruit's peel. The Old World style is perhaps a more civilized approach—I'm revealing my bias here—as it allows for a more relaxed pace of imbibing, and there's certainly nothing about a Negroni that should be hurried. But bartenders seem to be increasingly embracing this appeal, and are mixing Negronis to be enjoyed not only over the course of 20 minutes or so, but for a stretch of months. Bottle-matured Negronis—prepared en masse and rested in glass (sometimes with a shot of CO_2 for effervescence) for days or weeks before consumption—are increasingly in circulation, as are Negronis that have been aged in small oak barrels, a contribution to the current cocktail scene by London bartender Tony Conigliaro and his Portland, Oregon compatriate, Jeffrey Morgenthaler.

The Negroni is almost unrivaled in the degree to which it's been embraced, even fetishized, by craft bartenders and the cocktail devout.

You can buy your own barrel and play around with aging—or, if you'd rather not convert your garage to a rickhouse, it's worth the minimal effort to prepare a batch of Negronis and pour them into a bottle to let the mixture's flavor mature. I can't promise that this pre-bottled cocktail will taste better to you than a Negroni mixed *a la minute* from ingredients at hand—but having a bottle of Negronis kicking around the liquor cabinet or the fridge can make this most agreeable mixture a regular part of a cocktail regimen.

CHAPTER 4

STAYING POWER

Contemporary cocktails—and a few that just might be built to last

Crystal balls and tea leaves are notoriously unreliable, and just try divining the future with chicken blood without PETA climbing all over you. I can't swear that any of these drinks will actually stand the test of time—but after a decade of writing about cocktails, I've come to appreciate the taste of possibility.

There are more than 40 contemporary-ish cocktails in this chapter (along with a few oldies that are relevant to the points at hand). Some reflect the first sparks of creative promise in the late 1980s and '90s that later erupted into the conflagration of the cocktail resurgence. Most others, though, popped up over the past decade, as bartenders began to fully matriculate in the classics, and developed the confidence and skills to better play a role in the cocktail conversation.

Several of these drinks are inarguably solid bets for "future classic" status, while others, certainly, will provoke questions and the scratching of heads. Some of these drinks have hit the cocktail equivalent of the mainstream, being served in bars from San Diego to Singapore and appearing on menus everywhere from hushed neo-speakeasies to airport layover bars. Others may have flared out, and still others just never caught on (and some are simply personal favorites)—but regardless of the cards they've been dealt, each of these drinks is delicious enough to merit another look.

Of course, there are other cocktails out there today on bar menus around the world that I may not yet have even heard of, but are destined to become the century-old classics served in 2115. Maybe my great- or great-great-grandkids can sort out the details on those—or maybe they'll just take me out of my cryogenic chamber and thaw me in the microwave so I can have one more night on the town, and see what drinks truly had the stuff to stick around.

AÑEJO HIGHBALL

King Cocktail looks to Cuba, and we all win.

AÑEJO HIGHBALL

1½ oz. aged rum (Bacardi 8 recommended)
½ oz. curaçao
¼ oz. lime juice
2 dashes Angostura bitters
2 oz. ginger beer

Glass: highball

Garnish: lime wheel, orange slice

Method: Build first four ingredients in an ice-filled highball glass. Stir, and top with ginger beer. Garnish.

Dale DeGroff, New York City

Some contemporary cocktails are riveting in their modernity, prepared using equipment and philosophies honed in 21st century kitchens and in step with the changing tastes of the times. But other recent drinks—some of the best and most enduring, in my mind—are stirring in their simplicity, formulated in such a straightforward manner that you can't help but wonder, "How has this not been done before?"

File the Añejo Highball under Category B. Crafted by Dale DeGroff—the Dumbledore of the cocktail renaissance—the Añejo Highball has a rum-and-spice combo that is distinctly Caribbean in tone, and that makes itself welcome on sunny afternoons far from the 22nd parallel.

PLINY'S TONIC

What happens when the cocktail renaissance hits Texas? Habaneros, for a start...

PLINY'S TONIC

2 oz. gin (Citadelle recommended)
1 oz. lime juice
½ oz. rich simple syrup
2 mint sprigs, leaves only
¼-inch-thick slice cucumber
2 dashes habanero tincture

Glass: cocktail

Garnish: mint leaf

Method: Muddle cucumber in a shaker; add remaining ingredients and shake well with ice. Double-strain into a chilled glass; garnish.

Tip: Bittermens Hellfire Habanero Shrub will work for the tincture, or make your own by soaking a half-dozen seeded and stemmed habanero peppers in a cup of vodka for two weeks; strain before use.

Bobby Heugel, Houston

Early in the cocktail renaissance, when talented bartenders were swarming bars in New York, San Francisco, and Boston to start promising careers, Bobby Heugel headed south to Texas' Gulf Coast instead. Having recently completed grad school—a future in international relations beckoned—Heugel instead set his ambitious sights on what he could accomplish behind the bar in the bibulous then-backwater of Houston. He started documenting his work on a blog, Drink Dogma, and in 2009, together with a few friends, Heugel founded Anvil Bar & Refuge. Now, with partnerships in a handful of other bars and restaurants including Julep and The Pastry War—and having garnered a James Beard Award nomination along the way—Heugel is established as one of the most talented and influential bartenders in the country, and the Pliny's Tonic is a mainstay of Anvil's paradigm-shifting menu.

Not bad for a blogger.

A TASTE APART

FALERNUM

A citrus-spice combo that takes the cocktail shaker on a tropical tour.

A style of syrup (often lightly alcoholic) that originated in the Caribbean (and that's most at home in island-style punches and swizzles), falernum played a walk-on role as sidekick sweetener during tiki's 20th century heyday, then largely disappeared. Dale DeGroff was an early champion for falernum's return, and during my own early adventures with the cocktail shaker, kitchen experiments with falernum helped lead me down a pleasurably rum-soaked path.

Falernum's not the long-lost ingredient it once was, and once-forgotten drinks such as the Corn 'n' Oil (page 22) and the Royal Bermuda Yacht Club are now craft-cocktail standards. You can pick up a bottle of a commercial brand, or knock together your own version of my Falernum #10; see page 186 for recommended brands, and a recipe.

ROYAL BERMUDA YACHT CLUB

2 oz. aged rum (Barbados preferred)
¾ oz. lime juice
1 tsp. Cointreau
¼ oz. falernum

Glass: cocktail

Garnish: lime wheel

Method: Shake with ice to chill; strain into chilled glass. Garnish.

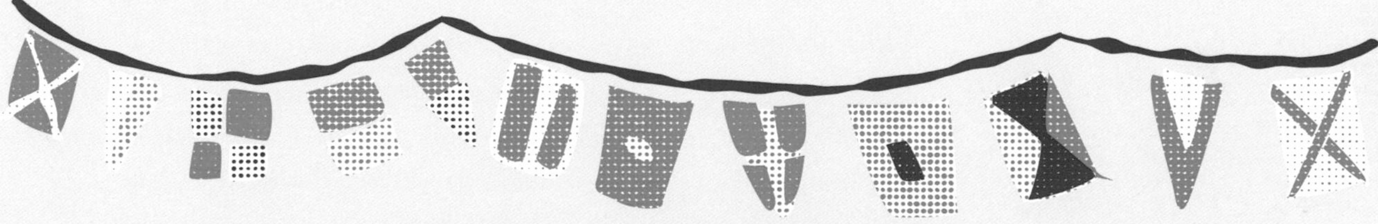

CHARTREUSE SWIZZLE

The Old World detours through San Francisco on its way to the tropics.

CHARTREUSE SWIZZLE

1½ oz. green Chartreuse
1 oz. pineapple juice
¾ oz. lime juice
½ oz. falernum

Glass: Collins

Garnish: mint sprig, fresh-grated nutmeg

Method: Add all ingredients to glass and fill with crushed ice. Use a barspoon to swizzle the mixture until frost forms on the outside of the glass. Top with crushed ice; garnish.

Marcovaldo Dionysos, San Francisco

Around the turn of the millennium, while New York and London were asserting themselves as the crown capitals of the cocktail renaissance, strange things were happening in San Francisco.

The Bay Area has been an essential stop on the cocktail circuit since Jerry Thomas first shook drinks at the El Dorado back in the Barbary Coast days. But while New York bartenders were shopping for tie-pins and arm garters to wear while mixing Prohibition-era cocktails, their colleagues in San Francisco were plundering the produce markets and creating stylistic mashups of the sort that would earn the city a place as the Pacific Coast parallel.

Marcovaldo Dionysos was a formative figure in the development of Bay Area cocktails, working in establishments ranging from Absinthe to Michael Mina's Clock Bar to his current roost at the tiki wonderland Smuggler's Cove. Marco's contributions to the modern cocktail canon are many (see the Uptown Manhattan, page 112), but chief among them is the Chartreuse Swizzle. Using a potent base of green Chartreuse—careful, at 120 proof, Chartreuse doesn't mess around—and matching its florid Old World herbaceousness against the rich, tropical-toned brightness of pineapple and falernum, the Chartreuse Swizzle is a hammock drink for the monastic set. Swizzles are supposed to be simple things—the drinks you leisurely stab with your straw during sleepy, sunny afternoons—but the Chartreuse Swizzle bumps the flavor complexity a dozen notches, while taking nothing away from the swizzle's life-of-leisure properties.

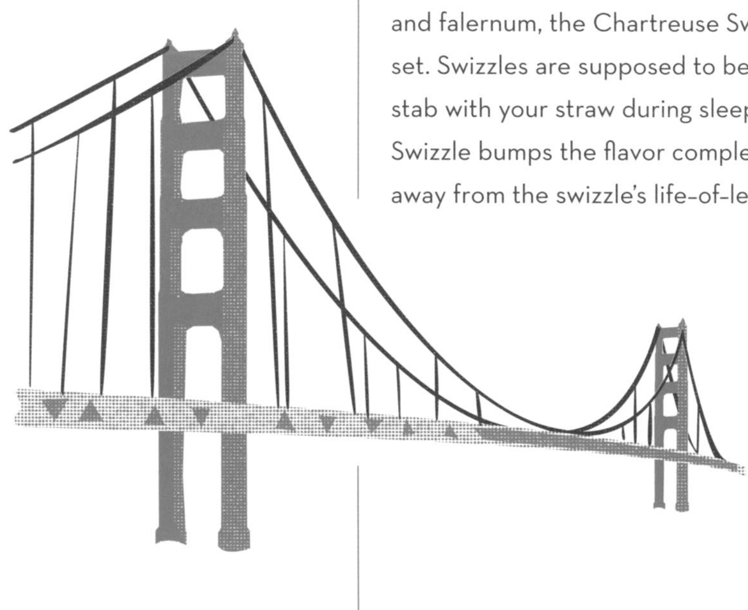

REVOLVER

After a couple of rounds, it's not the only thing that's loaded.

Bay Area bartender Jon Santer certainly wasn't the first to put bourbon in his coffee. But for the Revolver, Santer turned the equation around, using bourbon as the base and adding the familiar, fortifying tone of coffee liqueur. Don't overlook the citrus here: orange bitters help deepen the drink and add welcome touches of spice, and a big ol' orange twist at the end contributes an up-and-at-'em freshness. Think of these elements as the glass of OJ that accompanies spiked coffee during a hungover Sunday breakfast—a touch of sunshine amidst the ruggedness of life, a glimpse of light at the end of the rough-morning tunnel.

One note on mixing: for full firepower, use higher-caliber bourbon. Santer suggests 90-proof Bulleit bourbon, but anything between 90 and 101 proof should give you the bang you're looking for.

REVOLVER

2 oz. bourbon
½ oz. coffee liqueur
2 dashes orange bitters

Glass: cocktail

Garnish: flamed orange twist

Method: Stir with ice to chill, strain into chilled glass. Flame orange twist over drink (see page 27 for instructions) and use as garnish.

Jon Santer, Emeryville, California

RED ANT

A contemporary cocktail crosses the cultural divide.

The cocktail renaissance boosted the profile of two long-ignored spirits: rye whiskey—which had largely been absent from American glasses since Prohibition—and mezcal, the misunderstood Mexican spirit that didn't come into its own in the U.S. until the 21st century.

Rye and mezcal rarely meet in the mixing glass, but this drink from New York bartender Thomas Waugh—formerly of Alembic in San Francisco and later at NYC's Death & Co., before opening the Jules Verne-esque ZZ's Clam Bar in 2014—manages to straddle the divide. With sweetness from Danish cherry liqueur and a little funk from unaged cherry brandy, the Red Ant (named for the Rio Hormiga Colorada, or Red Ant River, in Oaxaca) is a borders-blurring cocktail with a rich, ethereal character.

RED ANT

1½ oz. rye whiskey
½ oz. Cherry Heering
½ oz. kirschwasser
1 tsp. mezcal (something smoky, like Del Maguey's Chichicapa or Vida)
½ tsp. cinnamon syrup (page 185)
2 dashes Bittermens Xocolatl Molé bitters

Glass: cocktail

Garnish: 3 cherries, speared on a cocktail pick to resemble an ant

Method: Stir with ice to chill, strain into chilled glass. Garnish.

Thomas Waugh, New York City

JASMINE

A bright precursor of a cocktail renaissance on the way.

JASMINE

1½ oz. gin
¾ oz. lemon juice
¼ oz. Campari
¼ oz. Cointreau

Glass: cocktail

Garnish: lemon twist

Method: Shake with ice to chill; strain into chilled cocktail glass. Garnish.

Paul Harrington, Emeryville, California/ Spokane, Washington

The cocktail renaissance didn't emerge from the fog at the turn of the millennium, a ship of Manhattans and high mixology suddenly sailing into sight of the thirsty masses.

Instead, the gestation of today's drinks culture was a long one, stretching back to the Kamikaze-soaked '80s. During those craft cocktail-starved years when Fuzzy Navels flowed like water, there were still a few bartenders around the world who were tinkering at their shaker tins in pursuit of bibulous beauty. Dale DeGroff was one, charting a path forward for New York City's bars; Dick Bradsell was another, doing much the same in London. And in the San Francisco Bay Area? That's where you found Paul Harrington, tending the bar in Emeryville while finishing his degree in architecture, and introducing the desperate few to civilized alternatives when Sex on the Beach was the call of the day.

Harrington's lasting contributions are numerous—his book, *Cocktail: The Drinks Bible for the 21st Century*, is an essential element of any serious cocktail library—but here's one that's fun to get on the outside of: the Jasmine.

Named for Matt Jasmin, a regular who had a taste for Campari, the Jasmine has few parallels as a bright and bitter refresher. Though Harrington only recently realized he'd been spelling Jasmin's name wrong all these years, the Jasmine cocktail makes no such missteps, its components performing in perfect balance. This is a great drink for the Campari averse—the cocktail almost perfectly replicates the flavor of grapefruit—and is particularly well-suited for breaking out on those spring and summer evenings when you prefer a short hoist to a long haul, but a Martini or Manhattan are just too ponderous for the moment.

COCKTAIL ESSENTIALS

TEQUILA & MEZCAL

Absent from the cocktail's first golden era, agave spirits are at the heart of the second.

First memories of tequila are often blurry. There may be a salt shaker involved, and a lime wedge—and maybe a bartender with a shot-glass bandolier, if you're in that kind of place, or a bottle of sketchy mezcal and a friend daring you to eat the pallid grub at the bottom, if you're in *that* kind of place.

But while tequila and mezcal may provide a rough introduction for many, agave spirits are among the most nuanced and delicate—and most deliciously intricate—on the shelf. Absent from pretty much every pre-Prohibition cocktail manual, and not taken truly seriously until the current millennium, tequila and mezcal are soaring to become the signature spirits of today's cocktail movement—assuming the industry that's grown up around them doesn't spoil everything first.

Let's look at the basics. Tequila and mezcal start out as agave, a type of bristly, slow-maturing plant with more than 100 species. Tequila is made exclusively from a single species, Blue Weber agave, and by law is made only in the Mexican state of Jalisco and in small parts of surrounding states. Once the agave has grown to maturity—which can take up to ten years—the piña at its core is harvested and cooked, and then chopped or crushed and fermented prior to distillation.

Blanco, or silver tequila may be rested after distillation for up to two months; reposado tequila is aged in oak for between two and 12 months; and añejo tequila is aged more than one year (there are also expanding classes of extra añejos and similar older tequilas, but these three styles are the ones most frequently encountered roaming about the cocktail bar).

Tequila's longtime reputation as a rough and rugged spirit was due largely to the preponderance of shoddy *mixto* tequilas, made by combining agave distillate with cheaper, neutral spirits. Mixtos are still

JAGUAR

1½ oz. blanco tequila
¾ oz. green Chartreuse
¾ oz. Amer Picon
3 dashes orange bitters

Glass: cocktail

Garnish: flamed orange twist

Method: Stir with ice to chill; strain into chilled glass. Flame orange twist over drink (see page 27). Garnish.

Tom Schlesinger-Guidelli, Boston

MAXIMILIAN AFFAIR

1 oz. single-village mezcal
1 oz. elderflower liqueur
½ oz. Punt e Mes
¼ oz. lemon juice

Glass: cocktail

Garnish: lemon twist

Method: Shake with ice to chill; strain into chilled glass. Garnish.

Misty Kalkofen, Boston

COCKTAIL ESSENTIALS

TEQUILA & MEZCAL *(continued)*

NOUVEAU CARRE

1½ oz. añejo tequila
¾ oz. Lillet blanc
½ oz. Bénédictine
¼ oz. brandy
5 dashes Peychaud's bitters

Glass: cocktail

Garnish: lemon twist

Method: Stir with ice to chill; strain into chilled glass. Garnish.

Jonny Raglin, San Francisco

AGUAMIEL

2 oz. blanco tequila
½ oz. Cynar
½ oz. pineapple gomme syrup
2 dashes Angostura bitters
1 pinch sea salt

Glass: cocktail

Garnish: lemon twist

Method: Stir with ice to chill; strain into chilled glass. Garnish.

Ryan Fitzgerald, San Francisco

the biggest sellers in tequila, but for every recipe in this book (and in your drinking life in general), you're much better off skipping the mixtos for 100-percent agave tequilas.

Spanish conquistadores introduced pot stills to Mexico beginning in the 1600s, but there are some agave advocates who trace the history of such spirits to a point centuries before European contact. According to these accounts, indigenous distillers in Oaxaca and surrounding regions had long been using primitive clay stills to produce prototypes of the spirit now known as mezcal.

The boom in tequila and mezcal is exciting, to be sure—but agave spirits are accompanied by a unique set of concerns.

Like tequila, mezcal starts as agave—but while tequila's parameters are narrow and rigidly defined by modern law, mezcal has more of a freewheeling nature (not to mention an element of rustic authenticity) that's made it a darling of many of today's bartenders and cocktail fiends. While tequila starts out as a Blue Weber agave, mezcal may be made from a much wider array of agave species; and while tequila's heart is in the northwestern state of Jalisco, mezcal's roots are in the coastal mountains and forests of Oaxaca, and in a handful of surrounding states.

These wider parameters mean mezcal can have a much more elaborate range of characteristics. And while tequila is today mostly the realm of global liquor conglomerates, mezcal is still largely produced on a much smaller basis. This means the particulars of the spirit's production—from the species of agave and the place and manner in which it's grown, to the often primitive, small-scale aspects of its

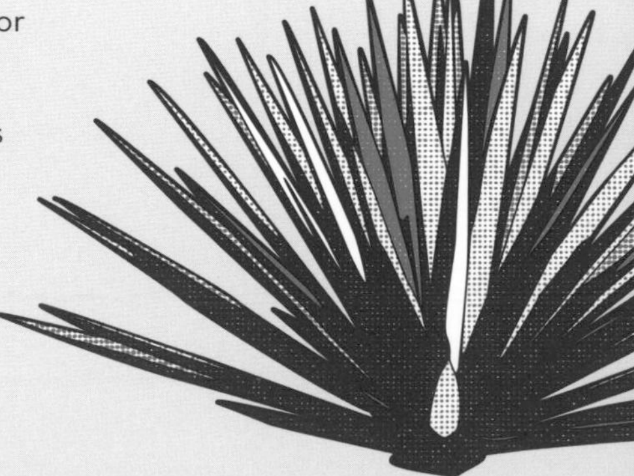

roasting, fermentation, and distillation—typically translate over into a flavorful, richly evocative spirit that's full of character. Such small-scale, or single-village mezcals can range from ethereally delicate spirits fragrant with wildflowers and brushed with the honeyed sweetness of agave, to deeply earthy, smoky spirits layered with flavors of slate, tropical fruit, and chocolate.

The category of tequila and mezcal is growing exponentially, with new brands from both massive companies and boutique producers joining the mix at dizzying speed. Suggested brands are in the Liqour Cabinet, page 177, but before you head for the liquor store, keep an important aspect of agave in mind.

The booming popularity of tequila and mezcal is creating serious concerns back home. From the ecological problems that accompany the intensive monoculture cultivation of agave for tequila, to the erosion of production and quality standards that come about as a traditionally made spirit hits the mainstream, agave spirits carry a unique set of baggage that shouldn't be discounted by the casual imbiber. In response to these concerns, Philadelphia-based restaurateur and tequila producer David Suro has banded together with craft-cocktail bartenders including Houston's Bobby Heugel, San Francisco's Ryan Fitzgerald, Boston's Misty Kalkofen, and New York's Philip Ward to form the Tequila Interchange Project (TIP), which advocates for the sustainable production of agave spirits and for economic fairness for those who make the spirit. There's much change afoot in the agave sector, and the questions can get complicated at times; but it's worth visiting TIP's website (TequilaInterchangeProject.org) before delving in on your own.

PALOMA

2 oz. blanco or reposado tequila

½ lime

4 oz. grapefruit soda (Jarritos works well)

1 pinch sea salt

Glass: highball

Garnish: lime wedge

Method: Squeeze lime half into glass and add tequila and salt; stir to combine. Fill glass with ice; top with chilled soda. Garnish.

Variation: No grapefruit soda? Instead, add 2 oz. fresh-squeezed grapefruit juice, 1 tsp. simple syrup, and 2 oz. club soda.

HARRINGTON COCKTAIL

A vodka cocktail for people who don't drink vodka.

HARRINGTON COCKTAIL

1½ oz. vodka
¼ oz. green Chartreuse
⅛ oz. Cointreau

Glass: cocktail
Garnish: orange twist
Method: Stir with ice to chill; strain into chilled glass. Garnish.

Paul Harrington, Emeryville, California/ Spokane, Washington

This drink's original name—"The Drink Without a Name"—was attached to it by its creator, Bay Area bartender-turned-architect Paul Harrington (see also the Jasmine, page 128). This original name had a couple of drawbacks: first, the drink could be easily confused with its many, many siblings sired by nomenclature-challenged bartenders around the world; and second, after a couple of rounds, guests start questioning the rationale and proposing their own alternatives, which only further muddies the matter and usually devolves into silliness. Rather than venture any further down that pointless path, bartenders began utilizing a more appropriate and common-sense title: the Harrington.

This is one of only a few vodka-based drinks in the book, and in this context, vodka's a good bet: its neutral character soothes the boisterous flavor of Chartreuse, and Cointreau helps smooth everything out into a mixture that doesn't really care what you call it, as long as you call for another.

MALECON

This suave London-born cocktail suggests a flash from the Daiquiri's past.

MALECON

1¾ oz. white rum
1 oz. lime juice
½ oz. ruby port
2 tsp. oloroso sherry
2 tsp. superfine sugar
3 dashes Peychaud's bitters

Glass: cocktail
Garnish: single ice cube
Method: Shake with ice to chill, strain into chilled glass, add ice cube.

Erik Lorincz, London

Constante Ribalaigua Vert worked in the tropical city of Havana in an era before modern air conditioning. He squeezed limes by hand and shook drinks by the dozen each night, yet photos seldom show him garbed in anything but the formal white jacket and tie preferred by the professional bar stewards of the era. *Classy. As. Hell.*

The Malecon is a Daiquiri variant, but it's not Constante's drink. It is, however, also classy as hell—with sherry and port in the mix, how could it not be—and it shares an additional quality with Constante's Daiquiri variants: it's unerringly delicious.

Slovakian barman Erik Lorincz, from the American Bar at the Savoy Hotel in London, is the master behind the Malecon (named for Havana's waterfront promenade), a drink that's gone on to be a favorite in the U.K., though still seeking traction in the U.S. Here's an opportunity to change that. . . .

THE CRAFT QUESTION

Ten years ago, the spirits world was a vast but arguably navigable realm. Pretty much all the gins, whiskies, rums, and other spirits you'd need for a cocktail were produced by a handful of companies—along with the vermouths, liqueurs, and bitters you'd need to round out the mixture.

Things change. In the past decade, scores of small distilleries have opened worldwide, with a vast concentration in the United States. As of mid-2014, the number of licensed craft distilleries in Washington State and in Colorado was approaching the triple digits, and bartenders in almost every state can reach for a locally made gin or vodka to mix the evening Martini.

Many of these distillers hew to traditional understandings of what spirits such as gin or bourbon should taste like, while others are pioneering new directions for what such spirits can be. Novelty can be a great thing—the gins from California-based St. George Spirits and brandies from Germain-Robin underscore the beauty that can be discovered while bushwhacking in unexplored terrain—but sometimes such changes can also be confusing when all you want is a basic Manhattan, and the local whiskey may be better suited to a much different task.

The boom in craft distilling is a splendid side effect of the renewed interest in spirits and mixology. But proceed with caution: as with any venture into new territory, some paths may lead to the riches of El Dorado, while others drop into the bibulous abyss. Visit a tasting room to get an idea of a new gin or rum's character, or query a local bartender for honest feedback on how a neighborhood whiskey truly fares in the mixing glass. The new world of craft spirits has its share of thorns, of which you should be wary—but don't let them dissuade you from seeking the roses in their midst.

OLD CUBAN

A mashup of venerable classics results in a drink destined to endure.

OLD CUBAN

1½ oz. aged rum (Bacardi 8 recommended)

¾ oz. lime juice

1 oz. simple syrup

2 dashes Angostura bitters

6-8 mint leaves

2 oz. chilled brut Champagne

Glass: cocktail

Garnish: mint leaf

Method: Gently muddle mint leaves with simple syrup in a cocktail shaker, and add everything else except Champagne. Shake with ice to chill, and double-strain into chilled glass. Top with Champagne. Garnish.

Audrey Saunders, New York City

Though the drink's name may summon images of the craggy, weather-worn Spencer Tracy as cast in Hemingway's *The Old Man and the Sea,* this most agreeable of modern cocktails has more of the clean-cut bearing of a dinner jacket-clad Alec Guinness in Graham Greene's *Our Man in Havana.*

Created by New York bartender Audrey Saunders while today's cocktail renaissance was still in its infancy, the Old Cuban is among the rarest of birds: an expertly structured cocktail that's full-flavored enough to satisfy even the most persnickety of cocktail nerds, yet bright, bubbly, and approachable enough to be embraced by those who insist they don't really go for the whole cocktail thing.

In a way, the Old Cuban is a masterful mashup of existing classics, reformulated into a cocktail well-suited for its own shot at bibulous immortality. The DNA of the Daiquiri and the Mojito are both to be found in the Old Cuban's rum-rich, mint-brightened mix, while the splash of Champagne is the flower in its buttonhole, a flourish that brings everything together and lightens the drink's texture and flavor, making it a choice cocktail for drinkers averse to (or seeking respite from) the big and the bold.

Use a mellow, buttery aged rum in this—Saunders calls for Bacardi 8—and remember that the sparkling wine will dry out the cocktail's flavor, so don't skimp with the simple syrup.

Hemingway and Greene built legacies for the ages upon, in part, their Cuba-inspired characters. With the Old Cuban, Saunders does the same for today's cocktail era, crafting a drink worthy of rediscovery when our great-grandkids head out for a night on the town.

A TASTE APART

SWIZZLES

Cold counters bold.

The Swizzle is the most onomatopoeic of drinks. The process and its product both share the "swizzle" name, as does a stick-style garnish gewgaw that, confusingly, has little if anything to do with the drink.

This all sounds quite complicated, but the swizzle is anything but. The growing ranks of Swizzles are descendants of a classic Caribbean style of drink in which rum (usually) is mixed with sugar or syrup, citrus, and—most importantly—a minor blizzard of crushed ice, then the mixture is all hand-blended into fragrant (and frozen) ambrosia through the use of a forked wooden *lele* twig.

Actual lele twigs can be hard to come by outside of the Caribbean, but there are plastic or stainless steel versions about (and a bar spoon can be deployed to the same swizzling task). The point of swizzling is to make a tall drink as cold as possible—and this often has the added benefit of taking what would otherwise be a hard-punching mix of (often high-proof) booze and its entourage, and converting it through the magic of ice-melt dilution into a more gentle companion.

Swizzles shouldn't be hurried—make the drink and let it rest a couple of minutes before your first sip—and they're well-suited to fragrant garnishes such as mint forests or splashes of bitters or aromatic spirits. Rum is a swizzle's traditional base, but there's no law against tossing some brandy in there, or some absinthe, or most anything else that goes well with ice, a straw, and a summer afternoon.

QUEEN'S PARK SWIZZLE

2 oz. Demerara rum
3/4 oz. fresh lime juice
1/2 oz. simple syrup
10-12 leaves fresh mint
2 dashes Angostura bitters

Glass: chimney

Garnish: mint sprig

Method: Combine ingredients in glass and fill with crushed ice. Use a bar spoon (or, ideally, a lele twig) to swizzle the drink until the outside of the glass is frosty (see page 26 for more on this method). Top with crushed ice. Garnish.

DOLORES PARK SWIZZLE

2 oz. rhum agricole blanc
1 oz. lime juice
1/2 oz. cane syrup (see page 186)
1/4 oz. maraschino liqueur
1/2 tsp. absinthe

Glass: chimney

Garnish: 1-2 mint sprigs, 4 dashes Peychaud's bitters

Method: Combine ingredients in glass and fill with crushed ice. Use a bar spoon to swizzle the drink until the outside of the glass is frosty. Top with crushed ice, dash bitters atop ice; and garnish.

Thad Vogler, San Francisco

BRAMBLE

London's lasting mark on the cocktail's latest round.

BRAMBLE

1½ oz. gin (Plymouth preferred)
¾ oz. lemon juice
½ oz. simple syrup
¾ oz. crème de mure (blackberry liqueur)

Glass: rocks

Garnish: lemon wheel, blackberries

Method: Build gin, lemon, and simple syrup in a rocks glass and fill with crushed ice, stirring to combine. Add more crushed ice if needed, and carefully drizzle crème de mure atop ice. Garnish.

Dick Bradsell, London

By the middle of August, summer seems like it'll last forever. Though the days have been gradually shortening since late June, August bursts into each day with a brightness and a sear of sun so intense that the cold and damp of winter seem like science-fiction fantasies about a gloomy far-off planet.

August's intensity brings some of the favorite flavors of summer, chief among them the dark mystery of the blackberry. An invasive species in parts of the U.S., and with varieties first introduced by horticulturalist Luther Burbank, the blackberry has a rugged richness and a tart bite perfectly in keeping with the plant's thorny character.

Blackberries make few appearances in the cocktail kingdom, but such spots can be legendary. London bartender Dick Bradsell developed the Bramble in the late 20th century formative years of the cocktail resurgence, and it's become a standard-bearing contemporary classic in the U.K. and much of Europe. Encountered more infrequently in the U.S.—a circumstance related to the scarcity of decent crème de mure, or blackberry liqueur, I'd surmise—the Bramble nevertheless inspires a degree of enthusiasm among bartenders and cocktail fiends with few parallels.

Simply a Gin Fix topped with a generous dollop of blackberry liqueur, the Bramble has such an evocative taste of summer—blackberries and boozy lemonade, served in a frosty package—that I'd nominate it as the signature drink of August (though I welcome it most any other time of year, as well).

COSMOPOLITAN

Do we need to take this outside?

Yes, I put a goddamn Cosmo recipe in this book. That pink-hued symbol of the "Sex and the City" era fell out of fashion years ago as everybody rediscovered things like rye whiskey and amari and so on, but as cocktail life cycles go, this one had a hell of a run.

The Cosmopolitan is everything that many cocktail geeks hate—it's pretty, and popular, and a vodka drink—and no doubt there are flinches of too-cool revulsion at its inclusion here.

But I invite you to spar about the Cosmo's qualities in person. Here's what to do: meet me in Brooklyn's Cobble Hill neighborhood next Thursday at dusk, at the corner of Atlantic Avenue and Henry Street. If I'm running late, wait inside the bar there—the Long Island Bar, a place that looks like an old diner. Tell the gangly looking guy who owns the place about your gripe with the Cosmopolitan, and that you're there to put a Cosmo advocate in his place. Then ask for a cocktail to sip while you wait, maybe let the guy mix something he's known for—and don't worry, I'll be along really soon.

COSMOPOLITAN

2 oz. citrus vodka
1 oz. Cointreau
1 oz. lime juice
1 oz. cranberry juice

Glass: cocktail

Garnish: lemon twist

Method: Shake with ice to chill; strain into chilled glass. Garnish.

Tip: If you don't feel like buying a bottle of citrus vodka just to make this one drink, it's likely nobody will rat you out if you reach for a citrusy gin instead. And yes, that's a 5 oz. drink (plus ice)—time to break out the oversized Martini glasses from the '90s.

Toby Cecchini, New York City

CLINT EASTWOOD

A bold and burly clock-cleaner that ends the evening right.

This is not the drink with which you begin your evening. As a way of wrapping up a night that grew late without warning, however, the Clint Eastwood works just dandy.

Hard-punching in both firepower and flavor, this bold and simple combo is the creation—nay, the responsibility—of Chicago bartender Mike Ryan, who first wielded the Eastwood's might at Violet Hour, and then helmed the bar at Sable. With the muscle of green Chartreuse and a surly stab of Angostura bitters built atop a base of rye whiskey—100 proof or better, please (this is not a place to hold back)—the Clint Eastwood is a nightcap with considerably more soporific power than a glass of warm milk.

CLINT EASTWOOD

1½ oz. rye whiskey
⅛ oz. green Chartreuse
⅛ oz. Angostura bitters
¼ oz. rich Demerara syrup

Glass: cocktail

Garnish: orange twist

Method: Stir with ice to chill; strain into chilled glass. Garnish.

Mike Ryan, Chicago

COCKTAIL ESSENTIALS

RUM

Yo ho ho, yourself—this globetrotting spirit's come a long way since Blackbeard's day.

ACE OF CLUBS

2 oz. amber rum
½ oz. lime juice
¼ oz. crème de cacao

Glass: cocktail

Method: Shake with ice to chill; strain into chilled glass.

LAND'S END

1½ oz. bold Jamaican rum (Smith & Cross)
¾ oz. lemon juice
¾ oz. raspberry gomme syrup
½ oz. curaçao

Glass: cocktail

Method: Shake with ice to chill; strain into chilled glass.

Adapted by Todd Smith, San Francisco

Between its pick as pirate's poison and the indignities of the Bahama Mama, rum has had a rough time over the centuries. Of course, if your name was frequently prefaced with "Demon" or followed by "and Coke," your reputation would likely be suffering a little, too.

Increasingly, though, bartenders are packing away the paper parasols and embarking on serious explorations of this most diverse of spirits. While the rules covering Cognac, bourbon, and tequila can be rigid, rum is a much more freewheeling style of spirit, as light and almost as crisp as vodka in some cases, and as dark and deep as crude oil in others.

Like the richest of rums, the spirit's history can be a bit opaque. Rum likely originated in the Caribbean in the 17th century—Barbados often argues its place as rum's birthplace—and, as rum expert Wayne Curtis notes in *And a Bottle of Rum*, his indispensable book on the spirit, rum was first manufactured ("crafted" is too generous a term) as a way to take the Caribbean's most prevalent form of industrial waste (molasses, a byproduct of the sugar industry) and convert it into something marketable, or at least buzz-worthy. This proto-rum was dubbed "kill-devil," which tells you pretty much all you need to know about its rough quality, and early descriptions read like one-star Yelp reviews: "rough and disagreeable," "a hot, hellish and terrible liquor" and "not very pleasant in taste."

> *From pirate juice to the spread of frozen Daiquiri machines, rum's received little respect over the years. But things change—and in rum's case, they're changing fast.*

But rum still carried a cheap bang, which is all that many look for, and it quickly caught on among sailors, and among slave owners who found it cheaper than food and almost as useful at wringing extra labor from those working in the harsh environment of the cane fields. Like cotton, cane sugar, and gonorrhea, rum was carried by sailors and ships to ports around the world, finding a favorite home in the American colonies, and in the cups and punch bowls of those who either couldn't afford or couldn't find preferred options such as brandy or port.

Much of rum's luster was lost during the American Revolution, when imports of Caribbean rum (and molasses for Massachusetts-based distilleries) were disrupted; in the years that followed, whiskey quickly moved into the vacuum. Late 19th century bar guides carry a few token rum drinks—mostly variations on Smashes and Sours that call for the mellowness of rum from "Santa Cruz" (St. Croix), or for a fragrant wallop from the funky rums from Jamaica—though by that era, rum had long been an essential component in punches, both party-size and single-serving. Rum's full utility as a cocktail spirit didn't become readily apparent to American drinkers until the 1920s, when Prohibition sent thirsty travelers scurrying to vacation in Havana, the cradle of the Daiquiri and its teeming brood (see page 102). This thirst for rum was only bolstered following Repeal, when the cheap and plentiful spirit proved appealing to pioneering bar owners including Ernest Raymond Beaumont Gantt, better known as Donn Beach, whose 1933 debut of his Don the Beachcomber bar in Hollywood set the tiki torch ablaze for countless customers seduced by his "rum rhapsodies" (for more on Beach, and the total tiki experience, see page 159).

Today's bartenders and cocktail fans have rediscovered rum (again), and the rum shelves present great opportunities (though sometimes they're hidden among the flavored spirits and gaudy colors). Rum-centric bars such as Smuggler's Cove, in San Francisco; Rumba, in Seattle; Hale Pele, in Portland, Oregon; and Lost Lake, in Chicago, are great places to matriculate an education in rum from freshman to post-grad level, and New Orleans offers two such opportunities, Cane & Table and Beachbum Berry's Latitude 29.

THE GETAWAY

1 oz. blackstrap rum
1 oz. lemon juice
½ oz. Cynar
½ oz. simple syrup

Glass: cocktail

Method: Shake with ice to chill; strain into chilled glass.

Derek Brown, Washington, D.C.

COCKTAIL ESSENTIALS

RUM *(continued)*

'TI PUNCH

2 oz. rhum agricole
1 tsp. cane syrup
Lime

Glass: rocks

Method: Pour syrup into rocks glass. Use a paring knife to cut a quarter-size disk from the side of a lime, getting a bit of the flesh along with the peel. Squeeze lime slice into glass and add disk to syrup. Add rum and stir to combine. Ice is optional—if using, add just before serving.

UNIQUE BIRD

2 oz. rhum agricole blanc
½ oz. lime juice
½ oz. pineapple gomme syrup
¼ oz. yellow Chartreuse

Glass: cocktail

Method: Shake with ice to chill; strain into chilled glass.

Connor O'Brien, Seattle

Foundation cocktails such as the Daiquiri welcome almost any type of rum in the shaker, but other drinks are constructed around a particular style (or styles—rum is the only spirit for which it's widely accepted for bartenders to mix multiple types together to create a particular character). Some rums respond better to the plug-and-play treatment than others; here's a very general overview of styles, and for recommendations for particular brands, turn to the Liquor Cabinet on page 177.

Cuban-style rums tend to be drier and crisper, and function as the base for the most thirst-quenching of Daiquiris. Amber aged rums range from the soft, buttery spirits from Barbados and the Virgin Islands to the brisk, bold rums from St. Lucia and Trinidad, and dark rums offer a spectacular spectrum, from the chocolatey richness of rum from Guatemala, to bold, brooding Demerara rums from Guyana, to the gnarly, seductive funk of pot-still rums from Jamaica. And as is true with pretty much everything else, the French have a different way of making rum, relying in this case on fresh sugarcane juice rather than molasses for the base of the distinctive *rhum agricole* from Martinique and Guadeloupe. (Haiti, once a French colony, also makes excellent cane-based rum that's similarly rich in character.) One of the particularly welcome outgrowths of the cocktail resurgence has been the introduction of Daiquiri-ready rums such as Caña Brava, and of rum blends that feature the best characteristics of multiple rum-making regions; rums such as Banks 5 Island (and its aged sibling, Banks 7 Golden Age) and Plantation 3 Stars make memorable Daiquiris, and function well in a variety of roles. And in 2014, one of the masters of the rum world began adding his own bottles to the liquor cabinet, as Ed Hamilton—who travels online and in life as the Minister of Rum—introduced Hamilton's rums, a line of superlative spirits that Hamilton sourced from distilleries in Guyana, St. Lucia, and Jamaica, with more islands and places being added over time.

Rum's past may be rugged, but its present and future are promising. Don't be afraid to experiment a little—the direction may not always be clear, but sometimes drifting off course can take you places you never knew you were looking for.

COCKTAIL ESSENTIALS

CACHAÇA

Brazil's signature spirit is a surge waiting to happen.

The first step in making rum is to start with sugarcane—either the fresh juice, as with rhum agricole, or the molasses leftover after making sugar, as with most other rum. But rum isn't the only spirit that comes from cane's sweet bounty.

Cachaça is Brazil's approach to rum, but its manner of production (and its flavor) is different enough that it's evolved into its own category of spirit. Like rhum agricole, cachaça starts as sugarcane juice (though a cooked-down syrup may also be used). Distilled in a somewhat different manner than most rum, cachaça can convey a crisper, grassier flavor, and aged cachaças—which can utilize a range of types of wood, though typically is aged in used bourbon barrels—can have a delicate balance of vanilla, toffee, and spice that makes them distinctively alluring.

There are thousands of producers of cachaça in Brazil (most unlicensed), but relatively few brands make it to the States; see page 179 for recommended brands. Aged cachaça is the standard style encountered in southern Brazil, but still a relative rarity in the U.S.; brands such as Novo Fogo are working hard to change this, and it's worth seeking out their excellent aged versions as part of a full cachaça education. Try the spirit in its signature drink, the Caipirinha; in a Batida, an agreeable guzzler that works well with most any type of fruit juice; or in a contemporary spin such as the Marmalade Sour, on page 153.

CAIPIRINHA

2 oz. cachaça
½ lime
1-2 tsp. superfine sugar, to taste

Glass: rocks

Method: Cut lime half into four equal-size chunks and add to cocktail shaker along with sugar. Crush fruit with muddler; add cachaça and a handful of ice. Shake well to chill, and pour (unstrained) into chilled glass.

BATIDA

1½ oz. cachaça
1 oz. coconut cream
1 oz. passion fruit juice

Glass: rocks

Method: Combine ingredients in a blender with 6 oz. crushed ice. Blend to combine; pour into glass. Garnish.

Variations: This recipe is just a template—swap condensed milk for the coconut, and almost any type of fruit juice for the passion fruit.

HONEY FITZ

Politics doesn't mix with liquor—but here's a possible exception.

HONEY FITZ

2 oz. dark rum (like Zacapa or Chairman's Reserve)

3/4 oz. grapefruit juice

3/4 oz. honey syrup

2 dashes Peychaud's bitters

Glass: cocktail

Method: Shake with ice to chill; strain into chilled glass.

Jackson Cannon, Boston

A favorite adage in the bar world is that bartenders are simply psychiatrists without the medical degree. But Boston bartender Jackson Cannon proves that just as often, the bartender functions as a diplomat.

Having grown up in the political sphere—his father, Lou Cannon, was the *Washington Post*'s chief White House correspondent during the Reagan years—Cannon became one of the most influential bartenders in Boston, one of the most influential cities in the cocktail's recovery. Always nattily dressed and with a diplomat's ready handshake and enthusiastic smile, Cannon has brought the best aspects of the political realm and placed them in the bar environment, raising the prestige of each.

Given his background, it's not surprising that Cannon reached into his city's political history—John F. "Honey Fitz" Fitzgerald was the silver-tongued mayor of Boston and the grandfather (and namesake) of President John F. Kennedy—when selecting a name for this fragrant drink, bold with rum and honey.

FORT WASHINGTON FLIP

Hearty enough for New England in November—tasty enough for anywhere, anytime.

FORT WASHINGTON FLIP

1 1/2 oz. applejack

3/4 oz. Bénédictine

1/2 oz. maple syrup

1 fresh egg

Glass: cocktail

Garnish: fresh-grated nutmeg

Method: Shake all ingredients without ice to combine, then add ice and shake again until foamy. Strain into chilled glass; garnish.

Misty Kalkofen, Boston

July 4th, 1776, may be recognized as the day the American republic was born—but in Boston, they got a head start.

By the spring of 1775, the rebellion in Massachusetts had developed to such an extent that the British found themselves surrounded in Boston, with no place to go except ocean. For 11 months, the Continental Army blocked all routes out of the city, and cemented their hold with Fort Washington, armed with big guns captured from Fort Ticonderoga. The fort proved so intimidating that the British abandoned the city.

Fort Washington is still there, and somewhere around the city you'll find this flip, created by Misty Kalkofen during her tenure at Green Street in Cambridge. With apple brandy, maple, and a whole egg, it's bold enough to sustain you through a New England winter night, making Boston a much more hospitable place than the British might remember.

TOMMY'S MARGARITA

Simplicity wins.

There's likely a special place in Hell reserved for those who relegate one of the world's most popular cocktails to afterthought status. That's where you'll probably find me in the great beyond for this meditation on the Margarita.

I have nothing against the Margarita—I actually love the little buggers, and I'd be a card-carrying supporter of the subculture that's grown up in Texas around the frozen Margarita, if they gave out cards for that sort of thing. But while I don't dispute the Margarita's inherent awesomeness, I'd be remiss if I didn't point out the Margarita's close, and perhaps even more quaffable relative.

At a time when cocktails are increasingly baroque, and complexities are layered one upon another, Tommy's Margarita suggests a degree of creative moderation, and cocktail civilization is the better for it.

The Margarita is basically a tequila-based spin on a classic Daisy—an old-timey style of drink crafted from a spirit, citrus, and orange liqueur—and is made in a near-identical manner to its Daisy-like cousin, the Sidecar. But at Tommy's Mexican Restaurant in San Francisco, barman and tequila evangelist Julio Bermejo took the classic Margarita one step back, giving it a life as a simple sour that was denied it in the earliest years of American mixology, when tequila was still mostly unheard of north of the Mexican border.

Mixed with tequila, fresh lime, and agave nectar, Tommy's Margarita is closer in style and format to the Daiquiri than to its namesake kin. This is a good thing—for while the classic Margarita is a Duke of the cocktail world, the Daiquiri is one of the kings. Sometimes, streamlining counts as progress.

TOMMY'S MARGARITA

2 oz. tequila (blanco or reposado, your call)

3/4 oz. lime juice

3/4 oz. agave syrup, to taste (see page 186)

Glass: rocks

Garnish: lime wedge

Method: Shake with ice to chill, strain into glass filled with fresh ice. Garnish with lime wedge.

Option: Before mixing drink, moisten the lip of the serving glass with a cut lime wedge, and rim the glass with coarse salt.

Julio Bermejo, San Francisco

MARGARITA

2 oz. blanco tequila

3/4 oz. lime juice

1 oz. Cointreau

Glass: cocktail or rocks

Garnish: lime wedge

Method: Shake with ice to chill; strain into chilled cocktail glass or rocks glass filled with fresh ice.

Option: Salt the rim, as above.

COCKTAIL ESSENTIALS

BITTERS

Taking a spin through the cocktail equivalent of the spice rack.

Plants that taste surly or scary on their own have a remarkable future in mixology.

Assorted roots, barks, and other botanicals can pack a brass-knuckle bitterness, nature's way of warning potential predators that only misery lies ahead. But when such bitter-edged plants as cinchona, gentian, and wormwood are compounded with other ingredients—including those that are a bit more agreeable, such as cinnamon, orange peel, or anise—then the balance can come across as more bracing than brawling, and can boost a little extra energy into the party going on in the glass.

Aperitif wines (page 63) and bitter liqueurs (page 154) tap the powers of bitter ingredients in ways to make them more palatable, but perhaps the most versatile use of these botanicals—and the most integral to the nature of cocktails—is when they're deployed in potent-flavored liquids best measured in drops and dashes, that function as all-around seasoning for drinks.

Originally used in drips and dashes, bitters are now flowing freely, each aromatic splash staking a larger claim on our liquid landscape.

Bitters were a core component of the original definition of a cocktail from 1804, and the category was relatively vibrant until Prohibition. Proprietary styles of bitters such as Boker's, Abbott's, and Peychaud's found their way into mixing glasses from New Orleans to New York, adding sparks of flavor and nuances of character to drinks.

It's often been said that bitters function in a cocktail like salt does in a soup—without it, there seems to be something missing, but if you can easily taste it, you've used too much. That's an imperfect analogy, because while bitters are certainly an all-purpose seasoning for drinks, adding their own touches to the mix, they also serve as binders of flavor, pulling the sometimes disparate characteristics together into a more fully integrated whole.

ALABAZAM

1½ oz. Brandy
2 tsp. Cointreau
2 tsp. simple syrup
1 tsp. lemon juice
1 tsp. Angostura bitters

Glass: cocktail

Method: Stir with ice to chill; strain into chilled glass.

Adapted by Jamie Boudreau, Seattle

SAWYER

2 oz. gin
½ oz. lime juice
½ oz. simple syrup
14 dashes Angostura bitters
7 dashes Peychaud's bitters
7 dashes orange bitters

Glass: rocks

Method: Shake with ice to chill; strain into chilled glass.

Don Lee, New York City

At the turn of the 21st century, almost all bitters except the paper-wrapped Angostura had disappeared from most bars; Peychaud's, from New Orleans, still held a regional appeal, and the Rochester, New York-based Fee Brothers company kept the bitter fires burning until the cocktail renaissance rolled around. But once the cocktail wheel started turning, bitters quickly rebounded, and today, the bitters market is booming with recreations of once-lost proprietary bitters, and with new (and often unexpected) styles.

A wander through a well-stocked store (or website) can turn up dozens of brands and styles of bitters, and it's rare to find a craft-cocktail bar that doesn't deploy at least one housemade style of bitters. Not all of these bitters are necessary, of course, though it's good to have options (see page 178 for a few recommendations)—producers including New Orleans-based Bittermens, from Avery and Janet Glasser; The Bitter Truth, from German bartenders Stephan Berg and Alexander Hauck; and Adam Elmegirab, in Aberdeen, Scotland, make some of the best of the current batch.

Though bitters are intended to be dispensed by the dropperful, bitters-loving bartenders are increasingly prying the dasher top off the bottle to make drinks that put these ingredients front and center. The Trinidad Sour, developed by New York bartender Giuseppe González while working the bar at Clover Club, is among the best of the bitters-forward mix, as is the Sawyer, developed by bartending brainiac Don Lee for New York's Momofuku Sszm Bar; in Seattle, bartender Jamie Boudreau shows his love for Angostura not only through drinks such as the Alabazam (adapted from an 1878 recipe from Leo Engels), but also via Boudreau's mahogany-and-birch bar at Canon, which was stained using cases of the Trinidad-made bitters.

TRINIDAD SOUR

1½ oz. Angostura bitters
1 oz. orgeat
¾ oz. lemon juice
½ oz. rye whiskey (100 proof or better works best)

Glass: cocktail

Method: Shake with ice to chill; strain into chilled glass.

Giuseppe González, New York City

PENICILLIN COCKTAIL

No prescription required.

PENICILLIN COCKTAIL

2 oz. blended Scotch whisky
3/4 oz. lemon juice
3/4 oz. honey syrup (see page 186)
2-3 quarter-size slices fresh ginger
1/4 oz. Islay single-malt Scotch whisky

Glass: rocks

Garnish: candied ginger

Method: Muddle ginger slices in shaker; add blended whisky, lemon, and honey syrup. Shake with ice to chill; double-strain into glass filled with fresh ice. Using a bar spoon, float Islay malt across top of drink. Garnish.

Variation: Substitute reposado tequila for the blended whisky and a smoky single-village mezcal for the Islay malt to make a **Peniciliana**.

Sam Ross, New York City

There may have been a time when a liquor-laden drink was genuinely considered an appropriate tonic for maladies of the body or soul, but for the most part, such notions are a part of the past.

That's not to suggest that the medicinal properties of the Penicillin Cocktail are purely speculative, or that this fortifying mixture of whisky, lemon, and ginger has no greater curative property than your average placebo. For while the touch of vitamin C may give a subtle pinch to the immune system, and the ginger/lemon/honey combo is familiar to anyone who's ever nursed a sore throat, the Penicillin Cocktail's true apothecarial prowess is in dispelling the gloom that can plague the afflicted (as well as the hale and hearty) during cold and flu season.

The bar is filled with bottles that hint at the medicinal. While this whisky-laced tonic may have all the painkilling oomph of a Percocet, it's as soft and as soothing a treatment as you're likely to find.

Crafted by Australian bartender Sam Ross, formerly of New York's Milk & Honey and now at Attaboy, the Penicillin Cocktail is one of the best bets among contemporary cocktails to attain longevity. The soft, soothing character of blended Scotch whisky is bolstered by the thunder and bombast of a smoky Islay malt, with the cold-cure flavors of lemon, ginger, and honey making it just what the doctor ordered.

It's important to not overlook the drink's possible preventative value—such a mixture shouldn't be saved just for when you're sick. Now, I can't prove that this smoky, spicy drink actually wards off rhinovirus or its infectious kin, but if laughter is still considered the best medicine, then a couple of these joy-inspiring cocktails enjoyed in good company may actually have medicinal merit after all.

WHO DARES WINS

A drink from Scotland that ventures off the whisky path.

When discussing U.K. bartenders' knack for craft cocktails, all too often it's London that gets all the love. But up north in Edinburgh, the gateway to Scotland's whisky wonderland, bartenders at places such as The Bramble and its sister bar, Last Word Saloon, show a keenly honed talent for turning out drinks with flavor that ranges far from the land's legendary malts.

Gin, lemon, and orgeat contribute a snappy, airy character to this drink from Bramble and Last Word co-owner Mike Aikman, but this twist on the classic Army & Navy adds notes of caraway and cumin via a light dose of kümmel. Bright and crisp meets ethereal and earthy—an endeavor that's as bold as its result is beautiful.

WHO DARES WINS

2 oz. gin
3/4 oz. lemon juice
1/2 oz. orgeat
2 tsp. kümmel

Glass: cocktail

Garnish: star anise

Method: Shake with ice to chill; strain into chilled glass. Garnish.

Mike Aikman, Edinburgh

THEOBROMA

Tequila keeps interesting company.

Chocolate gets a bum rap in the booze world. Sure, you scarfed down M&Ms as a kid (and maybe you're doing so now), and wafers of single-estate chocolate with a cacao-solid percentage cresting 80 are today's foodie ambrosia. But start putting that stuff in a cocktail shaker, and watch the clouds of doubt creep in.

I blame the chocolate martini, and the other sugar-laden alcopops that served as cocktails-with-training-wheels for young drinkers—that, and the substandard quality of many chocolate liqueurs (see Liquor Cabinet, page 177, for better alternatives). But chocolate can play a most alluring role in a cocktail when mixed with the right company.

I humbly submit my own interpretation of "chocolate and friends." Agave spirits have a preternatural affinity for the dark earthiness of chocolate, as does the ruggedness of an amaro rich with bitter orange. The result? A bold, elbow-throwing mixture that's unafraid to let its chocolate flag fly.

THEOBROMA

2 oz. reposado tequila
1/2 oz. Punt e Mes
1/4 oz. Bigallet China-China
1 tsp. crème de cacao
2 dashes Bittermens Xocolatl Molé bitters

Glass: cocktail

Garnish: orange twist

Method: Stir with ice to chill; strain into chilled glass. Twist orange peel over drink. Garnish.

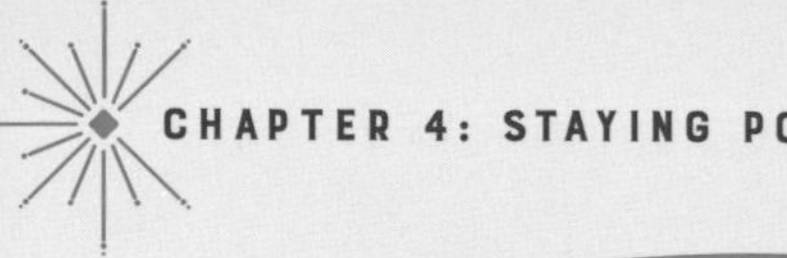

COCKTAIL ESSENTIALS

VODKA

A modest defense of the spirit cocktail nerds love to hate.

MOSCOW MULE

2 oz. vodka
½ lime
4 oz. chilled ginger beer

Glass: Moscow Mule mug or highball

Garnish: lime wedge

Method: Squeeze lime-half into ice-filled mug or glass and add remaining ingredients; stir and garnish.

The invasion came without warning. A sudden stab from the Soviet bloc to the heart of the West during the most frigid years of the Cold War, the incursion didn't carry the world-ending weight of an ICBM strike or echo with the thunder of Red Army tanks rolling though Bonn and Brussels. But vodka's advance into the U.S. and Western Europe had an impact from which today's bar culture (and craft cocktails) are still recovering.

Hyperbole? Hardly. In 1950, around 40,000 cases of vodka entered the U.S.; by 1955, that number was up to 4 million. In 1967, sales of vodka passed those of gin, and within a decade, vodka passed whiskey—*whiskey!*—to become the biggest-selling spirit in the country. Even today, as American drinkers have rediscovered their thirst for Daiquiris, Manhattans, and Negronis, vodka accounts for around a quarter of all liquor sales, and by volume still easily outpaces all competitors.

Vodka is the simplest of spirits. A modest mixture of high-proof ethanol and water that's largely defined (legally, anyway) by what it's not (flavorful and colorful), vodka has a robust history in Russia and Eastern Europe that stretches back to the Middle Ages. Traditionally made from rye, wheat, or potatoes, vodka can technically be made from pretty much anything that can be fermented, and while most of today's vodka still originates as grain-based neutral spirit, you can find vodkas on the shelf made from grapes, oranges, and apples.

With sales of the spirit still high, Americans clearly love vodka; but today's craft bartenders and cocktail enthusiasts just as clearly don't. (At a time when you could purchase vodkas made from milk or honey, it was frowned upon to order a vodka cocktail at Milk & Honey.)

Part of this is due to vodka's cultural baggage—who wants to sip bespoke beverages constructed from the same flavorless fuel that drives Kamikazes and that's often encountered in the company of Red Bull?—and part of it is due to vodka's perceived nothingness, its role in the lives of many drinkers as the transitional training pants that one must wear until a taste for big-kid booze like whiskey or gin is acquired.

But this is unfair. Despite vodka's *spiritus-non-grata* status, it has a short history as a cocktail base (about as long as tequila's, anyway), in drinks such as the Gypsy Cocktail, from the 1930s, and the Moscow Mule, which helped spark vodka's surge starting in the '50s. Bartenders who started their careers in the White Russian-sipping '80s and '90s recall vodka's ubiquity and its versatility; the Cosmopolitan (page 137), as refined by Toby Cecchini, put cocktail glasses in the hands of a generation of drinkers; Dick Bradsell's Vodka Espresso (which morphed into the Espresso Martini) is still a top-seller in parts of the world, decades after its debut; and Paul Harrington's eponymous cocktail (page 132) showcases vodka's talent at taking bold flavors and making them more approachable.

It's unlikely vodka will ever become a craft-cocktail favorite, but it presents a baby-bathwater scenario. Vodka brings more to the bar than its allegedly neutral character may imply; listen closely, and ignore the nattering cocktail-nerd peanut gallery, and vodka can remind you of the reasons it's still a big seller long after the Soviet Union went the way of the passenger pigeon.

VODKA ESPRESSO

2 oz. vodka
1 oz. espresso
½ oz. coffee liqueur
¼ oz. simple syrup

Glass: cocktail

Garnish: 3 coffee beans

Method: Shake with ice to chill; strain into chilled glass. Garnish.

Dick Bradsell, London

GYPSY COCKTAIL

2 oz. vodka
1 oz. Bénédictine
1 dash Angostura bitters

Glass: cocktail

Method: Stir with ice to chill; strain into chilled glass.

COCKTAIL STYLE

IN PRAISE OF DIFFICULT DRINKS

The best things don't always come easy.

RAMOS FIZZ

2 oz. gin (Old Tom works well, as does Plymouth)
1 oz. heavy cream
½ oz. lemon juice
½ oz. lime juice
½ oz. simple syrup
2 dashes orange-flower water
1 egg white
2-3 oz. chilled club soda

Glass: Collins

Method: Combine everything except club soda in a shaker and dry-shake to mix ingredients. Add ice, and shake long and hard until mixture is "ropy" and frothy—one minute at least, preferably two. Strain into chilled glass, and slowly add soda until the meringue-like head rises above the rim of the glass. Serve with a straw.

While I've tried to eschew the ongoing trend toward ever-more-elaborate preparations in this book, there are times when a complicated approach can return the appropriate reward.

Consider one of the hallmarks of classic New Orleans cocktails: the Ramos Fizz. Created by Henry Ramos around 1888 and the signature sip at his establishment, The Stag, the Ramos Fizz was the white-hot popular gourmet cupcake of its day. Rich with cream yet airy and light, and softly fragrant though packing a respectable punch, the Ramos Fizz was such an operation to prepare that Ramos required rotating teams of barmen to shake the drink to the desired frothiness—an exercise that often required many sets of hands (as many as 35 bartenders at Carnival's peak), and anywhere from two to 12 minutes of muscle-popping mixing.

The satisfaction to be found in a drink can be magnified by the sweat and effort it took to make it, the same way a scenic vista looks better when you've hiked or biked to the top than when you've driven to the summit in your Subaru.

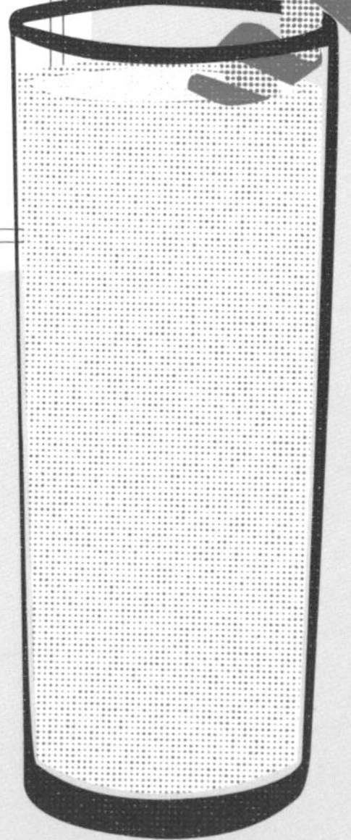

The Ramos Fizz had its heyday long before the Waring blender hit the scene, and while it's certainly possible to make the drink using such modern miracles (drinks writer Wayne Curtis has been known to shake Ramos Fizzes by the bucketload using a hardware-store paint mixer), something is arguably lost from such shortcuts of convenience. It may not be immediately evident—a mechanically manipulated Ramos Fizz is still a Ramos Fizz, which is a fine thing by default—but it lacks the satisfaction that comes with sweat and effort, the same way a scenic vista looks better when you've hiked or biked to the top than when you've driven to the summit in your Subaru. Such labor-intensive drinks harken back to less-hurried times, and sipping a laboriously prepared one offers its own sense of contentment. Life, briefly, slows down.

Of course, just because we're hip-deep in the Facebook era doesn't mean we've left PITA drinks behind for good. Throw a julep strainer in any direction and you're likely to hit a craft bartender making batches of foraged-flora bitters, sweet and tangy farmers-market shrubs and bespoke balsamic-fig gastriques. Some—okay, a bunch—of these drink ingredients are good. But as appealing as that recipe for dandelion-and-Seville-orange tincture may be, it's the kind of thing that can take weeks of preparation, but be so limited in range that it winds up only used once—twice, maybe, when cocktail-curious friends come over—and that stuff has a tendency of piling up, unwanted and unused.

Here's an exception. This one's awesome.

Don Lee is among the Mensa ranks of the cocktail cognoscienti. In 2007, during his time behind the bar at Jim Meehan's groundbreaking NYC watering hole PDT, Lee took the practice of fat-washing—basically, taking a fatty ingredient (such as bacon, or butter, or peanuts) and infusing the flavor into a spirit without the accompanying greasiness—and turned it to the power of good. Tapping the smoky beauty of Benton's bacon from pork maestro Allen Benton's Tennessee smokehouse, Lee added the swine's sultry nature to the ruggedness of bourbon, then crafted a simple twist on the Old Fashioned that's since populated craft-bar menus throughout the land.

Bourbon and bacon, together in a glass. C'mon, that's worth the trouble.

BENTON'S OLD FASHIONED

2 oz. bacon fat-washed bourbon (below)

¼ oz. maple syrup

2 dashes Angostura bitters

Glass: rocks

Garnish: orange twist

Method: Stir ingredients with ice; strain into rocks glass filled with a large cube of ice. Garnish.

Bacon fat-washed bourbon:

1 750ml bottle bourbon

1½ oz. rendered, melted bacon fat (it's essential to use good-quality smoked bacon, such as Benton's)

Combine liquid fat with bourbon in a nonreactive container; stir and cover. Let steep for 4 hours, then place container in the freezer and leave it undisturbed for 2 hours. Remove fat solids and strain through cheesecloth; bottle for use.

Don Lee, New York City

Safety Tip: Alcohol is a preservative, but it won't help you here. Fat-washed and other meat-treated spirits have a short lifespan; only make as much as you'll use over the course of a week or so, and keep it refrigerated.

FALLING LEAVES

What you'll be drinking in October.

Cocktails don't always require a load of liquor to make them excellent companions. Audrey Saunders, whose New York bar Pegu Club primed the palates of a thirsty public (and helped launch the careers of a generation of craft bartenders), devised this autumn-esque drink while at Bemelman's Bar, using a foundation of dry Riesling with just enough unaged pear brandy to push the drink into flavorful Nirvana.

In this drink, Audrey uses the pear brandy from Oregon's Clear Creek Distillery, which contributes the perfume-like fragrance of ripe Bartlett pears but not the fruit's sugar—leaving room for the richness of honey syrup and curaçao's touches of citrus peel and spice.

With its milder alcoholic payload and irresistible flavor combo, the Falling Leaves appeals to a broad audience—welcomed by dyed-in-the-wool cocktail nerds as well as by guests for whom a Martini is simply pass-out juice.

FALLING LEAVES

2 oz. dry Riesling

1 oz. pear brandy (use an unaged eau de vie)

½ oz. curaçao

¼ oz. honey syrup

1 dash Peychaud's bitters

Glass: cocktail

Garnish: star anise pod

Method: Stir with ice to chill; strain into chilled glass. Garnish.

Audrey Saunders, New York City

NORTHERN SPY

Apples and apricots bring cocktail hour to the orchard.

If Robert Frost can pen poems devoted entirely to October—"O hushed October morning mild, thy leaves have ripened to the fall" and all that—then it's not asking too much, when autumn rolls around, to mix a drink appropriate to the season.

Here's an autumn-imbued cocktail from Boston bartender Josey Packard: the Northern Spy.

Based on the crispness of American apple brandy—its apple-ness backed by a dose of sweet cider (use only a fresh cider, without preservatives) and its fruity brightness goosed up via apricot liqueur—the Northern Spy has the winsome flavor of the crisp days that pass as summer fades and winter advances. Serve with a cardigan and the first fire of the season.

NORTHERN SPY

1 oz. applejack

½ oz. unfiltered apple cider

¼ oz. lemon juice

¼ oz. apricot liqueur

2 oz. chilled brut sparkling wine

Glass: cocktail

Method: Shake first four ingredients with ice to chill. Strain into chilled glass; top with sparkling wine.

Variation: A dry, French-style sparkling (hard) cider is a nice substitute for the sparkling wine.

Josey Packard, Boston

A TASTE APART

JAM

A breakfast staple meets the cocktail shaker.

Between the Milk Punch and the Bloody Mary, there are plenty of ways to catch a buzz at the breakfast table. But this transaction also works in reverse: morning standards such as maple syrup and coffee long ago crept into cocktails, and eventually bacon (see page 151) and even sugary cereal found their way into the mixing glass. But for bridging the gap between breakfast and cocktail hour, the jam jar holds the greatest potential.

Jam is nothing more than fruit and sugar suspended in a luscious, pectin-rich mix, and fruit and sugar are the only things that distinguish many basic cocktails from a simple shot of booze. As cocktail historian Eric Felten noted, General Omar Bradley recognized the utility of jam in the drinker's arsenal; when fighting raged in Europe and North Africa and sugar and fresh fruit were scarce, Bradley added a dollop of marmalade to his whiskey for an impromptu twist on the Old Fashioned.

Apricot jam lends itself particularly well to cocktails, as does orange marmalade, which brings a bitter edge from the citrus peel that adds an extra dimension. Pectin can pose a problem when adding jam or marmalade to a shaker, resulting in a lumpy, chunky drink. This can be avoided by either dissolving the jam in an equal amount of hot water (à la honey syrup, page 186), or by first stirring or shaking the drink without ice to aid the jam's breakdown.

BREAKFAST MARTINI

1¾ oz. gin
½ oz. lemon juice
½ oz. Cointreau
1 tsp. orange marmalade

Glass: cocktail

Garnish: quarter-size circle of orange peel

Method: Combine ingredients in shaker and stir to dissolve marmalade; shake with ice to chill; strain into chilled glass. Squeeze orange peel over drink and use as garnish.

Salvatore Calabrese, London

MARMALADE SOUR

2 oz. cachaça
¾ oz. lemon juice
1 Tbsp. marmalade (mixed-citrus if you have it, orange if not)
1 tsp. simple syrup
2 dashes orange bitters
1 fresh egg white

Glass: cocktail

Method: Combine ingredients in shaker and shake, without ice, to dissolve marmalade and aerate egg white; add ice and shake hard to chill; strain into chilled glass.

Jamie Boudreau, Seattle

A TASTE APART

AMARI

Bitter liqueurs bounce from afterthought to omnipresent.

Cocktails are like conversations—a few interesting voices and a little back-and-forth are essential ingredients for a good one. And in the cocktail conversation, few voices are as commanding or as articulate as those provided by amari.

This broad class of bitter liqueurs—*amaro* is Italian for "bitter"—may have centuries of history behind it, but until the cocktail culture began to surge in force, it remained a mystery in most American bars. While many European countries (and increasingly, American craft distillers) have their own approaches to the complex, multi-layered bitterness found in these spirits—trans-Euro candidates include the Czech Becherovka, Unicum from Hungary, and Germany's gift to shot-pounding bros, Jägermeister—Italy is the font from which the most, and most memorable, amari flow.

It can be useful to think of amari as a particularly populous branch of the bitter family tree, with kin including wine-based aperitifs such as vermouth and quinquinas, and the intensely flavored cocktail bitters utilized in drops and dashes. As with vermouth and bitters, amari's roots trace to the apothecary's shop, with a wide range of botanical ingredients chosen for their believed utility at aiding digestion (hence their other familiar tag of *digestivi*) and calming an overindulged tummy.

This bitter family shares some ingredients—cinchona, gentian, and wormwood pop up across the board as bittering agents, and other flavoring ingredients can include a mix of sometimes dozens of botanicals, from cinnamon and saffron to ginger, mint, and thyme. But amari are also distinguished by a number of flavors and subclasses—these include the bitter-orange elements of Ramazzotti and Bigallet China-China Amer (from France, and useful as a substitute for Amer Picon); the artichoke-tinged Cynar; and subclasses such as nocino (an oil-black liqueur made with walnuts) and the menthol-tinged intensity of fernets, such as Fernet-Branca.

Unlike vermouth, most amari are spirits based, and are often made by macerating and/or distilling botanicals and then sweetening and sometimes aging the mix to create the desired balance between bitter, sweet, and

ITALIAN BUCK

1½ oz. Cynar
1½ oz. Amaro Montenegro
¾ oz. lime juice
3 oz. chilled ginger beer

Glass: Collins

Garnish: lime wheel

Method: Shake first three ingredients with ice to chill, strain into ice-filled glass. Add ginger beer; garnish.

Jamie Boudreau, Seattle

BITTER GIUSEPPE

2 oz. Cynar
1 oz. Carpano Antica Formula vermouth
¼ oz. lemon juice
6 dashes orange bitters (Regan's recommended)

Glass: rocks

Garnish: lemon twist

Method: Stir with ice to chill, strain into glass filled with fresh ice. Twist lemon peel over drink and use as garnish.

Stephen Cole, Chicago

boisterous. And unlike so-called "nonpotable" cocktail bitters, amari are pretty goddamn potable, and are designed to be drunk on their own, or with a little tonic or soda.

But bartenders doing what they do, it didn't take long for amari to make their way into the mixing glass along with whiskey, gin, and just about everything else around. The French Amer Picon and Italy's Fernet-Branca crept into drinks first mixed around the turn of the last century, but it wasn't until the 21st century craft-cocktail explosion that amari reached full representation. While many cocktail bars may have carried a dusty bottle of Fernet-Branca at one time, the token quickly became a torrent. Some bars now stock a score or more styles, from the cola-esque Averna to the chocolatey Montenegro to the burly alpine Braulio. And while originally deployed as a modifier, amari have come into their own as a base ingredient in drinks such as the Bitter Giuseppe from Stephen Cole at Chicago's Barrelhouse Flat and the Italian Buck from Seattle bartender Jamie Boudreau. And in New York City, Sother Teague and the team at Amor y Amargo have taken the trend and based an entire bar upon it, serving drinks such as the Black Rock Chiller.

The bitterness encountered in amari can range from a soft caress to a knuckle-studded wallop, and when they engage with whiskey or gin in the mixing glass, the alliance can defeat all rivals.

Amari have a talent at enlivening any number of cocktail conversations. Let 'em talk—at first encounter, it may occasionally be a challenge to determine what they're trying to say, but ultimately the conversation is never boring.

BLACK ROCK CHILLER

1 oz. reposado tequila
1 oz. Branca Menta
1 oz. Suze

Glass: rocks

Method: Build ingredients together and stir without ice. Serve at room temperature.

Note: You can substitute another gentian aperitif such as Salers, Aveze or Bittermens Amère Sauvage in place of Suze. This recipe also easily scales up—swap "750ml bottle" for "oz." in the above recipe, and you've got a bottled punch for your next party.

Sother Teague, New York City

RED HOOK & THE SLOPE

Riffs on the Manhattan that seem destined to stick around.

RED HOOK

2 oz. rye whiskey

½ oz. Punt e Mes

½ oz. maraschino liqueur

Glass: cocktail

Method: Stir with ice to chill; strain into chilled glass.

Enzo Errico, New York City

THE SLOPE

2½ oz. rye whiskey (Bulleit recommended)

¾ oz. Punt e Mes

¼ oz. apricot liqueur

1 dash Angostura bitters

Glass: cocktail

Method: Stir with ice to chill; strain into chilled glass.

Julie Reiner, Brooklyn

Not every advance has to have a moon-launch level of ambition. For every great leap on par with the mastering of fire or the advent of the Internet, there are countless nudges and tweaks that, together, move civilization forward (at least, one hopes).

The Manhattan was the cocktail equivalent of a moon mission, a step that crossed a then-invisible line dividing what came before from what followed. And while there have been many manipulations of the Manhattan from the railroad era to the YouTube age (see page 109), there are a couple of recent forays that deserve a closer look.

The middle of the 21st century's first decade saw the cocktail renaissance flare from glowing ember to blazing fire, as bartenders—those in New York and Boston excelled at this—took classic-cocktail models and refined them to their clearest essence, then expanded on the model in ways that ancestral bartenders would have recognized (and likely appreciated), but that also bore traces of contemporary genius.

"Genius" may be a heavy tag to hang on these two Manhattan relatives, but *damn*, if they aren't well-suited for liquid immortality. For the Red Hook, Milk & Honey barman Enzo Errico bolstered the vermouth's backbone by using Punt e Mes—a bolder, more bitter expression of a traditional Italian *rosso*—and dabbed the drink with maraschino liqueur, creating a robust mix with a bitter edge and a dry funk. Julie Reiner—owner of New York bars Flatiron Lounge and Clover Club, and for whom the "g" word is not hyperbolic praise—followed a similar path, but introduced apricot liqueur to the equation, making a drink both bold and bitter but also lusciously, decadently fun.

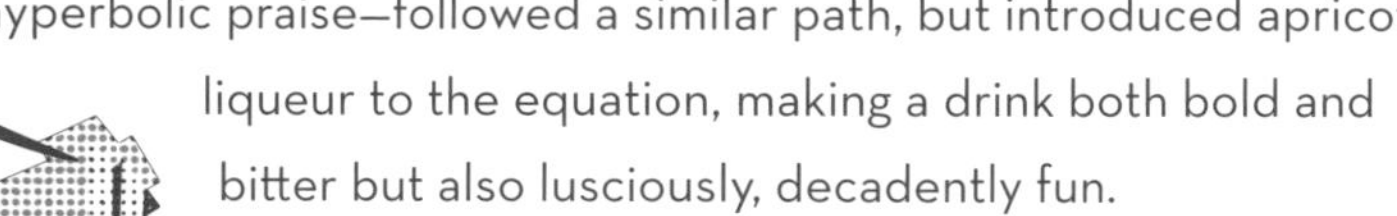

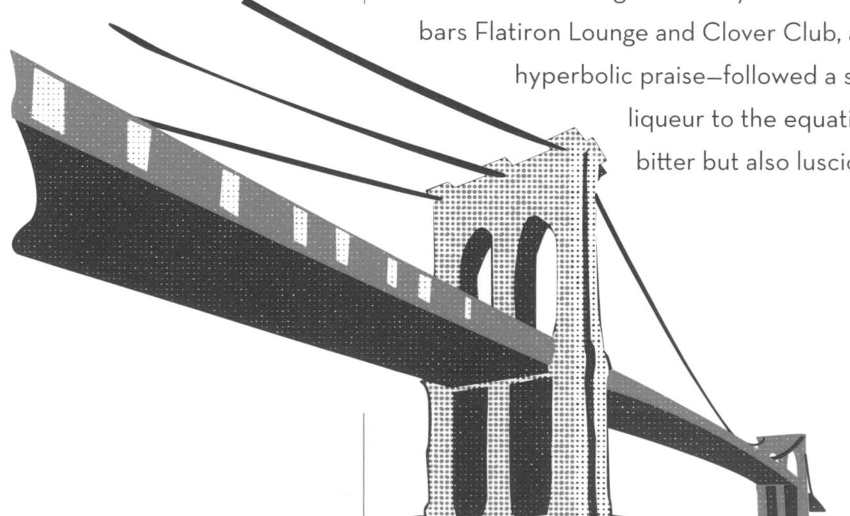

COCKTAIL ESSENTIALS

PISCO

This South American star steps beyond the iconic sour.

Remember Shakespeare's "A rose by any other name" folderol? Same goes for brandy and pisco. Pisco is a form of brandy, of course, but this South American standard puts a few New World twists on the Old World spirit.

Made from wine grapes in Peru and Chile—the countries have long sparred over pisco's true parentage—pisco can have a delicacy of aroma and a fine, nuanced flavor, much in common with its brandy kin. But pisco is its own creature, with a multitude of identities that can be alarmingly complicated for a pisco newbie. But here are a few basics to get you started:

Rules regarding pisco's production vary between Peru and Chile. In Peru, eight types of grapes may be used to make pisco, while Chile typically uses three (with Moscato the prevalent type). Peruvian piscos may not be aged (beyond a short post-distillation rest in a neutral container), and may be bottled as single-varietal *pisco puro*—Quebranta, an earthy spirit made from red-wine grapes, is the most prevalent Peruvian style, followed by the floral and fragrant Italia, from white-wine grapes—or as an *acholado*, a mix of two or more varieties. Most Chilean pisco is also bottled without barrel-maturation, though a few expressions spend a short time in oak.

America's expanding diversity and the rising popularity in Peruvian cuisine has helped fuel an interest in good pisco, and today is perhaps the best time ever to explore the spirit stateside. Suggested brands are listed in the Liquor Cabinet on page 177; try one out in a Pisco Bellringer from Jim Maloney's 1903 book *How to Mix Drinks*, or a contemporary drink such as the Cienciano from Seattle bartender Jay Kuehner.

CIENCIANO

1½ oz. pisco (Quebranta recommended)
½ oz. amontillado sherry
½ oz. Ramazzotti
¼ oz. cachaça

Glass: cocktail

Garnish: orange twist

Method: Stir with ice to chill; strain into chilled glass. Garnish.

Jay Kuehner, Seattle

PISCO BELLRINGER

2 oz. pisco
½ oz. lemon juice
½ oz. simple syrup
2 dashes orange bitters
2 dashes Peychaud's bitters
1 tsp. apricot liqueur

Glass: cocktail

Garnish: lemon wheel

Method: Shake first five ingredients with ice to chill; rinse chilled cocktail glass with apricot liqueur, discarding excess, and strain drink into apricot-rinsed glass. Garnish.

DIVISION BELL & NAKED & FAMOUS

Birds of a feather from two of NYC's best bartending minds.

DIVISION BELL

1 oz. mezcal
3/4 oz. lime juice
3/4 oz. Aperol
1/2 oz. maraschino liqueur

Glass: cocktail

Garnish: grapefruit twist

Method: Shake with ice to chill; strain into chilled glass. Garnish.

Philip Ward, New York City

NAKED & FAMOUS

3/4 oz. mezcal
3/4 oz. lime juice
3/4 oz. Aperol
3/4 oz. yellow Chartreuse

Glass: cocktail

Method: Shake with ice to chill; strain into chilled glass. Garnish.

Note: Go smoky with the mezcal—Simó uses Del Maguey's Chichicapa, and Vida is also a good bet.

Joaquín Simó, New York City

When Murray Stenson made his Lazarus move on the long-dead Last Word (page 39), he didn't just send countless bartenders scrambling to recreate the resurrected drink—he put their mental wheels in motion as they riffed on the original, some coming back with truly distinctive drinks. The Paper Plane (page 98), from New York bartender Sam Ross, is one Last Word relative worth discovering; here are two more from New York bartenders Philip Ward and Joaquín Simó.

Mezcal and lime are longtime companions in Mexico, but when the bright bite of Aperol and expressive European liqueurs get involved, the combo's flavor starts to roam far from its original home.

While tending bar at Pegu Club, Ward first tinkered with the Last Word by coming up with his eponymous Last Ward, with rye swapped in for the gin and lemon for the lime. But after opening the agave bar Mayahuel in 2009, Ward began working with other equal-parts drinks (sometimes tweaking the proportions), an effort culminating with the Division Bell. The smoky earthiness of mezcal takes center stage, backed by citrus and the bright bitterness of Aperol, with the softening funk of maraschino performing as mediator for the mix.

It's an excellent variation, and one related to a drink that returns to the Last Word model: the Naked & Famous, from Ward's fellow Death & Co. alumnus Joaquín Simó, lately of Pouring Ribbons. Mezcal, lime, and Aperol continue their contrapuntal performance in Simó's drink, but instead of maraschino's mellowness, Naked & Famous turns to the honeyed herbaceousness of yellow Chartreuse.

COCKTAIL STYLE

THE TRIUMPH OF TIKI

Putting flavorful fun back into cocktails, one Mai Tai at a time.

Tropical drinks are the Lost Boys of cocktails. Like rum-slugging Peter Pans, they refuse to give up their taste for adventure or their grip on the fantastical brightness of possibility in an otherwise dour Dry Martini world.

The escapist element introduced by exotic drinks—which have worn a number of nomenclatural hats, none of them fitting perfectly: tiki drinks, Polynesian drinks, tropical, or (more appropriately) faux-tropical drinks—came at a suitable time. In 1934, soon after Prohibition's repeal, New Orleans-bred bartender and traveler Ernest Raymond Beaumont Gantt opened Don the Beachcomber bar in Hollywood. He stocked the menu with drinks based on rum—which, unlike American-made spirits like bourbon, was a product in ample supply, and which, unlike imported brandies and gin, was still a remarkable bargain for a cash-strapped entrepreneur—and decorated the place with assorted nautical ephemera collected during his rambles.

The result was a blowout: Gantt (who soon rechristened himself "Donn Beach") struck upon a perfect formula during the escape-thirsty years of the Depression, his decor suggesting the possibilities of island paradise while his robust drinks—"rum rhapsodies" in Beach's view—helped wash away the grey drudgery of those grim years. Not that Beach's guests were spending their days on the soup line: Howard Hughes, Clark Gable, Charlie Chaplin, and Joan Crawford were among his clientele. Soon enough, so was Bay Area restaurateur Victor Bergeron, who took Beach's formula and replicated it with his own imprint, adopting the "Trader Vic" moniker and launching a tiki empire that eventually had outposts in New York, London, and Dubai.

MAI TAI

1 oz. dark Jamaican rum
1 oz. aged rhum agricole
1 oz. lime juice
1/2 oz. curaçao
1/4 oz. orgeat
1/4 oz. simple syrup

Glass: rocks

Garnish: lime shell, mint sprig

Method: Shake with crushed ice to chill; pour (unstrained) into glass; garnish.

DONGA PUNCH

1½ oz. aged rhum agricole
1½ oz. Don's Mix (see below)
3/4 oz. lime juice

Glass: Collins

Method: Shake with crushed ice to chill; pour unstrained into glass; add more crushed ice to fill.

Note: Don's Mix is among the secret formulae that Berry decoded from Beach's old bars; mix it by combining 4 oz. grapefruit juice with 2 oz. cinnamon syrup (see page 185 for a recipe).

COCKTAIL STYLE

TIKI *(continued)*

TEST PILOT

1½ oz. amber Jamaican rum
¾ oz. white rum
½ oz. Cointreau
½ oz. falernum
½ oz. lime juice
1 dash Angostura bitters
6 drops Pernod or absinthe
1 cup crushed ice

Glass: rocks

Garnish: cherry

Method: Combine ingredients in blender and add crushed ice. Blend at high speed for 5 seconds; pour into glass; garnish.

The drinks crafted by Beach, Bergeron, and the hordes of pith-helmeted, Hawaiian-shirt-wearing followers took the oil-paint artworks of essential island drinks such as the Planter's Punch and the Daiquiri and blew them up into sprawling Technicolor productions. Beach imbued his drinks with traces of his New Orleans heritage—dashes of Herbsaint or Pernod and Angostura are common touches in his recipes—and Bergeron repeatedly riffed on the Daiquiri in forms that may have even been recognizable to Constante Ribalaigua, whose Havana bar Vic ventured to while researching plans for his restaurant empire.

Tiki's torch burned for decades, illuminating the post-War 1940s and '50s in a rum-fuelled glow—but the aesthetic was almost extinguished as its Polynesian-styled extravagance devolved into Gilligan's Island-style goofiness.

Beach and Bergeron were notoriously secretive about their recipes, hoping to frustrate the efforts of imitators (the irony was apparently lost on Bergeron). They had good reason: drinks such as the Zombie, introduced by Beach in 1934, and the Mai Tai, debuted by Bergeron a decade later, were the trend-setting Cronuts of their era. They tasted great, too—island-hopping blends of rums frequently made their way into such drinks, taking the light-on-its-feet crispness of a Cuban white rum, for example, and playing it against the mellow depths of an aged Jamaican rum, as seen in drinks such as the Test Pilot. Essential combinations were also discovered: Beach revealed grapefruit's preternatural affinity for the flavor of cinnamon and pre-mixed the combo, dubbed it "Don's Spice," and utilized it in drinks such as the Donga Punch (page 159). And true to a style of drinks that firmly belonged in the jet-setting 20th century, these improvisations took the flavors of multiple continents and added them to a single drink, with tropical flavors such as pineapple, guava, and papaya playing against an international array of spirits and liqueurs.

Tiki's torch burned for decades, illuminating the post-War 1940s and '50s and fitting right in with the freewheeling early '60s. Eventually, though, tiki's carefree abandon devolved into *Gilligan's Island*-style goofiness, and the luau lights were snuffed out. The years also weren't kind to the creations of Beach and Bergeron: lacking a recipe to replicate, imitators simply made up their own drinks and appropriated the established names, so a drinker enraptured by the depth of rum flavor in a Mai Tai or the delicate interplay of tropical flavors in a Zombie would ask for one or the other at a competing bar, and wind up with something much different—not infrequently, some half-assed riff on rum mixed with pineapple juice and grenadine, with a tiny, sad umbrella up top just to rub in the indignity. These drinks weren't only disappointing to the customer—they were so lousy that they wound up sullying the entire realm.

2070 SWIZZLE

1 oz. aged rum (Angostura 1919 recommended)
1 oz. 151-proof Demerara rum
½ oz. Demerara sugar syrup
½ oz. honey syrup
¼ oz. allspice liqueur
4 drops Pernod or absinthe
2 dashes Angostura bitters
Grating of fresh nutmeg

Glass: Collins

Garnish: mint sprig

Method: Combine ingredients in glass and fill with crushed ice; swizzle to chill (see page 26), and add more crushed ice to fill. Garnish.

Martin Cate, San Francisco

THREE DOTS AND A DASH

1½ oz. aged rhum agricole
½ oz. Demerara rum
½ oz. honey syrup
½ oz. lime juice
½ oz. orange juice
1 dash Angostura bitters
¼ oz. falernum
¼ oz. allspice liqueur
¾ cup crushed ice

Glass: Collins or tiki mug

Garnish: 3 cherries and a short pineapple stick, speared together on a cocktail skewer

Method: Combine ingredients in blender, adding ice last. Blend at high speed for 5 seconds; pour into glass or tiki mug. Garnish.

Such was the cultural crapper tiki was in, and where it likely would have remained, had it not been for Jeff Berry, a scholarly thrift-store spelunker with a taste for rum. A Southern Californian with childhood memories of visits to Polynesian-style restaurants (and of the preponderance of the tiki aesthetic in everything from Chinese restaurants to motels and trailer parks), Berry began digging into dusty cookbooks and magazines—and later, tracking down retired bartenders who'd worked alongside Beach, coaxing from them the secrets hidden in Beach's recipes. Today, traveling under the

COCKTAIL STYLE

TIKI *(continued)*

ZOMBIE (1934)

1½ oz. dark Jamaican rum
1½ oz. white rum
1 oz. 151-proof Demerara rum
½ oz. falernum
½ oz. Don's Mix
(see page 159)
¾ oz. lime juice
1 dash Angostura bitters
6 drops Pernod or absinthe
2 tsp. grenadine
¾ cup crushed ice

Glass: chimney

Garnish: mint sprig

Method: Combine ingredients in blender and add crushed ice. Blend at high speed for 5 seconds; pour into glass, adding ice cubes to fill. Garnish.

Don the Beachcomber, adapted by Jeff Berry

nom de booze Beachbum Berry, Jeff is the authoritative master of an entire realm of popular culture, and his books (starting with *Beachbum Berry's Grog Log*, co-authored with wife Annene Kaye—aka Mrs. Bum—in 1998, and continuing through his most recent, 2014's *Potions of the Caribbean*) have set the blades of thousands of Waring blenders spinning. Bartenders and drinks enthusiasts replicate now-classic concoctions that had been out of circulation sometimes for decades, such as the Test Pilot, Three Dots and a Dash—and, notably, the Zombie, the original 1934 recipe for which had long been thought lost, until Berry deciphered a notebook once owned by one of Beach's early bartenders.

The tiki torch is now carried at a growing cadre of bars that blend the craft-cocktail movement's dedication to precision and quality with the laid-back tiki air. Bars such as Smuggler's Cove in San Francisco; Lost Lake and Three Dots and a Dash in Chicago; the Shameful Tiki Room in Vancouver; El Camino in Louisville; and Hale Pele in Portland are burnishing Beach and Bergeron's legacies, and bartenders such as Brian Miller—who tended the bar at Death & Co. before swapping his vest and tie for face paint and a piratical bandanna—are leading the charge via tiki pop-ups and regular tiki nights at even the most buttoned-down of cocktail bars. Along the way, they've dusted off classics such as the Scorpion Bowl and the Sidewinder's Fang,

as well as refurbished or created tropical-style drinks of more recent provenance. The Jungle Bird—a relative newcomer, having first popped up in 1978—enjoys a certain degree of fanaticism in the craft-cocktail bar, thanks in part to New York bartender Giuseppe González's recipe tweak that amplified the rum's robustness; and Smuggler's Cove owner Martin Cate, one of the fez-crowned practitioners of the craft, demonstrated the swizzle's enduring appeal via his bespoke 2070 Swizzle (page 161). And as the crowning orchid on this comeback, Jeff Berry entered the bar game himself in late 2014, opening Beachbum Berry's Latitude 29 in his adopted hometown of New Orleans.

The tiki drink enters its ninth decade showing a little wear, to be sure. But despite its AARP-worthy age, the tiki bar is still the earthly equivalent of Neverland, a place where drinks (and the people who love them) still resolutely refuse to grow up.

JUNGLE BIRD

1½ oz. blackstrap rum
¾ oz. Campari
½ oz. lime juice
½ oz. simple syrup
1½ oz. pineapple juice

Glass: rocks or tiki mug

Garnish: pineapple wedge

Method: Shake with ice to chill; pour into tiki mug (or strain into glass filled with fresh ice). Garnish.

Adapted by Giuseppe González

THE GRADUATE

A simple sip from one of the masters of cocktail complexity.

THE GRADUATE

1 oz. sweet vermouth
¾ oz. blended Scotch whisky
½ oz. curaçao
½ oz. tonic water

Glass: rocks

Garnish: lemon twist

Method: Build first three ingredients in ice-filled glass and stir to combine. Add tonic; stir again. Garnish.

Daniel Shoemaker, Portland, Oregon

The world needs more drinks like this: simple, quaffable, and just so goddamned delicious.

Daniel Shoemaker—the owner of Teardrop Lounge in Portland, Oregon—doesn't particularly specialize in simplicity: house-blended spirits, bespoke tinctures and gastriques, and reverse-engineered, housemade amari are more his typical stock in trade. But a couple of years ago, I took perverse pleasure in asking Shoemaker for an original drink that used only items from a select (and small) list of ingredients. His response? A touch of panic, at first—nothing good comes easy, you know—and then, brilliance.

Vermouth, buttressed by blended scotch—a bold move. Tonic water? Because you need both brightness and bittering in a drink, and this delivers on both fronts. And orange liqueur, for plushness—because we're not just booze-seeking animals; we also come to cocktails seeking a little soothing.

BRAVE COMPANION

Bourbon, vanilla and chocolate add up to liquid fun.

BRAVE COMPANION

2 oz. bourbon
¾ oz. lemon juice
½ oz. crème de cacao
½ oz. vanilla syrup (see page 185)

Glass: rocks

Garnish: lemon wheel

Method: Shake with ice to chill, strain into ice-filled glass, garnish.

Erick Castro, San Diego

Vanilla and chocolate? Yeah, I was apprehensive, too, at first—but what works great with strawberry in the middle in Neopolitan ice cream, also works smashingly with bourbon and a lacing of lemon.

When coming up with the opening menu for his San Diego bar Polite Provisions in 2013, Erick Castro shook the contemporary trend toward ever-more-complicated drinks, aiming instead for simplicity. No centrifuge-clarified juices or gelatin-firmed foams were to be deployed—rather, straightforward and delicious were in. We are the richer for it.

RÉVEILLON COCKTAIL

It's how you say "Merry Christmas" in New Orleans.

Not every keen cocktail-tuned brain is positioned behind a professional bar. New Orleans native Chuck Taggart started his Gumbo Pages blog in the formative years of the Internet, cataloging his cooking and drinking and general carrying on from his current hometown of Los Angeles.

It was after reading a Gumbo Pages post at some point that I decided to take a shot at the blogosphere in 2005. While Chuck's writing ranged from political posts to kitchen projects, with frequent forays to the liquor cabinet, I turned solely in a boozy direction. But over my years of blogging, I frequently came back to Chuck's site, in search of recipes or liquid wisdom that I could try out on my own.

I'm glad I did. In 2005, Taggart put together this liquid tribute to a New Orleans Yuletide, drawing the seasonal flavors of apples and pears together with the holiday spark of allspice and the general deliciousness of a robust vermouth.

Named for the traditional Christmas Eve dinner party that's still celebrated in formerly French New Orleans, the Réveillon Cocktail is now a holiday favorite in Chuck's house (and in mine), as well as in bars such as Arnaud's French 75 in New Orleans. And the Réveillon isn't just delicious—it packs enough punch to sooth you through the annual holiday endurance test with the in-laws.

RÉVEILLON COCKTAIL

2 oz. applejack or Calvados

1/2 oz. pear brandy (use an unaged eau-de-vie)

1/2 oz. allspice liqueur

1/4 oz. Punt e Mes

1 dash aromatic bitters

Glass: cocktail

Garnish: star anise pod

Method: Stir with ice to chill; strain into chilled glass. Garnish.

Note: For the aromatic bitters, Angostura works well; The Bitter Truth or Abbott's work better.

Chuck Taggart,
Los Angeles/New Orleans

COCKTAIL ESSENTIALS

AQUAVIT

Scandinavia's savory spirit has a walk-on role in the cocktail renaissance.

TRIDENT

1 oz. aquavit
1 oz. dry sherry (manzanilla or fino work well)
1 oz. Cynar
2 dashes peach bitters

Glass: cocktail

Garnish: lemon twist

Method: Stir with ice to chill; strain into chilled glass. Garnish.

Robert Hess, Seattle

Savory flavors often get short shrift in cocktails. Aside from the Bloody Mary and such questionable bygone drinks as the Bullshot (beef boullion and vodka—yes, really), cocktails that skew savory rather than to the safer waters of sweet, sour, or bitter are rarely encountered.

Make that past tense. Aquavit—the traditional spirit of Norway, Sweden, and Denmark, that can be flavored with botanicals ranging from cumin and caraway to dill and fennel—has been making inroads in American bars (and craft distilleries) during the cocktail boom.

Not that aquavit was ever exactly scarce; Scandinavian immigrants brought a taste for the booze from back home westward as they settled in regions ranging from Wisconsin and Minnesota to the Pacific Northwest. Chicago, Seattle, and Portland, in particular, have always held somewhat fast to a taste for aquavit, a fondness now reflected in domestic brands including North Shore Distillery's Private Reserve Aquavit, House Spirits' Krogstad Festlig Aquavit, and Old Ballard Liquor Company's expanding range of regional-style aquavits, from a classic Norwegian Riktig to a southern Swedish Älskar.

Though aquavit is usually consumed straight in its home countries—the better to wash down bites of *lutfisk* and *smørrebrød*—bartenders are deploying aquavit's spicy, savory notes in drinks such as the Trident from Seattle cocktail evangelist Robert Hess, which takes the uber-Italian Negroni on a tour of Scandinavia.

SINGLE VILLAGE FIX

A 21st century combo lavishes mezcal with some 19th century-style love.

Our contemporary cocktail world is one filled with boutique bitters, carbonated and custom-bottled cocktails, and barrel-aged everything. But even as creativity in the craft-cocktail movement has gone supernova, some of the most memorable (and, arguably, most enduring) drinks from today's bartenders are among the simplest and most approachable.

San Francisco bartender Thad Vogler built a resumé filled with some of the most significant bars and restaurants in the Bay Area (Jardiniere, Slanted Door, Bourbon & Branch, and his own places: Bar Agricole in the Mission District, and Trou Normand downtown). But even as Vogler has worked at the forefront of San Francisco's cocktail culture, his approach has always skewed to the simple. Here's one of the most ridiculously delicious drinks to come out of the city's cocktail scene, from Vogler's original menu at Beretta: the Single Village Fix.

Like the classic 19th century Fixes, Vogler's drink is built using stark simplicity: booze, citrus, and a fruity syrup, in this case a traditional pineapple gomme. But while classic Fixes were based on brandy, whiskey, or gin, Vogler reached for the smoky, ethereal character of single-village mezcal to craft this bold-flavored, yet delicate descendant.

Pioneering bartenders such as Jerry Thomas and Harry Johnson never had the opportunity (or, perhaps, the interest) to play around with Mexican spirits like tequila and mezcal. But with this drink, Vogler took such classical approaches and applied them to the ruggedly rustic flavor found in good mezcal.

Smoky and earthy, with the brightness of fresh lime and the deep lusciousness of pineapple gomme, the Single Village Fix gives agave spirits their deserved moment in the classic-cocktail spotlight.

SINGLE VILLAGE FIX

1½ oz. single-village mezcal
¾ oz. lime juice
¾ oz. pineapple gomme syrup

Glass: cocktail

Method: Shake with ice to chill; strain into chilled glass.

Thad Vogler, San Francisco

GIN BASIL SMASH

A simple drink from Germany hits the global big time.

GIN BASIL SMASH

2 oz. gin
3/4 oz. lemon juice
3/4 oz. simple syrup
3-4 sprigs fresh basil

Glass: rocks

Garnish: basil leaf

Method: Muddle basil in shaker; add remaining ingredients. Shake with ice to chill; strain into ice-filled glass. Garnish.

Jörg Meyer, Hamburg

The renewed taste for good cocktails is not strictly an Anglo-American phenomenon. While New York, San Francisco, and London positioned themselves early as capital cities of the cocktail renaissance, good drinks quickly found a home in Germany. Bartenders such as Mike Meinke, in Berlin, quickly honed their cocktail-crafting talents, and Munich bartenders Stephan Berg and Alexander Hauck helped put the global mixology machine in motion via their Bitter Truth line of superlative bitters and liqueurs.

In Hamburg, Jörg Meyer opened a bar and helped spark a larger cocktail revolution across the continent. Le Lion, Meyer's impeccably elegant watering hole, quickly rose to the highest echelons in the bar world after its 2007 debut. Le Lion's success is due not only to Herr Meyer's high standards of service, but also to one of the more unlikely—and endearing—drinks to come out of the early 21st century.

The Gin Basil Smash has a Julep-like straightforwardness that belies the airy complexity of its bright, refreshing flavor. Fresh basil by the handful is incorporated into the drink, lending a summery herbaceousness to what's otherwise a basic Gin Sour. But from such modest approaches magnificence takes root, and the Gin Basil Smash became not only Germany's signature contribution to the early years of the cocktail renaissance, but an ocean-crossing export that's equally at home in craft-cocktail bars in California, Colorado, and Texas.

Le Lion is now a long-in-the-tooth veteran in an increasingly crowded bar world, and the Gin Basil Smash is fully at home in the ranks of drinks likely to pop up as recognized classics when the next cocktail renaissance rolls around.

LOUIE LOUIE

A prime city in the cocktail's resurgence continues to lead the way.

There are cocktail ingredients that have natural affinities for one another, and then there are those that have soul mates. Rum and lime, and rye whiskey and sweet vermouth, obviously fit this latter category—another match, and an unlikely couple, is the bitter love Campari has for the sultry flavor of pineapple, as evinced in this cocktail from an early menu at Trick Dog in San Francisco.

Campari is an Italian aperitivo, as Old World in its resolute bitterness as any amaro in the clan. And pineapple? The sweet, tropical fruit so at home in Caribbean punches? Always open to new experiences, pineapple has many loves—I've mentioned its *amor* for Chartreuse (page 126), its madness for mezcal (page 167), and its overall agreeable nature (page 89), but Campari? Campari is the bitter brightness to pineapple's relaxed lushness, and the combo is as surprising as it is engaging every time it's encountered.

LOUIE LOUIE

1 oz. bourbon
1 oz. Campari
1 oz. pineapple juice
1 tsp. lime juice
1 tsp. rich simple syrup
Five drops saline solution (see below)

Glass: cocktail

Method: Shake with ice to chill; strain into chilled glass.

Saline Solution: Mix 1 tsp. sea salt with 10 tsp. water; stir to dissolve.

Morgan Schick, San Francisco

CUMBERLAND SOUR

Canada's bartenders go heavy in the cocktail game.

North America's devoted cocktail adherents pinball between New York, San Francisco, Chicago, New Orleans, and a road atlas's worth of cities in search of bibulous bliss. But those who fail to venture north of the border have, well . . . failed.

Canada's cocktail culture may have been slower to develop than that of their southern neighbor, but bartenders in the land of toques and poutine are making up for lost time. British Columbia, in particular, has nurtured an appetite for cocktails, and bartenders such as Shawn Soole and Nate Caudle in Victoria, and Shaun Layton, Lauren Mote, and Danielle Tatarin in Vancouver, are making the Manhattan feel right at home in maple leaf territory.

This one's from Jonathan Smolensky at Hawksworth in the Hotel Georgia, a brilliant bar, restaurant, and hotel in Vancouver's city center. A classic Whiskey Sour is fleshed out with the shadowy bitterness of nocino and sweetened with—what else—maple syrup.

CUMBERLAND SOUR

1¾ oz. bourbon
¾ oz. lemon juice
½ oz nocino
1 tsp. maple syrup
1 egg white
2 dashes aromatic bitters

Glass: rocks

Garnish: aromatic bitters

Method: Dry-shake all ingredients until foamy, then shake again with ice to chill. Strain into glass containing a single large cube of ice; garnish with dashes of bitters.

Jonathan Smolensky, Vancouver

CHAPTER 5

BOTTLES, TOOLS & TIPS

Making cocktails at home isn't much different from cooking: you need a few basic tools and ingredients to get started, along with a general idea of how to use them.

There's no need to dive into the deep end right from the start. Pick a recipe or two from the preceding pages—perhaps a couple that share a common ingredient—and start stocking your bar from there. Or, if you've already got a head start on acquiring the liquor, bar tools, and other accessories needed to start mixing, this chapter also provides info on a few ingredients that may be worth making yourself, or spending the time and effort to track down.

Save yourself some aggravation by investing in decent liquor, mixers, and tools (I've specified brands where suitable). The initial outlay may be more expensive, but the results will be much more satisfying, and the experience more enjoyable. After all, cocktails are supposed to be fun.

ICE

What heat is to cooking, ice is to drinking: the instrument through which the fair-to-middling is transformed into the sublime. A mini-industry has sprung up around bars and restaurants and their designated ice programs, but for the average at-home mixer, it's doubtful you'll need the industrial ice truck to come around very frequently.

You can prepare a perfectly serviceable cocktail using the product from the built-in ice machine on your refrigerator. But there are a few things you can do to up your cocktail-ice game without investing in a massive upgrade of your freezer.

Ice puts the rattle in the shaker and the clink in the glass—along with enough cooling power to bring a cocktail to life, and a dab of dilution to soften a drink's sharp edges.

Fresh ice is essential—using the stuff that's been roosting at the back of your freezer for a month along with the pack of Trader Joe's fish sticks will have reliably unpleasant results; make it a habit to keep ice no longer than five days. And this may seem obvious, but keep your ice cold, so the surface is dry to the touch—warmer, wetter ice can result in watery drinks.

Silicone or food-grade rubber ice-cube trays come in various sizes for cocktail use. You can replicate your favorite bar's Kold-Draft ice (without the frequent and expensive maintenance calls) by using trays that make 1¼-inch cubes. There are also trays that enable you to add a 2-inch cube to your Old Fashioned, or a 2-inch globe to your bourbon. Kitchen stores such as Sur la Table have a range of options for trays and ice molds, and Cocktail Kingdom has ice tools to suit all home needs.

Ice-crushing equipment is covered in the Gear section (page 173), and should you choose to go full-geek with your home ice program—dedicating your refrigerator's freezer to the preparation of large blocks of crystal-clear ice that you can then saw, chip or pick to your heart's content—check out drinks writer Camper English's frozen shenanigans at Alcademics.com.

COCKTAIL GEAR

As with every job from neurosurgery to unclogging a toilet, things tend to turn out better when you're using the right tools. There are easy work-arounds for mixing drinks, but if you're holding this book, you're probably looking for something a little more serious. There was a time when assembling a decent cocktail kit required some focused shopping; online retailer (and producer/importer) Cocktail Kingdom (CocktailKingdom.com)—run by certified cocktail nerds Greg Boehm and Don Lee—made that a thing of the past, and its website can be a one-stop shop for quality barware. Other excellent retailers include Boston-based The Boston Shaker (TheBostonShaker.com), Cask in San Francisco (CaskStore.com), the Bar Shoppe in Seattle (TheBarShoppe.com), and Bar Keeper in Los Angeles (BarKeeperSilverlake.com).

Cocktail Shaker

The basic three-piece cobbler shaker probably looks familiar—a metal (sometimes glass) canister fitted with a rounded, perforated top for straining, and a cap to fit over the strainer part. These shakers are ubiquitous and relatively easy to use, but they have their downsides—cheaper versions sometimes leak, the strainer is rarely suited to the task, and the little cap tends to get stuck (or lost). Should you opt for this style, spend a few extra bucks for a quality model—those from Usagi are preferred among Japanese bartenders, and are durably built for frequent use; they're available from Cocktail Kingdom.

Another option is the two-piece Parisian shaker, which resembles a cobbler shaker except the top is a solid piece; these are preferred by many European bartenders. Basic stainless-steel models can be found at retailers such as Amazon and BarProducts.com, or you can go with a sleeker model from Cocktail Kingdom.

If cocktails are your thing, you'll want to try out a Boston shaker—the style commonly seen in American restaurants and bars, with a 16-oz. tempered-glass base fitting into a slightly larger metal tin—or a set of paired shaking tins. You can pick up a two-piece Boston-shaker set from most kitchen stores or from retailers such as Amazon—the German-made WMF Loft is a nice package—or you can head for your local restaurant-supply store or an online outlet like BarProducts.com for a more affordable generic-style set. Shaker tins are similarly available at BarProducts.com, though the Koriko weighted tins from Cocktail Kingdom are professional grade and still reasonably priced.

Mixing Glass

You'll need this for stirred drinks. A basic 16-oz. tempered-glass pint glass, available everywhere, is perfectly adequate for your needs; if you're looking for more than adequate, consider a Yarai mixing glass, much en vogue among craft-cocktail bartenders, or one of its (usually) Japanese-made kin. They're more expensive than a pint glass, but they look awesome and have more of a professional feel; available at Cocktail Kingdom.

Bar Spoon

In a pinch, a chopstick will accomplish many of the tasks asked of a bar spoon, but this tool is essential for regular cocktail sessions. Bar spoons are useful not just for stirring drinks, but as a basic measure (the bowls of most hold around 5ml, or 1 tsp., though it's worth double-checking your model just to make sure). The basic twisted-stem spoons with a red-plastic cap are ubiquitous, and crappy; you'll get a better feel and balance from a piece of equipment designed for professional use. My favorite is the German-made Rösle long bar spoon, which has a smooth stem and a natural balance (available from Amazon and other online and specialty retailers), but most bartenders aim for twisted-stem models such as the Hoffman or Teardrop models from Cocktail Kingdom.

Strainers

A Hawthorne strainer resembles a small, perforated paddle with a spring around the edges, and may have a handle; the cheap models at many restaurant and kitchen stores are shoddy and should be avoided. A basic model that's reliably good is from OXO, available at kitchen-supply stores such as Sur la Table and via online retailers like Amazon; the British-made Bonzer strainers also work well, and are available from Amazon. Cocktail Kingdom also sexies up the strainers, with options ranging from utilitarian stainless steel to elegant vintage-style and gold-plated models, and the Koriko strainer was designed by Don Lee to take the 19th century-style Hawthorne into the 21st.

Be careful when purchasing julep strainers—cheaper models may not fit mixing glasses properly. The julep strainer from Australia-based Uber Bar Tools is attractive and sturdy (though its rounded-triangle shape takes some getting used to) and available via Amazon, and Cocktail Kingdom features several reliably good strainers.

A conical fine-mesh strainer also comes in handy for double-straining drinks, and for making syrups and other ingredients. Your local kitchen store or favorite online retailer should be able to hook you up.

Knife & Cutting Board

A good knife is essential for cutting citrus and garnish. Your basic paring knife will do, but it's a better bet to have a dedicated knife for bar purposes. I like the Zyliss stainless-steel utility knife, which has a cover for when you need to transport your bar kit to a party, but my new favorite is from Boston bartender Jackson Cannon, who worked with R. Murphy Knives on a style of knife best-suited for bar needs; it's available from RMurphyKnives.com, and from retailers such as The Boston Shaker (TheBostonShaker.com).

A small, dedicated cutting board is also an essential item for cutting citrus and garnish—you don't want your Ramos Fizz tasting like the onions you chopped for last night's dinner. Sold everywhere.

Citrus Juicer

You can always just give your lemon or lime a fierce squeeze when mixing your evening Daiquiri, but that's inefficient (not to mention slow and messy). There are all kinds of citrus-juicing tools about; unless you're running a restaurant or bar (or really, really like fresh juice), investing in an electric model doesn't make sense. Instead, opt for the simple lever-style handheld juicers found in kitchen stores (the gear-operated Chef'n FreshForce boosts the power of such juicers, and is available from Amazon), or—if your budget and kitchen space allow—try a countertop model (such as those from Vollrath) that uses a hand lever to quickly express a cocktail party's worth of juice.

Measures

Jiggers and their calculating kin are vital for mixing drinks well. Jiggers typically come with a measured cone at each end—1 oz. and 1½ oz. is pretty common—though there's some variation, so be sure to check. Much less attractive though way more useful are the angled measuring jiggers from OXO, available in stainless steel or plastic; these provide more finely tuned modes of measurement, from 5ml (1 tsp.) up to 2 oz., and the tools are both cheap and sold everywhere. Or, split the middle by going for one of the "banded" Leopold jiggers designed and sold by Cocktail Kingdom; structured with the aesthetic appeal of a vintage-style jigger, it still offers handy measurement guides, though not as detailed as the useful (if ugly) OXO model.

Muddler

A wooden kitchen spoon or the end of a rolling pin will suffice for many muddling needs, but a dedicated muddler isn't out of place in a well-stocked home bar. Wood works best, and avoid models that are varnished or that don't feature food-safe finishes; a basic muddler from Sur La Table or Cocktail Kingdom work well, though Chris Gallagher's hardwood PUG Muddlers are not only formidable, but they have a great feel; available from The Boston Shaker or WNJones.com/Pug.

Peeler

Sawing off chunks of orange peel with a kitchen knife isn't advisable after your second Negroni; instead, opt for a standard Y-shaped vegetable peeler, which performs the same job faster and with less risk. You can buy an expensive model (or just use whatever's lying around your kitchen), but my hands-down favorite is the bargain-basement Kuhn Rikon peeler from Switzerland—it's sold everywhere, costs about $4, shaves peel at the perfect thinness for a cocktail, and when it breaks or goes dull, is cheap and easy to replace.

Ice-Crushing Equipment

You can't make a Mint Julep without breaking a few cubes. The most low-tech way to go is to purchase a Lewis bag (basically a thick canvas sack) from Amazon, Sur la Table, or pretty much any kitchen store, fill it with cubes from the freezer, and then whack the hell out of it with a rolling pin (or, if your cocktail needs the full Thor experience, you can purchase a dedicated Schmallet Wood Mallet from Cocktail Kingdom). An ice crusher performs the same trick with slightly less noise and drama (and can produce the satisfying pebble-size ice needed for Cobblers); I use the hand-cranked Metrokane model, though like Dylan at Newport, you can go electric if you don't mind the ridicule from the old-schoolers. Or, to make a bunch of crushed ice for a party, just toss a few trayfuls of cubes into a Cuisinart food processor and pulse until your ears ring.

Microplane Fine Grater

You'll need a microplane for grating nutmeg atop drinks or for shaving citrus zest for homemade syrups and cordials. Check your local kitchen store, or there's always Amazon.

LIQUOR CABINET

With the growing interest in cocktails and the rise of craft distillers, the liquor selection has exploded in recent years. The suggestions provided here should be taken with a grain of salt; recommendations are based on my taste and personal experience, and as the saying goes, your mileage may vary. For better utility to the reader (as well as my own sanity), I'm prioritizing widely available selections over regional craft spirits—but this is merely a starting point. Try the brands that are available to you in restaurants and bars, and let your taste and your interest lead the way.

Absinthe

Absinthe's return was accompanied by brands both exceptional and execrable; much of the chaff has since fallen away, but it's still worth being wary. Ted Breaux's Jade line of absinthes (including Edouard, Nouveaux Orleans and Verte Suisse, among others) is still a gold standard; Emile Pernot Vieux Pontarlier is a very good brand with wide distribution, and domestic brands including Absinthe Marteau and Pacifique are reliably excellent. Pernod's eponymous absinthe is widely available, and servicable for cocktail use.

American Whiskey

You can get by with a single, favorite brand of bourbon for most cocktail needs, but I like to keep a few options around. Buffalo Trace is a good choice as a utilitarian, cocktail-ready bourbon, and for sours and other drinks where you still want some bourbon presence but don't want to break the bank, aim for steals such as Evan Williams (the single barrel is one of the best deals in bourbon), Four Roses Yellow Label or the 100-proof Old Grand Dad. Wheated bourbons such as W.L. Weller, Larceny, and Maker's Mark are my picks for bourbon-forward drinks such as Old Fashioneds and Mint Juleps, that invite you to recline in the whiskey's soft embrace.

Much rye whiskey currently on the shelf comes from a single distillery in Indiana, sold in bulk and bottled under a variety of labels, including Templeton Rye, Bulleit Rye, and others. It has a mashbill that's 95 percent rye, and the whiskey's not bad—try it out, and use it if you like. I prefer rye whiskeys that have more of a grain mixture in the mash, and find they suit my taste better in cocktails. The 100-proof Rittenhouse is still the rock star of rye whiskey, and Sazerac rye and the 101-proof Wild Turkey rye are also great picks. Knob Creek's rye is very good, and is essentially a higher-proof interpretation of the Jim Beam Distillery's venerable Old Overholt rye, which is also a solid go-to whiskey.

Apple Brandy & Calvados

Despite their mutual base of apples, Calvados and applejack (or American apple brandy) aren't fully interchangeable. Laird's still makes the widest-distributed applejack in the country, though the product sold under that name is tamer in flavor than it once was; the go-to spirit now for applejack drinks is Laird's Bonded Apple Brandy, a 100-proof spirit that's made entirely from apples and offers lotsa fun. Clear Creek Distillery in Oregon makes a good young apple brandy well-suited for cocktails, and Huber's Starlight Distillery in Indiana also makes a pleasant applejack; with the recent rise in craft distillers, these ranks are sure to swell. Calvados may require a bit of independent research (the fun, drinking kind)—my preferred brand for cocktails is Chateau du Breuil Fine Calvados; it's reasonably priced, vivacious in spirit, and doesn't mind mixing it up in the cocktail glass, and the spirits from Busnel, Christian Drouin, or Boulard are dependably good.

Aquavit

There's not a huge selection in the U.S. of this signature Scandinavian spirit; Aalborg and Linie are solid choices, or go domestic with Krogstad Festlig Aquavit from Oregon.

Bitters

There are literally dozens of styles of bitters now available, with new launches all the time. Many of the new styles are nice, but in terms of necessity, here's where to get started:

- Angostura bitters are essential, period.
- Orange bitters have many available brands; I like Angostura's orange bitters for all-around utility, though the cardamom spiciness of Regan's Orange Bitters No. 6 and the brightness of Fee Brothers Orange Bitters also have their appeal.
- Peychaud's bitters are a distinctly pink style of bitters with a light fragrance of anise, and are called for in many New Orleans cocktails, as well as in drinks that better benefit from a gentle nudge than a sharp poke.
- Other styles of aromatic bitters are also very useful, and are interchangeable with Angostura in most recipes. The Bitter Truth Aromatic Bitters are excellent, and the aromatic pimento (that is, allspice) bitters from Dale DeGroff are absolutely divine.
- Boker's Bitters is a defunct brand of cardamom-rich aromatic bitters from the 1800s; Scottish bartender Adam Elmegirab's Boker's Bitters is an excellent reproduction that's well worth having around. Another long-defunct proprietary brand from the cocktail's Golden Age is Abbott's Bitters; the reproduction from Tempus Fugit is wonderful, and a great substitute for Angostura in many drinks.
- Grapefruit bitters have occasional use (a dash in a Martini or Gin & Tonic is not out of place); Bittermens is where you need to go.
- Celery bitters have a natural affinity for gin and an on-again, off-again thing for tequila; The Bitter Truth's version is excellent.
- Peach bitters have limited but tasty use; Fee Brothers makes a decent version, and The Bitter Truth's peach bitters are awesome.
- Chocolate, or molé bitters, go great with tequila- or rum-based cocktails; Bittermens Xocolatl Molé Bitters largely set the standard, and should cover all your needs.

Brandy

Don't blow the budget on buying brandies for cocktails—but at the same time, don't skimp and wind up with distilled plonk. VSOP grade or better is desirable from the large Cognac brands; among the big Cognac houses, I have a weakness for Martell VSOP. But the smaller houses seem better suited for cocktail use; the exuberantly fruit-forward Pierre Ferrand Ambre and Pierre Ferrand 1840 make excellent bases for cocktails, as does the 106-proof Louis Royer Force 53, and the VSOPs from Hine and Hardy always pull at my cocktail shaker's heartstrings. Armagnac shouldn't be overlooked as a cocktail brandy—in some cases, its dry ruggedness is better-suited to the cocktail task than Cognac. Marie Duffau Napoleon Bas Armagnac is a good starting point, but the category selection is still shallow in the U.S.; keep an eye on it.

Unaged fruit brandies may have limited utility in cocktails, but having a couple of good products on hand can add some razzle-dazzle to your drinks. Consider grabbing bottles of Poire William (or Williams pear) brandy, and a kirschwasser for certain drinks. Trimbach and Purkhart are estimable European brands, and among American producers, Oregon's Clear Creek Distillery and California's St. George Spirits have got you covered. Aged peach brandy was as scarce as unicorn tears only a few years ago; Peach Street Distillers in Colorado is among the craft distillers who've helped change that—tasty stuff.

Cachaça

Novo Fogo is reliably excellent, and is available in an aged as well as a white version, and brands such as Leblon, Avuá, and Sagatiba should suit your needs.

Champagne

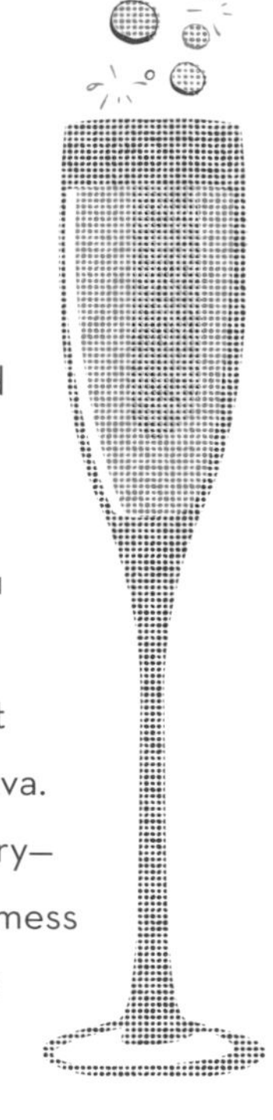

Rule No. 1: Don't blow the mortgage. Rule No. 2: Don't drink crap. There's plenty of decent stuff to be had for cocktails; if the "C" word scares you, seek out the advice of your local wine shop, or opt for Cremant du Bourgogne (which is merely Champagne from a different ZIP code), or a good, dry Cava. And always go for brut, or dry—honestly, you don't want to mess with anything sweeter when cocktails are involved.

Genever

Bols is the category's building-block genever; Diep 9, from Belgium, is also worth its fair turn in the shaker.

Gin

You can mix most of the gin drinks in this book with a single brand of gin, but that doesn't mean you should—the gin world is wide enough to warrant exploration. A basic London dry-style gin is essential; Tanqueray and Beefeater are the mainstays here, and are useful in a wide range of drinks; lesser-known (though damn desirable) selections include Sipsmith and No. 3 Gin. The earthiness of Plymouth Gin is particularly welcome in spirit-forward gin drinks such as the Martini and its ilk; in addition to the eponymous brand, try Ford's Gin—technically not a Plymouth-style gin, but close enough for cocktail work. Old Tom gin is still a relative rarity; Hayman's Old Tom is spectacular, and Ransom Old Tom, from Oregon, is an intriguing aged gin. You could spend years trying the different Contemporary gins, especially with the explosion of those from craft distillers; ones I like, and that have some utility, include the superlative Botanivore and Terroir gins from California-based St. George Spirits; Junipero, from San Francisco's Anchor Distilling; The Botanist Gin, from Scotland; and Blue Gin, from Austria.

Irish Whiskey

Ubiquitous brands like Jameson and Bushmills are fine for most cocktail purposes, and Powers brings a certain charm. For something with more staying power, consider upgrading to Green Spot or Red Breast, and keep on eye on newcomer brands such as Teeling's.

Liqueurs

The basic rule for all spirits goes doubly for liqueurs: beware the bottom shelf. Fortunately, the selection of superlative liqueurs has blossomed in recent years, so it no longer takes an international plane ticket to stock the liquor cabinet.

- **Apricot liqueur** long suffered under the "apricot brandy" label, but the brands worth seeking out dispense with the confusing moniker. Rothman & Winter season their liqueur with actual apricot brandy (the unaged eau de vie), and it has a fresh, natural flavor unburdened by excessive sweetness. Giffard's Abricot du Roussillon flits closer to the flavor of apricot jam, which brings a certain lusciousness to a drink.

- **Bitter liqueurs** are a wide category worth diving into. Amer Picon is mostly absent from U.S. bars (except for suitcase imports by folks who pack bottles home from France); Bigallet China-China Amer is a preferred substitute, as is Bittermens Amer Nouvelle. You should also lay in a stock of bitter liqueurs including Fernet-Branca, Aperol, Campari, and Averna, and Cynar and Amaro Montenegro are dandy things to break out on occasion.
- **Cherry liqueur** is largely defined by Peter Heering Cherry Liqueur (aka Cherry Heering), from Denmark, and it's the style called for in the recipes in this book, though Rothman & Winter's cherry liqueur is nothing to sneeze at.
- **Coffee liqueur** is a good category to search among the craft distillers, many of whom work with local roasters. Firelit Spirits Coffee Liqueur is made by St. George Spirits using beans from Bay Area roasters, and House Spirits in Portland, Oregon features Stumptown beans in a rum base.
- **Crème de cacao** comes in two versions: white and dark, and yes, there's more of a difference than simply the color. Giffard's white cacao is a good bet, and for dark, Tempus Fugit is excellent.
- **Crème de mure** is a French blackberry liqueur not often used in the States; Briottet is a very good brand, as is Giffard. Clear Creek Distillery's blackberry liqueur is also quite nice.
- **Curaçao** is among the most venerable (and versatile) of liqueurs; Pierre Ferrand makes the best option beyond compare.
- **Elderflower liqueur** was long the province of a single brand, St. Germain.

There are now others on the shelf—many good, but they vary in flavor and intensity. St. Germain was the brand in hand when the cocktails in this book were developed, so if in doubt, go with the obvious choice.

- **Maraschino liqueur** tastes nothing like the candy-red cherries; Luxardo is the preferred brand, though Maraska ain't half bad.
- **Nocino** is an Italian-style liqueur with the bitter flavor of green walnuts; Nux Alpina, from Austria, is a good choice.
- **Pear liqueur** can be ethereally delicious; I like the Austrian-made Pür Likor Williams Pear, and the pear liqueurs from Clear Creek Distillery and Rothman & Winter are also very good. And the Spiced Pear Liqueur from St. George Spirits is amazing stuff.
- **Sloe Gin** was long ruled by bottom-shelf brands; thanks to makers including Plymouth, Hayman's, and Bitter Truth, the spirit's reputation has been restored.
- **Triple Sec** is drier and crisper than curaçao, and essential to Sidecars and classic Margaritas. Cointreau is still the heavy hitter here, though Combier's orange liqueur and Giffard's Triple Sec are also very good.

Mezcal

The mezcal selection has metastasized in recent years, and the category shows no sign of shrinking anytime soon. Ron Cooper's Del Maguey line helped define today's mezcal world, and Mezcal Vida remains useful as a flavorful (and approachably priced) cocktail mezcal. A few bucks more gets you a bottle of Chichicapa or Tobala, and it's worth playing the field a little—the mezcals from El Jolgorio, Vago, Pierde Almas and Fidencio are all solid.

Pisco

Ten years ago, the selection of pisco available in the U.S. was somewhat depressing; today, all that's changed. For cocktail use, consider starting with a good acholado, or blend of Peruvian piscos; Campo de Encanto is a solid bet designed for cocktails, and acholados from Barsol and Macchu Pisco are excellent choices as well. Pisco Porton is also a good brand for basic cocktail use.

Rum

Unlike gin or bourbon, where a bottle or two can cover most of your needs, rum requires a little stockpiling—but fortunately, it's still a relative bargain in the booze world. White rum is a basic building block for most Daiquiri-style drinks; Bacardi Superior and Havana Club (still absent from the U.S. due to the decades-long Cuban embargo) long defined the category, but recently, white rums with a bit more of a flavorful backbone have come into play—Plantation 3 Stars, Caña Brava and Banks 5 Island are all great options, and the white rums from Flor de Caña and El Dorado are good workhorse spirits. The rum category expands a bit more when you get into aged rums; Bacardi 8 is a good all-around aged Cuban-style rum, Appleton Estate Signature Blend has utility as an aged Jamaican rum, and the Barbados rums from Plantation and Cockspur serve a number of needs. And then there are the bolder, more specialty-oriented rums; a hard-punching bunch of Jamaican funk is sometimes needed in cocktails, and is best provided by brands including Smith & Cross and Hamilton's Jamaican Pot Still Black Rum, as well as the overproof bucket-of-knuckles known as Wray & Nephew. Scarlet Ibis is a dry, slightly higher-proof rum that's excellent in cocktails; the rich, chocolatey rums from the Spanish Main such as Ron Zacapa occasionally enter the picture; and the Trinidadian rums from Plantation are good cross-category mixers. Cane-based rums and rhum agricole are a whole different story; the Haitian rum from Barbancourt can be a good introduction to the category—the 8-year-old 5-star is scrumptious, and affordable. Once you're ready to dive in, aim for the rhum blancs from Martinique—Neisson, La Favorite, and Rhum J.M. are all great—and for aged rhum agricole, the *eleve sous bois* from Neisson is a sure winner, as is Rhum Clement's Canne Bleu.

Scotch Whisky

A basic blended Scotch will take care of 90 percent of your cocktail needs; Famous Grouse is a dependable go-to, or for a few bucks more, shell out for Compass Box's Asyla. Smoky Islay malts come into play from time to time; go with your favorite, or grab some Laphroaig or Ardbeg—they'll conquer pretty much any challenge you throw their way.

Sherry

Don't use the styles interchangeably—there are different kinds for a reason. Regardless of if you need a dry-as-bone fino, a nutty amontillado, a ponderous oloroso, or a gently sweet Pedro Ximenez, Lustau and Hidalgo are prominent brands of all, with reliably decent results.

Tequila

Tequila is tricky; the category is booming with new brands, but many come from the same handful of distilleries, and are produced using methods more akin to factory farming than to artisanal craftsmanship. That said, there's a good selection of excellent brands (and of course, these are all pure-agave tequilas), such as the spirits from Siete Leguas, Tequila Ocho, Tapatio, Don Julio, Fortaleza, Siembra Azul, Tequila Cabeza, and Olmeca Altos.

Vermouth

The major brands—Martini & Rossi and Cinzano for the sweet Italian *rosso* style, and Noilly Prat for the French dry style—have a reason they've been around for centuries: they're all good, and work well in cocktails. Those looking to upgrade a bit can shift to Dolin dry and Cocchi Vermouth di Torino rosso with excellent results, and Dolin's blanc is hands-down the best of the style. Carpano Antica Formula has an indulgent richness that became a favorite during the cocktail renaissance; it's a bit heavy for all-around use, but works excellently in many Manhattan variations and vermouth-forward drinks, and Punt e Mes—an extra-bitter vermouth—is a delicious requisite for some cocktails. New World vermouth producers are still coming into their own; Imbue Petal & Thorn, Sutton Cellars' California vermouth and the creative interpretations from New York's Atsby and Brooklyn's Uncouth Vermouth are good places to start.

Vodka

I'm admittedly not much of a vodka aficionado, and the category is anything but small. For all-around cocktail use, clean-and-crisp vodkas from the big brands—Absolut, Russian Standard, etc.—as well as smaller boutique brands including Square One, Aylesbury Duck and Hangar One are safe bets. If actually digging into vodka is your aim, some good places to start include the potato vodkas from Karlsson's.

COCKTAIL KITCHEN

In addition to buying the booze, there are other provisions you should stock or prepare in order to be fully cocktail-ready.

Citrus

All fruit isn't created equal. When shopping for citrus for your cocktails, aim for organic, unwaxed fruit, as the peel often becomes an active participant in the process. Lemons are pretty straightforward; early incarnations of the Daiquiri were intended for use with smaller, sweeter key limes rather than today's more-prevalent Mexican limes, so that's worth a diversion when key limes are in season. Yellow grapefruit has more of a bitter, sour flavor than the familiar ruby red—and it's that edgier flavor you're looking for when mixing grapefruit into a cocktail, so opt for yellow grapefruit if you can. Navel oranges have a bright, colorful peel that's good for garnishing, but the juice is bland and insipid; use Valencia or Cara Cara oranges for juice, or blood oranges when they're in season. Store citrus fruit at room temperature and wash before use.

Sugar

In almost all cases, you're better off using simple syrup (below), but some recipes beg for the straight stuff. For both syrup-making and general mixing, you can go with normal granulated, but a better option is superfine (also sold as baker's sugar). This is not the same thing as powdered confectioner's sugar—that stuff has cornstarch in it, which will make your cocktails lumpy and gross—but a more finely ground sugar, which dissolves easier in liquid. You'll also want to lay in a stock of Demerara sugar, for making rich simple syrup (also below), as well as some sugar cubes (basic white or Demerara—your call), for Old Fashioneds and the like.

Syrups

Simple Syrup: This is nothing more than sugar dissolved in water, for ease of mixing into drinks. Any recipe in this book calling for "simple syrup" intends a 1:1 ratio of sugar to water. You can mix over heat, as with rich simple syrup below, but at this concentration, superfine sugar (and even regular granulated) easily gives itself up to the water. Simply measure 8 oz. sugar (or 16 oz., or whatever) with the same amount of water in a covered container, and shake until the sugar dissolves. Take a hint from pastry chefs: weigh your ingredients on a digital kitchen scale before mixing, rather than relying on measuring cups or other volume measures—this provides a more reliable standard of measurement. Simple syrup keeps in the fridge for several weeks (to lengthen the lifespan, follow the stovetop method for rich simple syrup), and don't limit your use to cocktails—it's also great for sweetening coffee, tea, lemonade, bitter attitudes, and the like.

Rich Simple Syrup: Some cocktails require a more intense sugar nudge without the added dilution from water; that's when you aim for a 2:1 sugar-to-water ratio. This is best prepared using heat, to ensure the sugar dissolves: Weigh 16 oz. of sugar and combine in a saucepan with 8 oz. of water, and whisk over medium heat until the sugar has completely dissolved. Demerara sugar makes a rich, toffeelike syrup using this method, and rich Demerara syrup is called for in several recipes in this book.

Cinnamon Syrup: Tiki drinks and punches can benefit from a little spice. You can purchase cinnamon syrups—the one from B.G. Reynolds (BGReynolds.com) is quite good—or make your own. To prepare, mix a rich simple syrup (as above), and once the sugar has dissolved, add several coarsely crushed sticks of cinnamon (three cinnamon sticks for 8 oz. water and 16 oz. sugar should work fine). Let simmer for five minutes, then cover and remove from heat. Let cool to room temperature, and strain before use.

Vanilla Syrup: B.G. Reynolds also makes a nice vanilla syrup, or make your own in the same manner of cinnamon syrup, above, substituting 2 split vanilla pods for the cinnamon sticks.

Gomme Syrup: Gomme (or "gum") syrup is a traditional 19th century-style bar ingredient. Gomme is nothing more than rich simple syrup that has gum arabic (also called acacia gum) added as an emulsifier. Gum arabic not only gives the syrup a much heavier viscosity; it lends a rich, silky lusciousness to cocktails made with it. San Francisco-based Small Hand Foods (SmallHandFoods.com) makes a gomme syrup (both the plain and the fruit syrups eschew the French spelling, and are sold as Gum Syrup), or you can mix your own using Portland bartender Jeffrey Morgenthaler's easy-peasy method: You'll need some food-grade gum arabic (available at natural-food stores or at FrontierCoop.com) and either Demerara or superfine sugar. Combine 2 oz. gum arabic with 2 oz. water in a small container, and stir to combine; cover and let sit until the powder has completely dissolved, about 48 hours. Mix 12 oz. sugar with 6 oz. water in a saucepan over medium heat, and whisk to dissolve the sugar. Add the gum arabic mixture and stir to combine, then remove from heat and let cool. Bottle for use, and keep refrigerated.

Fruit Syrups: Small Hand Foods has you covered for authentic, naturally flavored pineapple and raspberry gum syrups, or it's a snap to make your own using either rich simple syrup or gomme syrup. Take a pint of fresh, washed raspberries (or you can use frozen—I won't tell) and place in a bowl, then cover with 12 oz. of rich simple syrup or gomme syrup. Crush the fruit with a wooden spoon or potato masher and cover; let the berries macerate overnight, or up to 24 hours. Strain through a fine-mesh strainer, pressing the fruit to extract as much liquid as possible. Keep refrigerated and use within one week. Follow the same process for pineapple syrup, except use one trimmed, peeled pineapple that's been cut into wedges and 12 oz. of gomme or rich simple syrup.

Honey Syrup: Honey adds a great flavor to some cocktails, but it's too viscous to mix without some modification. To make honey syrup, mix 8 oz. hot water with 8 oz. honey, and whisk until fully combined; keep refrigerated.

Agave Syrup: Follow the directions for Honey Syrup, using agave nectar in lieu of bee juice.

Sugarcane Syrup: 'Ti Punches and some swizzles can be made with basic simple or gomme syrup, but for the full character, grab some sugarcane syrup such as Petite Canne; available at Amazon, and elsewhere.

Falernum

This Caribbean-born sweetener plays a role in many (mostly rum-based) cocktails. Velvet Falernum is a widely available brand, and B.G. Reynolds makes a good version, as well, though it's also easy and relatively cheap to make your own. Use 6 oz. overproof rum (Wray & Nephew preferred); the zest of nine limes; 40 whole cloves; 1½ oz. peeled, chopped fresh ginger; 1 oz. blanched, slivered almonds; 14 oz. rich simple syrup; and 4

½ oz. fresh lime juice. Dry-toast the almonds in a hot pan until golden, then soak them in the rum along with the spices and lime zest for 24 hours. Strain through cheesecloth, pressing to extract the liquid. Add the syrup and lime juice, and bottle for use; store in the refrigerator.

Grenadine

This ruby, pomegranate-based syrup has gone to hell and back in the past half-century. Avoid any brands that don't start with pomegranate juice and sugar, or that have ingredients that seem alien (dabs of other fruits or flavorings may be fine, but once HFCS or Red #5 come into play, it's time to keep looking); Small Hand Foods has you covered once again, B.G. Reynolds makes a tart hibiscus-hued grenadine, and Jack Rudy Cocktail Co. in South Carolina makes a fine grenadine. If needed, make your own: start with 8 oz. pomegranate juice (make your own by pulsing fresh pomegranate seeds in a blender and then straining the juice, or use a bottled, unsweetened 100-percent pomegranate juice), and place it in a saucepan with 16 oz. superfine sugar. Whisk over medium heat until sugar is fully dissolved, then let cool. Some like to add an ounce of vodka or gin to the grenadine for preservative power, and/or a teaspoon of orange-blossom water for aromatics—these are optional, so proceed as you desire. Keep refrigerated.

Orgeat

This French almond syrup has been a part of the cocktail realm for more than 150 years. There are recipes online for homemade orgeat, but I've always found them more hassle than they're worth, especially when there are decent commercial brands available. Jennifer Colliau's Small Hand Foods makes a superlative orgeat with an earthiness from apricot kernels, and B.G. Reynolds makes an orgeat designed for use in tiki drinks. Once you've opened the bottle, though, use it quickly—fresh orgeat has a limited life span. If you need something to keep in the cabinet for the long term, the French brand Giffard makes a good candidate.

Maple Syrup

Mrs. Butterworth's has no place near your cocktail shaker—always go for pure maple syrup. The darker, heartier Grade B has more richness of flavor than the lighter Grade A, and is preferred for drinks.

Lime Cordial

Rose's is the biggest-selling brand of lime cordial, but its flavor leaves much to be desired. Fortunately, Chicago bartender Todd Appel cracked the code for making a fantastic fresh version in a remarkably simple way. First, use a zester to remove the green zest from eight organic, unwaxed limes. Cut the zested limes in half and squeeze for juice. Strain the lime juice and weigh it on a digital kitchen scale—you should have around 8 oz. of juice, depending on your limes—and add the juice along with an equal amount of sugar (by volume) to a small saucepan. Heat over medium, whisking steadily; when the mixture is hot but not boiling (175°F on a candy thermometer) and the sugar has dissolved, remove from heat and let cool to room temperature. Add the reserved lime zest to the syrup and let steep in the refrigerator overnight, or up to 24 hours, before straining. Bottle for use, and keep refrigerated. For more citrus-cordial fun, check out Todd's other recipes at ToddAppel.com.

Cold-Brew Coffee

This coffee concentrate isn't only tasty in drinks like the Black Jack (page 54), but it's also a summer standby. Many roasters sell packaged cold brews, or you can make your own quite easily. Measure 3/4 cup of coffee beans—I like Stumptown's Holler Mountain blend, or choose your favorite from a local roaster—and grind at the coarsest setting your grinder allows. Mix with one quart water and let steep at room temperature for 8-9 hours, to taste; strain and refrigerate. Use it in cocktails or simply serve over ice.

Orange Flower Water

This perfume-like essence is integral to Middle Eastern cuisine, and to cocktails like the Ramos Fizz. French brands like A. Monteaux are much more potent than Middle Eastern brands like Al Wadi; if using the latter, you may wish to increase the amount called for in the drink.

Mint

Spearmint is the preferred style of mint for Juleps, Smashes, and the like, though other varieties may merit exploration. Go as fresh as you can—grow your own if you have the option (mint has all the tendencies of a weed, growing with little encouragement and nearly impossible to kill)—or buy fresh bundles from the farmers market. To keep your mint fresh, unwrap it and rinse, then wrap small, cigar-size bundles in lightly moistened paper towels. Place the bundles in a plastic bag (don't seal it closed—it needs a little air) and keep refrigerated.

Cherries

Skip the neon-colored supermarket orbs; instead, opt for legitimate maraschino cherries from Luxardo, or the tart, dark candied Italian Amarena cherries available from brands such as Toschi. In either case, rinse the cherries before use. Check your favorite specialty food store, or there's Amazon.

Eggs

The importance of freshness can't be over-emphasized; short of buying a chicken, start hitting up your local farmer's market for the best-possible eggs. Combat sulfurous odors by storing the eggs in a container along with a few lemons; eggshells are porous, and the fruit's fresh aroma will

permeate the shells and brighten the smell of the eggs. The potential hazards of consuming raw eggs are minimal, and can be further reduced by washing the eggs before use, and by maintaining proper sanitary conditions while handling the eggs and mixing your drinks.

Club Soda

The spreading ubiquity of at-home soda devices like Soda Stream has made it possible to have a steady supply of sparkling water on hand. For commercial brands, Q Soda makes a club soda that's surprisingly good.

Tonic Water

Good brands of commercial tonic waters have proliferated recently; I like those from Fever-Tree. Tonic syrups are also increasingly in circulation; simply mix with gin and club soda to make a G&T. The Yeoman Tonic Syrup from Small Hand Foods is my favorite, but Tomr's Tonic, from New York bartender Tom Richter, and Jack Rudy Tonic Syrup, from South Carolina bartender Brooks Reitz, are also very good.

Ginger Beer

Ginger ale is usually boring; most drinks benefit from the extra spiciness of ginger beer. There are some fresh brands available in certain cities—Rachel's Ginger Beer in Seattle is a notable example—but for bottled, widely distributed brands, Blenheim has a super-spicy quality that can be addictive, Bundaberg is an Australian brand that has plenty of bartender devotees, and Fever-Tree has a spark well-suited for cocktails.

RESOURCES

As I mentioned way back at the beginning, this book is just enough to get you started. The cocktail star has gone supernova in the past decade, and there are a number of options for those who wish to explore this rapidly expanding realm.

Books & Magazines

David Wondrich is the Grand Poobah of the cocktail renaissance, and his book, *Imbibe!* (Perigee Trade, 2007) is largely responsible for throwing gasoline on the fire. Read it if you haven't, or read it again if you have—an updated edition was released in 2015.

Jeff "Beachbum" Berry was charting a cocktail course into the unknown when he first started chronicling his studies of tiki drinks in the 1990s. His books *Beachbum Berry's Sippin' Safari* (SLG Publishing, 2007) and *Beachbum Berry Remixed* (SLG Publishing, 2009) are useful guides for a deeper exploration of the tiki universe, and *Beachbum Berry's Potions of the Caribbean* (Cocktail Kingdom, 2013) covers details on drinks such as the Daiquiri and its multitudes of rum-kissed kin.

Vintage bar guides can still surprise even the most seasoned of cocktail geeks. Original copies are increasingly rare and expensive, but Cocktail Kingdom (CocktailKingdom.com) has republished some of the best and most influential. My picks as must-haves include the reprints of Jerry Thomas *How to Mix Drinks: A Bon Vivant's Companion*, Harry Johnson's *Bartender's Manual*, Charles H. Baker, Jr.'s *The South American Gentleman's Companion*, and David Embury's 1948 work, *The Fine Art of Mixing Drinks*.

Two books I encountered early in my own cocktail adventures put me on the proper course, and continue to serve as inspiration and sources of information. William Grimes' *Straight Up or On the Rocks* (North Point Press, reissued in 2002) is a good, thorough survey of America's drinking past and the evolution of the cocktail, and Ted "Dr. Cocktail" Haigh's *Vintage Spirits and Forgotten Cocktails* (Quarry Books, reissued in 2009) turned every bartender wannabe (myself included) into an amateur historian.

There's been a wave of recipe books from those who've helped guide the cocktail boat; among the best are *The PDT Cocktail Book* (Sterling Epicure, 2011), from Jim Meehan, and *Death & Co.: Modern Classic Cocktails* (Ten Speed Press, 2014), from Dave Kaplan and Alex Day, with Nick Fauchald.

I've avoided including many of the complex preparations and painstaking procedures encountered in the cocktail world nowadays—partially in an effort to make this book more user-friendly, but also because entire books exist that are devoted to these practices. *The Bar Book: Elements of Cocktail Technique* from Jeffrey Morgenthaler and Martha Holmberg (Chronicle Books, 2014) delves into the multitudinous minutiae of ingredients and preparation. London bartender Tony Conigliaro goes deep on the science of molecular gastronomy–inspired mixology in his book, *The Cocktail Lab* (Ten Speed Press, 2013), a move reflected by Dave Arnold in his excellent book on drinks science and technique, *Liquid Intelligence* (W.W. Norton, 2014). Some ingredients deserve their own works: two good ones to have on hand are *Bitters* (Ten Speed Press, 2011), by Brad Thomas Parsons; and *Shrubs* (Countryman Press, 2014), from Michael Dietsch.

And I'd be remiss if I didn't include *Imbibe* magazine (ImbibeMagazine.com). Full disclosure: I've written for *Imbibe* (and more recently, have edited it) since its first issue in 2006. The magazine and website provide regular, informed insight into the current movements in the cocktail world. It's just what we do.

Online Shops

Cocktail Kingdom (CocktailKingdom.com) is a one-stop shop for the cocktail devout, selling bar gear, bar books, glassware, bitters, and assorted paraphernalia for the serious cocktail aficionado.

Small Hand Foods makes some of the best, most authentic syrups in the bar world, prepared by a bartender with a deep sense of integrity. Buy them—SmallHandFoods.com.

Buying booze online can be tricky (or illegal, depending on your state); some of the stores with selections well-suited to the cocktail curious include New York-based Drink Up NY (DrinkUpNY.com) and AstorWines.com, and California-based Hi Time Wine (HiTimeWine.net. If you're looking for specialty spirits, Cask Store (CaskStore.com) is a good option.

The Boston Shaker (TheBostonShaker.com) is another good outlet for bar tools, books, and paraphernalia.

Websites

The Cocktail Chronicles website (CocktailChronicles.com)—c'mon, I can't not include my own website. That's where this whole thing started, and where I'll continue to chronicle my boozy explorations.

I wrote nearly 400 posts over a four-year stretch for Serious Eats (SeriousEats.com), and the site continues to have some of the more interesting and up-to-date content about today's bar world.

PUNCH (PunchDrink.com) is essential reading for any cocktail nerd, and offers great insight into the boozy zeitgeist.

Camper English's Alcademics (Alcademics.com) provides regular news updates about drinks, as well as insight into bar events and assorted details of the cocktail world. If you're looking for deep nerdery about ice, this is a good site to visit.

Fred Yarm has maintained the Cocktail Virgin blog (CocktailVirgin.blogspot.com) for many years now, regularly documenting the drinks he encounters in Boston, replete with recipes.

Apps

Smartphone and tablet apps have been slow to reflect the burgeoning cocktail renaissance; two apps released in 2014 by New York-based cocktail fiend Martin Doudoroff's MixologyTech are changing that. Beachbum Berry's Total Tiki was assembled in partnership with Jeff Berry, and features recipes and details about a vast archipelago of tropical-style drinks; and Martin's Index of Cocktails & Mixed Drinks is a thorough chronicling of drinks recipes from bar guides starting in the mid-19th century. In 2015, Doudoroff partnered with PDT founder Jim Meehan to put together a comprehensive PDT cocktail app that extends the range of Meehan's book. These apps were released for iPhone and iPad; check mixologytech.com for updates and details.

Events

Drinking is a social sport—get out and make some friends. Tales of the Cocktail (TalesOfTheCocktail.com) is an annual event in New Orleans that regularly draws thousands of bartenders and cocktail enthusiasts for five days of seminars, parties, and all-around carrying on.

ACKNOWLEDGEMENTS

Here we are, at the back of the book—and like the last hour before closing time after sitting in a bar for way too long, I'm starting to get a little misty and preparing to proclaim my deep and abiding love for everyone.

Way back when I was still a novice blogger, I'd pull up a barstool at Seattle's Zig Zag Café and, if I'd posted a recent recipe that he liked, then-head bartender Murray Stenson would quote back something I'd written and ask me, "So, when are you gonna write a book?" This went on for years, and along the way he mixed (and I drank) many of the recipes collected here. Thanks, Murray—and in reply to your question, here it is.

Murray is only one among many who provided me first with inspiration and awe, and later with friendship, support, and steady urging to finally sit down and write the damn thing. Ted Haigh—Dr. Cocktail in the booze world—was among the most ardent and supportive, and David Wondrich—without whom I'd likely have little interest in cocktails, not to mention a career—is also owed a great debt of thanks. Jeff "Beachbum" Berry has also always been invariably supportive, ever since our first encounter in New Orleans in 2006. Thanks, gents—many beers are owed.

Imbibe magazine publisher Karen Foley took a chance on a no-name blogger in 2005, hiring me to write for her startup publication's first issue, and then keeping me in whiskey money ever since, and *Imbibe's* staff have always been my biggest boosters over the years—their support and patience have been much needed at times, and always much appreciated.

I collected material for this book almost from the moment I started blogging and writing professionally about drinks in 2005. Many bartenders, bloggers and other cocktail enthusiasts have helped me along the way, and some, in particular, helped me with ideas for the drinks selection in this book. Thanks go to Erik Adkins, Jacques Bezuidenhout, Jamie Boudreau, Jacob Briars, Derek Brown, Erick Castro, Martin Cate, Jennifer Colliau, Daniel Djang, Philip Duff, Ryan Fitzgerald, Simon Ford, Chris Hannah, Brian MacGregor, Duggan McDonnell, Jeffrey Morgenthaler, Casey Robison, Mike Ryan, Dave Shenaut, Chuck Taggart, Keith Waldbauer, Angus Winchester, Fred Yarm, and Naren Young.

Over the years of writing about drinks, I've had the great pleasure of building a cadre of colleagues who also double as friends, and who've been ever-supportive of my sometimes naïve questions. I owe much thanks—and more beers—to many, including Anu Apte, Brooke Arthur, Greg Boehm, Andrew Bohrer, Jared Brown & Anistatia Miller, Jackson Cannon, Wayne Curtis, Alex Day, Dale DeGroff, John Deragon, Martin Doudoroff, H. Joseph Ehrmann, Chris Elford, Andrew Friedman, Alexandre Gabriel, Erik Hakkinen, Robert Hess, Bobby Heugel, Misty Kalkofen, Guillaume Lamy, Don Lee, Jim Meehan, Ben Perri, Jim Romdall, Audrey Saunders, Jared Schubert, Eric Seed, Thad Vogler, Neyah White, and Rocky Yeh.

Working as a drinks writer can be a hell of a lot of fun, but it's sometimes a challenge to live with one. In addition to the deadline crunches and roller-coaster cash flow that are parts of any writer's household, drinks writers also accumulate vast hoards of booze and books, which fill closets and cabinets and cover everything in sight. My wife, Leonora, puts up with this stuff, as do my kids, Isaac and Stella (Rose). Thanks for your patience and support, guys—I'll get those bottles out of the way in a little bit.

ABOUT THE AUTHOR

Paul Clarke is a journalist specializing in spirits, cocktails, and the culture of drink. The executive editor of *Imbibe* magazine, he has spent the past decade researching and writing about drinks for *Imbibe*, the *San Francisco Chronicle*, the *New York Times*, Serious Eats, Tasting Table, and many other publications and websites, and is a member of the editorial board for the *Oxford Companion to Spirits and Cocktails*.

Since 2005, Clarke has documented his exploration of fine spirits and mixology on The Cocktail Chronicles, one of the first exclusively spirits and cocktail-related blogs on the Internet, and he's the founder and moderator emeritus of Mixology Monday, a monthly online cocktail party that's attracted scores of participants and thousands of readers since its 2006 debut.

A regular speaker at events including Tales of the Cocktail, Portland Cocktail Week, and the Manhattan Cocktail Classic, Clarke has received a Spirited Award from Tales of the Cocktail for Best Cocktail Writing, and a Bert Greene Award from the International Association of Culinary Professionals for his drinks journalism.

He lives in Seattle.

Paul can be found on Twitter and Instagram as @cocktailchron,
on Facebook at facebook.com/CocktailChronicles, and
at his online home since 2005, CocktailChronicles.com.

BASE INGREDIENT INDEX

Drinks are categorized by the base spirit or ingredient; recipes that split the base between two or more spirits, or that have alternate preparations, are included in all relevant categories.

INDEX

INDEX *(continued)*

INDEX *(continued)*